London Lights

A History of
West End Musicals

Compiled for *This England* by Edmund Whitehouse

This England acknowledges the help and assistance of many enthusiasts, without whom it would have been difficult to compile and check the enormous amount of material contained in this book. In particular, the Appendices took more than four years to research and much conflicting information was found during that period. It is hoped, however, that even though they inevitably contain statistics open to debate, they will still present a valuable record and overall picture for the future, never previously available at a glance.

The help of the following people is kindly acknowledged with a special vote of thanks to Alex Gleason who spent much valuable time tracking down obscure data: David Ades, Jude Balen, Percy Bickerdyke, British Dance Bands E-Mail Group, Terry Brown, Cheltenham Reference Library, Paul Collenette, Peter Dickinson, Stephen Garnett (Stanley Holloway article), Richard Havers, Trevor Hill, Eric Holmes, Philip Lane, Barry McCanna, Iris McCanna, Joe Moore, Philip Scowcroft, Ned Seago, Richard Stevens, Angeline Wilcox (Joyce Grenfell article), Peter Wallace, Ken Wilkins, Andrew Williams, and Adrian Wright. In addition, *This England* is pleased to recognise the staff production and design team whose dedicated work made it possible to piece everything together:- Paul Makepeace, Christine Manifold, Ann Augur, Keren Bowers, Maureen Compton, Roger Knapp, Shirley Collins and Peter Worsley.

We apologise to anyone we have missed out!

*Queueing for the **Black and White Minstrel Show** at Shepherds Bush.*

THIS ENGLAND

Published by This England Books,
Alma House, 73 Rodney Road, Cheltenham,
Gloucestershire, GL50 1HT. Tel: 01242-537900

Printed in Great Britain by Polestar Wheatons Ltd., Exeter

ISBN 0 906324 54 8

CONTENTS

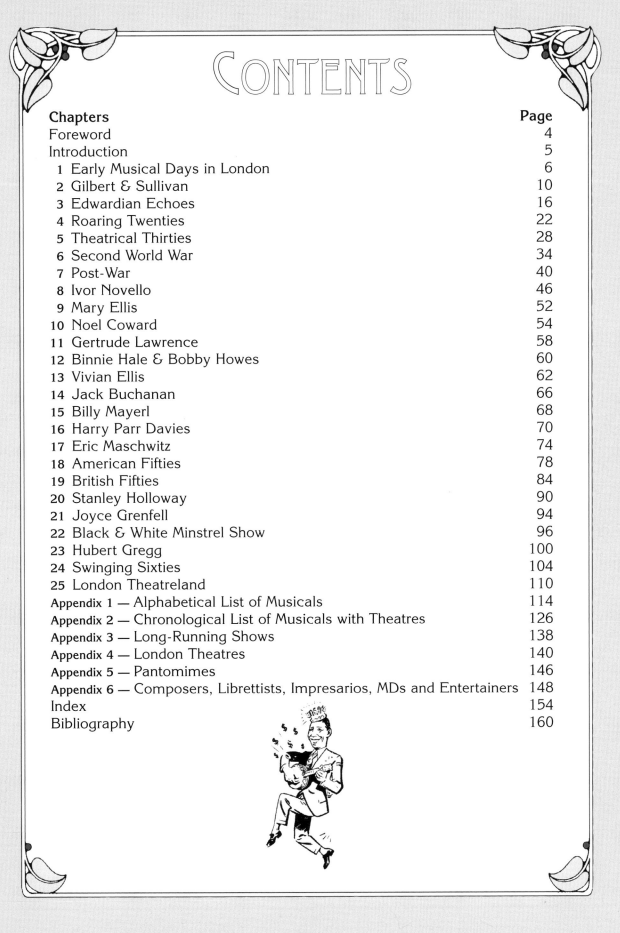

FOREWORD

I was fortunate enough to have a grandmother who loved the theatre and when I was a boy she took me to suitable shows such as *Peter Pan* — I actually remember Jean Forbes-Robertson in the title role — and some delightfully unsuitable entertainments including a girlie revue called, I think, *Beauties of the Night* at the Metropolitan Theatre of Varieties in London's Edgware Road, not far from my grandmother's house in Paddington. Soon I became a Gilbert and Sullivan fanatic, spending many happy hours in the gallery queue at Sadler's Wells whenever the D'Oyly Carte company came to town. Peering in through the stage door once I caught a glimpse of Pooh-Bah in full Japanese rig enjoying a cigarette and thought how exciting life backstage must be.

Thus began what for me has been a lifelong love affair with the theatre. In my young days I did a stint in Rep, playing Shakespeare and Shaw and Pantomime and Charley's Aunt, so I got a taste of what theatrical life was really like. As things turned out I was destined to make my living from Radio and Television, and very grateful I am: but from these everyday media the indefinable ingredient of magic is missing.

You will find that ingredient in abundance in this delightful book. Here is a history of London's musical theatre, and here are close-ups of the stars who made that history what it is: Noel Coward and Gertrude Lawrence, Ivor Novello and Jack Buchanan, Stanley Holloway and the Crazy Gang to name just a few. And there's room for creative off-stage figures such as Eric Maschwitz and Billy Mayerl, Vivian Ellis, Hubert Gregg, and Joyce Grenfell's brilliant partner Richard Addinsell. And all along the way there's an abundance of evocative pictures to bring the glamorous past to life.

Yes, it is an exercise in nostalgia. But why not linger for a little in the theatre of the past when, thanks to a book like this, it can still offer us so much pleasure in the present day?

Ring Up the Curtain!

Richard Baker

Richard Baker OBE

INTRODUCTION

It is humbly believed this book will fill a gap in the history of London Musicals. Its main aim is to paint a broad canvas from the Victorian times to the late-20th century but concentrating unashamedly on the older rather than the newer. In this manner it hopes to rekindle many long-forgotten memories for "silvertops" while opening up a new vista for younger readers.

Many contemporary volumes have been published down the years but none has previously attempted to pull all the strings together. In addition it is hoped that the Appendices, which have taken more than four years to compile, will prove a valuable source of reference for years to come.

When the book was first suggested by Richard Stevens of Angel Radio on the Isle of Wight, it was intended to be a compilation of the articles published in *This England* magazine under the title of "London Lights". This colourful series ran from Summer 2000 until Winter 2003 but research on this volume began long before it ended. Nobody, however, could possibly have imagined it would end up listing more than 2,000 Musicals, 350 theatres, and the dates of more than 1,200 famous people — not to mention nearly 300 photographs and illustrations. Whilst the extensive Appendices do not claim to be comprehensive — nor can they ever be guaranteed 100% accurate — nothing like them has ever been attempted before. Anyone able to plug any of the gaps, however, is most welcome to contact the author.

All the chapters stand alone, but they are also inter-linked. Occasional repetition was therefore necessary to complete individual stories but the overall pattern is well established.

It has become fashionable in recent years to denigrate the past but that is to completely miss the point. Everything in history is a product of time and space, and relevant only when seen in context. Popular music never stands still and identical words of a love song today can mean something very different to what they meant 100 or even 50 years ago. Celebrity status is also nothing new but what *has* changed is that the media now creates them artificially whereas most of the stars in this book achieved fame through sheer wealth of talent. There was no short-cut to the top in those days!

Read on and enjoy the unfolding story of the London Musical. When it began it was very much subservient to the London Play, but after more than a century it has now finally taken over as the dominant partner in the West End. *Long may it continue!*   EDMUND WHITEHOUSE

EARLY MUSICAL DAYS IN LONDON

Musical theatre did not really become a popular art form in England until mid-Victorian times, prior to which grand opera and other musical soirées were largely the province of the urban aristocracy. The common man was irretrievably wedded to his village and local events until the Industrial Revolution came along, but even when towns mushroomed in size there was little organised entertainment for the masses outside the music hall, which was more like an indoor fairground. It was only when the emerging middle class began to frequent such places as London's Vauxhall Pleasure Gardens on the south bank of the River Thames that the musical theatre began to take shape.

On the Continent it was the likes of the Strauss family in Vienna and Jacques Offenbach in Paris who set the ball rolling. Between them, the former produced countless numbers of waltzes while the latter, by the time of his death in 1880, had notched up no fewer than 100 operettas.

In London, Gilbert and Sullivan concocted a peculiarly English type of show which quickly spread to North America. As the 20th century began to unfold so the musical blossomed with London's West End and New York's Broadway becoming the focal points for the best of English-speaking productions. Although many have now disappeared, others live on, if only in the form of a single song which has withstood the test of time.

One such offering came from **The Bohemian Girl**, a mid-19th century work by the Irish composer Michael Balfe. In a tale of gypsy love, intrigue and mistaken identity *"I Dreamt That I Dwelt in Marble Halls"* is sung by a beautiful kidnapped princess sadly ruminating about her early life. She falls in love and, despite the malevolent intentions of the gypsy queen, finally marries the young man who saves her from a wild animal. He also turns out to be of noble birth, but from another country disguised as a gypsy because the princess's father had been hunting him as an enemy soldier. Everyone is eventually reunited, except the queen who is accidentally shot dead by the man she hires to kill the young lovers. The show thus ends on a happy note and became a popular success well ahead of its time. It was also a forerunner of modern operetta.

In 1893 **A Gaiety Girl** was one of the first of the many "Girl" musicals to appear in the Metropolis. Based on the society lives of four young ladies, one of whom is falsely accused of theft at a garden party, the show predictably finishes happily in romance. It should have been staged at the Gaiety Theatre itself but such was the success of other contemporary productions there that it had to be moved to the Prince of Wales

Edward German (1862-1936) (left) wrote much serious music but is best remembered for his patriotic 1902 operetta **Merrie England**.

Michael Balfe (1808-1870) (right) wrote 26 operas including **The Bohemian Girl** *which opened at Drury Lane in 1843.*

◁One of the most successful Edwardian musical writers was Lionel Monckton (1861-1924). Educated at Charterhouse and Oxford University, he was called to the Bar in 1885 but quickly established a name outside the legal profession. He composed the melodies for more than 20 shows, of which **The Arcadians** was the most successful, running for more than 800 performances. He is seen here with his wife, Gertie Millar (later the Countess of Dudley), for whom he wrote many of his best songs.

cess that Broadway immediately revived it and subsequently turned it into a film. Also imported with the show was its star Edna May, who sang *"When We Are Married"* and *"They All Follow Me"*. Edna became a big name over here and after deciding to adopt England as her home, appeared in many more musicals, including the 1909 production of **Our Miss Gibbs**, the story of a young flower-girl from Yorkshire who comes to London and becomes romantically entangled with a member of the aristocracy. It also starred George Grossmith Jr., Gertie Millar, Ruby Miller and Gladys Cooper.

But it was the turn-of-the-century production of **Florodora** which caused everyone to sit up and take notice of its revolutionary combination of early jazz rhythms and syncopated dances. With the hit song *"Tell Me, Pretty Maiden"* performed by parasol-waving ladies and straw-boatered

where it ran for 413 performances.

Five years later London took over the ailing American production of **The Belle of New York** and turned it into such a box-office suc-

◁Edna May (1878-1948) and G.P. Huntley in **The Schoolgirl** (1903). Five years earlier Edna had made her name in the London production of **The Belle of New York** and, although an American, she enjoyed England so much that she stayed here and remained a firm favourite with theatre-goers for many years afterwards.

▷Edmund Payne (left) and George Grossmith Jr. (1874-1935), in the 1909 production of **Our Miss Gibbs**, the romantic story of a Yorkshire flower-girl in London. Grossmith, son of a famous Gilbert and Sullivan Savoyard, was a fine performer in his own right and is best-remembered for the hit song from this show, "Yip-i-addy-i-ay".

△ *This bustling late-Edwardian street scene at the junction of London's Strand and Aldwych can be accurately dated because the recently-opened Gaiety Theatre is advertising* **Our Miss Gibbs**, *a musical which began an unbroken run of 636 performances in January 1909. The first Gaiety theatre, erected nearby in 1866, was closed in 1903 for road improvements and its successor surprisingly suffered the same fate just before the last war. Ironically, it then survived the Blitz and was not actually demolished until 1957, long after the traffic scheme had been superseded. This traffic scene was also shortly to become a thing of the past with horse-drawn buses ousted by the new-fangled motor car.*

gentlemen, it set the musical pattern for years to come and was revived many times at home and abroad. Prominent among the performers was black-faced American dancer, Eugene Stratton, who had stayed over here following a visit with a troupe of minstrels. When the show transferred to New York it strongly influenced the writing of several future legendary musical giants, including Jerome Kern, Richard Rodgers and George Gershwin.

For pure Englishness one need look no further than the rustic dances and patriotic songs from Edward German's **Merrie England**. Set in Elizabethan times the story revolves around a romantic plot involving, among others, Sir Walter Raleigh, the Earl of Essex, and "Good Queen Bess" herself. Surprisingly, it ran for only 120 performances but this was largely because of its similarity to Gilbert and Sullivan, who had finally terminated their partnership only a few years earlier and who were temporarily out of fashion. The production was appropriately staged at the Savoy Theatre — specially built for "G & S" by Richard D'Oyly Carte — and

included the famous Savoyards Henry Lytton, Richard Passmore and Rosina Brandram. Despite its initial poor reception, however, the show soon came back to prominence and much of the beautiful score can still be heard regularly today. Among the more famous songs are *"Every Jack Should Have a Jill"*, *"The Yeomen of England"* and *"Dan Cupid Hath a Garden"* better-known as *"English Rose"*.

Another quite brilliant pre-First World War musical score came from the pen of Lionel Monckton — **The Arcadians** being as melodic as any show from the Edwardian period and most thereafter. The story concerns an intrepid balloonist named James Smith, who crash-lands in the fictitious Utopian land of Arcady where he surreptitiously adopts the name of "Simplicitas". But when his secret is discovered some of the Arcadian citizens decide to travel to London with the aim of saving it from decadence. They fail — but gloriously! The plot is so far-fetched and absurd that it makes the music all the more endearing. Two songs in particular, *"Pipes of*

8

Pan" and *"Charming Weather"*, have remained all-time classics and will endure for generations to come, the overture being particularly popular.

Monckton also contributed musical scores to several other successful shows including **The Shop Girl, The Circus Girl, The Geisha, The Runaway Girl, The Messenger Boy, Kitty Grey, The Toreador, The Country Girl, The Orchid, The Cingalee, Spring Chicken, The Girls of Gottenberg, The Quaker Girl, Mousmé, The Dancing Mistress, The Belle of Bond Street,** and **The Boy,** plus several lively revues staged to boost the morale of troops and civilians during the First World War. His marriage to the aforesaid famous music hall actress and singer Gertie Millar, however, foundered when he failed to give her a leading role in **The Arcadians.** After his death she became a Countess by marrying the Earl of Dudley.

Much has been written about the Edwardian period (1901-1914) when almost everyone went to the theatre or music hall because few people owned a gramophone and radio had yet to become a commercial proposition. The advent of the First World War, however, made a dent in the nation's finances and swept away the heyday of live performances for ever. Fortunately, popular music survived, battered and bruised but still intact.

△ *Marie Studholme, Kate Cutler and Louie Pounds are seen here in the original 1893 production of* **A Gaiety Girl***, forerunner of more than 40 "Girl" musicals which thrilled London audiences for decades. Despite their copious covering they were regarded as beauties.*

Early London theatres were largely dangerous wooden affairs and situated more towards the east with many falling victim to the ravages of fire. Some were rebuilt but many new lavish edifices were erected in late-Victorian and Edwardian times by when the West End had become the indisputable focal point of the capital's music and drama productions. Theatres such as the Adelphi, Duke of York's, Royal Opera House (Covent Garden), Gaiety, Haymarket, Wyndham's, Empire, Prince's, Pavilion, Drury Lane, Coliseum, Winter Garden, Hippodrome, Lyric, Shaftesbury, Strand, Prince of Wales's, Savoy and Victoria Palace are just some of the exciting names which trip off the tongue and which, a century later, still conjure up colourful musical images of yesteryear.

◁ *Eugene Stratton (1861-1918) was born in America but came to England with a troupe of minstrels at 19. He decided to settle down here and built up a fine reputation as a black-faced singer and soft-shoe dancer. As a gentle music hall crooner he had few equals and is best-remembered for several famous songs, including "Little Dolly Daydream", "Lily of Laguna", and "I May Be Crazy but I Love You".*

GILBERT & SULLIVAN

Of all artistic combinations, Gilbert and Sullivan (G & S) has been the most enduring. The two men's work is almost as popular today as it was more than a century ago and yet they hardly ever met socially, each living a totally independent existence.

Much has been made of their public disagreements but they knew inwardly that each depended on the other. In 1903, three years after Sullivan's death, Gilbert finally confessed that his writing was not much use without a Sullivan and that he could no longer find one! Sullivan, in his turn, tried desperately hard as a composer of serious music but, while many thought he succeeded admirably, he always considered himself to be a failure in this respect.

Both men were born in London, William Schwenk Gilbert in 1836 and Arthur Seymour Sullivan in 1842. Gilbert originally trained to be a soldier and barrister but his love of humorous writing and the spoken word, some of it quite acerbic, caused an abrupt change of career. Also a competent illustrator, some of his early words and pictures appeared in *Punch* magazine, and his comic ballads were just a short step away from those of a fully-fledged playwright.

Sullivan was a more impressionable young man and, after serving as a chorister at the Chapel Royal, trained at the Royal Academy of Music where he became Professor of Composition during his twenties, also performing as resident organist at the Royal Opera House. His musical career appeared to be clearly mapped out but like many other would-be classical performers, including Eric Coates and Albert Ketèlbey, his economic future lay in lighter music.

Sullivan's first sortie into the theatre came in 1867 with **Cox and Box**, the action of which takes place in a single room which the landlord secretly lets out alternately night

Sir William Schwenk Gilbert (1836-1911)

Sir Arthur Seymour Sullivan (1842-1900)

MAD MARGARET.
RUDDIGORE.

△ **Ruddigore** or *"The Witch's Curse"* brought to life ancestors from huge portraits on the wall but it came hard on the heels of **The Mikado** *which was a hard act to follow.*

▽ **Iolanthe** *was produced in 1882 and subtitled "The Peer and the Peri". It was a biting satire on peers in the House of Lords who "did nothing in particular, and did it very well".*

THE DUKE OF DUNSTABLE.
PATIENCE.

△ **Patience** *poked fun at the aesthetics of the time. With the sub-title of "Bunthorne's Bride", it contains some fine melodies and has remained popular ever since.*

THE MIKADO OF JAPAN.
THE MIKADO.

△ *Conceived at a time when the country was "Oriental mad",* **The Mikado** *remains the best-loved of all G & S operas, with some of the finest tunes and lyrics ever written.*

MARCO & GIUSEPPE PALMIERI.
THE GONDOLIERS.

△ *Marco and Giuseppe are the two* **Gondoliers** *who mistakenly think that one of them is betrothed to a foreign princess. A typical Gilbertian plot decides otherwise, however.*

▽ *Jack Point is the tragic hero in* **The Yeomen of the Guard**. *Based on complicated events in the mediaeval Tower of London, the opera ends on both sad and triumphal notes.*

A sure sign of popularity was to have a series of cigarette cards designed in your favour. These pictures are from a second set of 50 released by John Player and Sons in 1927.

IOLANTHE.
IOLANTHE.

MAJOR-GENERAL STANLEY.
THE PIRATES OF PENZANCE.

△ *One of the best G & S patter songs is from Major-General Stanley in* **The Pirates of Penzance**. *A group of cowardly policemen try to protect his unmarried daughters.*

PRINCESS IDA.
PRINCESS IDA.

△ **Princess Ida** *has not really withstood the test of time. Subtitled "Castle Adamant", its contemporary story of women's liberation has been largely overtaken by events.*

JACK POINT.
THE YEOMEN OF THE GUARD.

△ *The Savoy Theatre during the original production of* **Patience**. *The newly-installed and revolutionary electric lighting can be seen and the increased visibility must have created a sensation.*

and day to two men named Mr. Cox and Mr. Box. They eventually chance upon each other and discover they are actually long-lost brothers engaged to the same girl!

Four years later (1871) came the first production of the famous G & S partnership. To mixed receptions, **Thespis** ran for 63 performances at the Gaiety Theatre but can no longer be revived because the music has disappeared, although some of it was probably reworked into later operas. Subtitled "The Gods Grown Old", the action takes place on Mount Olympus in mythical ancient Greece.

Influential impresario Richard D'Oyly Carte was highly impressed and arranged for Gilbert and Sullivan's one-act **Trial by Jury** to be performed at the Royalty Theatre in 1875. The plot, relatively simple by later standards, involves a court scene trying a breach of promise in which the judge becomes romantically entangled with the female plaintiff.

In the same year, Sullivan's **The Zoo**, subtitled "A Musical Folly", another romantic tale but not written by Gilbert, was performed at St. James' Theatre. It never reached the heights of **Trial by Jury**, however, and nor did any of Sullivan's other later light operas with-

out Gilbert's witty librettos, namely **Haddon Hall** (1892), **The Chieftain** (1895), **The Beauty Stone** (1898), **The Rose of Persia** (1899) and, posthumously completed by Edward German, **The Emerald Isle** (1901). **Ivanhoe** (1890) was a traditional grand opera which went the same way.

In 1877 came **The Sorcerer**, the only full-length G & S opera without a subtitle. The wizard in question is John Wellington Wells, "a dealer in magic and spells" who is hired to concoct a potion which causes couples to fall madly in love. Unfortunately the wrong people become paired off, causing much mirth and despair until the plot is finally unravelled and all ends happily. The new venue was the Opera Comique, reached via an underground passage and sharing a back wall with the Globe Theatre next door — not an auspicious setting but greater things lay in store.

HMS Pinafore, or "The Lass Who Loved a Sailor", opened in 1878, and its nautical cousin **The Pirates of Penzance**, subtitled "The Slave of Duty", two years later. They were both performed at the Opera Comique but in order to avoid plagiarism and breach of copyright law, the latter was first produced in New York together with a one-off performance at the Bijou Theatre in Paignton, Devon, where the D'Oyly Carte Company happened to be on tour. The ploy was successful and avoided **The Pirates** from being "pirated". Both operas cast persons in varying ranks of life and introduced us to the famous "patter" song, memorably *"I Am the Very Model of a Modern Major General"* from **The Pirates**. Less taxing but scarcely less noteworthy is *"I am the Monarch of the Sea"* from **HMS Pinafore**.

The Gilbert and Sullivan die was now well and truly cast, and for both men it became a serious business. As part of his preparation for the new nautical offering, Gilbert went down to Portsmouth and was rowed around various ships searching for a suitable location. He finally settled on the quarter-deck of *HMS Victory* which he obtained permission to sketch and model in detail.

Patience was first performed at the Opera Comique in 1881 but was soon transferred to D'Oyly Carte's splendid new purpose-built Savoy Theatre, making it the first of the so-called "Savoy Operas". Lit by new-fangled electricity and with a queueing system for unreserved seats, the Savoy was an instant success. Could Gilbert and Sullivan match its splendour with attractive stage productions?

△ *Richard D'Oyly Carte (1844-1901), was a theatrical entrepreneur who spotted the potential of Gilbert and Sullivan's musical partnership and as a result built the ultra-modern Savoy Theatre in the Strand which became home to the Savoy Operas.*

They could and they did. **Patience**, subtitled "Bunthorne's Bride", was a parody of the upper-class Victorian aesthetic movement and poked fun particularly at Oscar Wilde and Algernon Swinburne. Its delightful music combined beautifully with the clever libretto.

The following year **Iolanthe**, or "The Peer and the Peri", mimicked the government of the day and the House of Lords in particular. The opera was widely advertised as being called **Perola** but, in order to outwit any rival illegal productions, was deliberately renamed a short time before the first night. In 1884 **Princess Ida** was based on a wealthy royal female rejecting her betrothed and all male-dominated society by retreating into a specially-created all-ladies academy called "Castle Adamant", the subtitle of the opera. Although highly enjoyable, the relatively weak plot has caused it to become one of the lesser-performed Gilbert and Sullivan operas.

Only a year later came the most famous, and arguably the best of all the partnership's masterpieces. The contemporary Victorian craze for everything Oriental was an ideal platform and the results were spectacular.

△ *Sullivan as a chorister at the Chapel Royal.*

△ It was Henry Lytton, seen here with Rhoda Maitland as Elsie Maynard, who first decided that Jack Point should drop down dead at the end of **The Yeomen of the Guard***. Gilbert had originally planned a conventional ending but his capacity for the unusual caused him not to intervene and henceforth the opera had a dramatic and sad finale.*

Without doubt **The Mikado**, or "The Town of Titipu", was the right opera in the right place at the right time. The romantic entanglements are acted out to the full with witty stings-in-the-tail to satisfy every member of the audience. The lyrics are brilliant and the music outstanding. It has rightly remained popular ever since but was a hard act to follow.

In 1887 **Ruddigore**, or "The Witch's Curse", was on a hiding to nothing and did not measure up to the audience's high expectations. Ghostly ancestors coming to life and walking out of their giant picture frames was a clever idea but not quite imaginative enough at the time. Nevertheless, the opera is still regularly performed. What would the duo think of next?

The inspiration came unexpectedly the following year when Gilbert was reputed to have been travelling on the London Underground and spotted a poster depicting a beefeater. **The Yeomen of the Guard** was born. Centred on the Tower of London in mediaeval times, it ends with the expected meeting of principal leads in a happy embrace, but with one notable exception —

the court jester, Jack Point, dying at the feet of his lost love after hopelessly pleading his cause. In the original production Jack pretended to be dead but then wiggled his leg to show he was only acting, much to the audience's amusement.

The famous Henry Lytton, however, apparently with Gilbert's full approval, decided that a dramatic ending would be better and set the pattern for all future productions, with a dead Jack Point ringing down the final curtain. It is not unknown for the actor concerned to work himself up into such a frenzy that he is quite unable to take part in the following curtain calls. "The Merry Man and His Maid" was an apt subtitle for this melodramatic work.

In 1889 the action moved to Italy for **The Gondoliers**, a highly colourful and successful production based in Venice. Subtitled "The King of Barataria", the plot is woven around two young princes, one of whom, but neither knows which, is betrothed to a beautiful infant princess. In the usual dramatic twist it turns out to be someone completely different

△ "Savoyard" was the name given to early players of G & S at the Savoy Theatre. One of the most famous was George Grossmith, seen here in the role of Sir Joseph Porter "The Ruler of the Queen's Navy" in **HMS Pinafore***. Attending him is Jessie Bond in the role of Hebe, one of his "cousins — whom he reckons up by dozens".*

△ *In later life Gilbert became quite a social figure and is seen here as the Deputy-Lieutenant of Middlesex.*

and the princess marries her childhood sweetheart who had been secretly switched to avoid kidnapping while still a baby. It was another box-office triumph but the pair's legendary inspiration suddenly began to falter, added to which Gilbert was outraged when he discovered a large sum of the partnership's money had, without his knowledge, been spent on new carpets prior to the production.

Eventually D'Oyly Carte managed to reunite them but neither of the two remaining Savoy Operas is regularly seen today. **Utopia Limited**, or "The Flowers of Progress", was first performed in 1893 and was a parody of everything Victorian. Set on the South Sea island of Utopia, the inhabitants rebel against perfection and decide that a little corruption is the best antidote. Many contemporary reviews were scathing although a recent revival has shown much of the production to be very agreeable.

Less favoured has been the final offering, **The Grand Duke** of 1896, which proved to be the parting of the waves for two very disparate characters. Subtitled "The Statutory Duel", the action takes place in the fictitious Bohemian Duchy of Pfennig Halbpfennig where a plot is hatched to get rid of the ruling Grand Duke. Gilbert was unhappy with the result and an ailing Sullivan finally lost patience with his partner who regularly and

rigorously rehearsed the cast to perfection, even if it took all night. Gilbert had also become extremely bad-tempered on account of his painful gout. The two geniuses never collaborated again.

It upset Gilbert when, in 1883, his partner received a knighthood from Prime Minister Gladstone and that Queen Victoria allegedly enjoyed Sullivan's music more than his own librettos. On the other hand it rankled with Sullivan that when he visited the Queen she often insisted on tunes from the Savoy Operas rather than his more serious compositions. In fact the Queen enjoyed both Gilbert's dialogue and Sullivan's more serious music, which suggests it was probably a matter of petty jealousy on both sides. Genius often rankles with others of equally great intellect!

Sullivan died first, in 1900, and was buried in St. Paul's Cathedral. Gilbert, a successful independent playwright, and owner of the Garrick Theatre which opened in 1889, was eventually knighted in 1907. Four years later he too was dead from a heart attack, sustained while rescuing a young lady from drowning on his estate. His remains were interred at Great Stanmore in Middlesex.

Whatever their faults, Gilbert and Sullivan were a peerless combination of brains and creativity, responsible for a unique slice of English musical history. On any given date, throughout the length and breadth of the country, dozens of G & S societies can be found planning and rehearsing their next show. Despite many attempts at modernisation, it is still the original productions which continue to give the most pleasure. Thoroughly English in character, in "love, laughter and song" (Sir Henry Lytton), long may they continue.

△ *Grim's Dyke, where Gilbert died after rescuing a young lady who had got out of her depth in the lake.*

EDWARDIAN ECHOES

As the Edwardian period drew to a close so a Continental influence became apparent in London's theatreland. Franz Lehar's 1907 tuneful production of **The Merry Widow** ran for 778 performances at Daly's Theatre — starring Lily Elsie in the title-role opposite American, Joseph Coyne. It was followed three years later by **The Chocolate Soldier**, Oscar Straus's setting of George Bernard Shaw's book *Arms and the Man*. In 1911 Lehar again held sway at Daly's with an Anglicised version of **The Count of Luxembourg**.

All three shows were extremely colourful with **The Merry Widow** having a major effect on world fashions in Europe and America where it became the done thing for middle-aged and elderly society ladies to wear "Merry Widow" hats and clothes. **The Chocolate Soldier** ran for 500 performances at the Lyric Theatre and involved a cowardly combatant who preferred eating chocolates to fighting. He later, however, outsmarted a dashing officer rival for the hand of the leading lady. Much of **The Count of Luxembourg** was rewritten by Adrian Ross and Basil Hood (1864-1917) who between them also penned the librettos to many other musicals.

Other successful shows of the time included Lionel Monckton's **The Quaker Girl** (1910), featuring the composer's wife, Gertie Millar — despite the fact that they had just fallen out! In January, 1909, Gertie had starred in her husband's production of **Our Miss Gibbs** but three months later came his biggest success, **The Arcadians**, to which Gertie naturally expected to be transferred. Lionel, however, disagreed!

Three profitable shows in two years was a rare achievement for anyone but it was shared by one of Monckton's many collaborators, Ivan Caryll. In a career spanning more than 30 years, he scored several operettas including no fewer than eight of the **Girl** musicals. His contemporary, Paul Rubens (1875-1917) also wrote several hit musicals, includ-

◁ ▷ *Few couples have ever made such an impact as husband-and-wife team, Jack Hulbert (1892-1978 — far left) and Cicely Courtneidge (1893-1980 — right). They met in 1913 at London's Shaftesbury Theatre when Jack was engaged to appear opposite Cicely by her father, Robert, the producer of the show. Stars of stage, screen and radio, and married for 65 years, they thrilled audiences for decades. Jack's equally famous brother Claude — second left — invariably played the part of the silly ass, both on-stage and on-screen but also on radio and records. All three enjoyed solo careers in addition to their partnerships. In addition to everything else, Jack and Cicely are well remembered for Saturday night appearances on BBC radio when they enacted out a mini-drama which had all the listeners guessing right up until the end.*

△ Gertie Millar in **Our Miss Gibbs** at London's Gaiety Theatre in 1909. She was disappointed not to receive a title role in **The Arcadians** later the same year.

△ Lily Elsie (1886-1962) and Joseph Coyne (1867 - 1941) in the leading roles from **The Merry Widow** (1907), a production which took both Europe and North America by storm, leading to a new fashion craze in ladies' clothes and hats.

△ Huntley Wright and Ethel Irving in Lionel Monckton's **A Country Girl** (1902) which ran for 729 performances at Daly's Theatre.

△ Percy Fletcher (1879-1932) was an outstanding musician and composer who made his living as musical director at several London theatres, many at the same time! He was also the genius and orchestrating brains behind the hugely popular **Chu Chin Chow** which ran for 2,238 performances between 1916 and 1921.

▷ James Blakeley, a star in the 1903 production of **The Schoolgirl**, which opened at the Prince of Wales Theatre on 9th March — another of the many successful "Girl" shows which ran all across the country.

Adrian Ross (1859-1933), real name Arthur Reed Ropes, wrote the librettos to a large number of musicals, 16 of which enjoyed more than 400 performances.

Belgian-born composer Ivan Caryll (1860-1921) quickly settled down in London where he became an integral component of the late-Victorian and Edwardian musical scene.

ing **Miss Hook of Holland, The Sunshine Girl, Tonight's the Night, After the Girl,** and **The Balkan Princess.** Sidney Jones (1861-1946) was another noteworthy British composer who penned **The Medal and the Maid, The Bugle Call, The King of Cadonia** and **The Persian Princess.** Equally active Frank Tours (1877-1963) trained as a classical organist at the RCM but also scored several Edwardian musicals, including **The Dairymaids, The New Aladdin, The Dashing Little Duke** and **Girl o'Mine.**

One of Caryll's many "Girls" was **The Pearl Girl** (1913), in which a promising young actor was engaged by producer Robert Courtneidge to perform opposite his daughter at the Shaftesbury Theatre. Jack Hulbert and Cicely Courtneidge soon married and forged perhaps the greatest husband-and-wife team of the 20th century, playing brilliantly together in countless musicals, films, revues, plays and shows in a glittering joint-career which lasted more than 50 years. They also appeared regularly on radio.

SOME POPULAR EARLY LONDON MUSICALS

1893	A Gaiety Girl	
1894	The Shop Girl	
1896	The Geisha	
	The Circus Girl	
1898	The Belle of New York	
	A Runaway Girl	
1900	Florodora	
1902	Merrie England	
	A Country Girl	
1903	The Orchid	
	The Schoolgirl	
	The Cherry Girl	
1906	The Belle of Mayfair	
1907	Girls of Gottenberg	
	The Merry Widow	
	Tom Jones	
1909	Our Miss Gibbs	

	The Arcadians
	Houp-La!
1910	The Chocolate Soldier
	The Quaker Girl
	The Girl in the Train
1911	The Count of Luxembourg
1913	The Pearl Girl
	The Girl from Utah
1915	Bric-a-Brac
1916	Chu Chin Chow
	Follow the Crowd
1917	Maid of the Mountains
1918	The Lilac Domino
1919	Kissing Time
1920	The Beggar's Opera
1921	The Rebel Maid
1922	Lilac Time

△ *The Theatre Royal, Drury Lane, is the oldest in the land, receiving its regal charter from King Charles II as long ago as 1662. Three years later it witnessed the first stage appearance of Nell Gwynn. Later notable performers included David Garrick (1717-1779) and R.B. Sheridan (1751-1816). Twice burnt down, it has been rebuilt several times — once to a design by Sir Christopher Wren. Over the years it has hosted numerous gala occasions and popular musicals, and maintains a friendly rivalry with its neighbouring royal theatre, Covent Garden.*

Although the Edwardian era was extremely glamorous it was also relatively short-lived because the new monarch was almost 60 when he acceded to the throne in 1901. His death nine years later was all too soon followed by the outbreak of the First World War when musicals, like everything else, underwent a drastic and radical reappraisal. Reduced personnel resulted in a smaller number of shows, but **Chu Chin Chow** (1916) astonished everyone by becoming the biggest ever box-office draw, its run remaining unsurpassed for more than three decades, until **Salad Days** overtook it.

In retrospect it is easy now to see exactly why the show became so popular. When **Chu Chin Chow** opened at His Majesty's Theatre on 31st August, 1916, the First World War was at its height and for soldiers on leave it was a rare treat and a breath of fresh air. In a drab world of khaki and associated gloom when travel to foreign parts meant only one thing — armed combat — being able to lose oneself in the make-believe world of the theatre, if only for a few hours, meant everything to those who never knew if they would see their family again. So successful was this colourful production that it survived the war and continued to play to packed houses for a total of five years, during which time it enjoyed an unbroken run of 2,238 performances, chalking up viewing figures of nearly three million — a feat unequalled until the Fifties. As its name suggests the story was one of Oriental intrigue, complete with Ali Baba and the 40 thieves, slave traders, beautiful women, rich sultans and a treasure-filled cave accessible only by the words "Open Sesame". Oscar Asche's exciting story and Frederic Norton's lively music combined to make the perfect kaleidoscopic backdrop to a dismal period of history. The music retains its charm and much of it is still well-known, especially *"March of the Robbers"* and *"The Cobbler's Song"*. Another notable musical, with 1,352 performances, again at Daly's Theatre, was **The Maid of the Mountains**. Scored by Harold Fraser-Simson and James W. Tate, it opened on 10th February, 1917, and included the show-stoppers *"A Bachelor Gay Am I"* and *"Love Will Find a Way"*. It also created a new star in Jose Collins (1887-1958), whose mother Lottie sang the famous music hall ditty *"Ta-ra-ra-boom-de-ay"*.

Other shows came and went but the last really great contemporary musical before the "Roaring Twenties" arrived was **The Lilac Domino**, which touched down in London by way of Leipzig, Vienna and New York. Staged at the Empire Theatre, it opened on 21st February, 1918, and ran for 747 performances. Like **Chu Chin Chow** it provided much-needed escapism from the ghastly effects of the Great War.

In 1920 **The Beggar's Opera**, originally written by John Gay in 1728, was adapted by Frederic Austin and took nearly 1,500 curtain calls at the Lyric Theatre, Hammersmith. Schubert too, became rehabilitated and, almost 90 years after his death in 1828, Vienna staged a successful musical précis of his tragically short life. In 1921 the score was rewritten and appeared on Broadway as **Blossom Time**. It was then modified for British audiences by the Australian composer, G.H. Clutsam and, retitled **Lilac Time**, ran for 626 performances at the Lyric Theatre on Shaftesbury Avenue.

One other show is worthy of mention but not because of its long run. In 1921 the London Empire put on **The Rebel Maid**, a delightful operetta by the fine light music composer, Montague Phillips. It should have done well but, unfortunately for both composer and theatre alike, it coincided with a national coal strike which meant very few late-night trains and buses operating out of the Metropolis. The production lasted for only four months but its most famous song, *"The Fishermen of England"*, has survived intact.

Despite all the many political and economic upheavals, the early-Twenties was about to witness a new era of British musicals which were more international in outlook and also coincided with a large increase in popular record sales.

△ *Starting in the mid-Victorian era and running through to the Second World War, there was a rash of musicals using the word "Girl" in their title, both on Broadway, New York, and in London's West End. This picture shows Hayden Coffin leading the male chorus in the song "The land where the best man wins" from* **The Girl Behind the Counter** *which opened at Wyndham's Theatre in 1906.*

SOME OF THE MORE IMPORTANT LONDON "GIRL" SHOWS

The Bohemian Girl (Balfe operetta)	1843	Drury Lane 27.11.1843
The Girl He Left Behind Him	1881	Vaudeville 29.11.1881
The Dancing Girl	1891	Haymarket 15.1.1891
The Prancing Girl	1891	Prince of Wales 26.11.1891
The Nautch Girl	1891	Savoy 30.6.1891
A Gaiety Girl	1893	Prince of Wales 14.10.1893
The Shop Girl	1894	Gaiety 24.11.1894
My Girl	1896	Gaiety 13.6.1896
The Circus Girl	1896	Gaiety 5.12.1896
The Girl from Paris (Gay Parisienne)	1896	Duke of York's 4.4.1896
The Telephone Girl	1898	Drury Lane
A Runaway Girl	1898	Gaiety 21.5.1898
The Casino Girl	1900	Shaftesbury 11.7.1900
The Girl From Up There	1901	Duke of York's 23.4.01
A Country Girl	1902	Daly's 18.1.02
The Girl from Kay's	1902	Apollo 15.11.02
The Cherry Girl	1903	Vaudeville 21.12.03
The Earl and the Girl	1903	Adelphi 10.12.03
The Schoolgirl	1903	Prince of Wales 9.5.03
The Girl Behind the Counter	1906	Wyndham's 21.4.06
The Girl on the Stage (The Little Cherub)	1906	Prince of Wales 13.1.06
The Girls of Gottenberg	1907	Gaiety 15.5.07
The Girl From Over the Border	1908	Kings,Hammersmith 18.5.08
The Girl in the Train	1910	Vaudeville 4.6.10
The Quaker Girl	1910	Adelphi 5.11.10
The Girl in the Taxi	1912	Lyric 5.9.12
The Sunshine Girl	1912	Gaiety 24.2.12
The Pearl Girl	1913	Shaftesbury 25.9.13
The Girl Who Didn't	1913	Lyric 18.12.13
The Girl on the Film	1913	Gaiety 5.4.13
The Girl from Utah	1913	Adelphi 18.10.13
After the Girl	1914	Gaiety 7.2.14
The Only Girl	1915	Apollo 25.9.15
The Bing Girls Are There	1917	Alhambra 24.2.17
The Girl in the Bath	1918	Kings, Hammersmith 22.4.18
The Girl Behind the Gun	1919	Winter Garden 20.5.19
The Girl for the Boy	1919	Duke of York's 23.9.19
A Little Dutch Girl	1920	Lyric 1.12.20
The Little Girl in Red	1921	Gaiety 10.12.1921
The Cabaret Girl	1922	Winter Garden 19.9.22
His Girl	1922	Gaiety 1.4.22
The Girl Friend	1927	Palace, 8.9.27
The Girl from Cook's	1927	Gaiety 1.11.27
That's a Good Girl	1928	Hippodrome 5.6.28
Lucky Girl	1928	Shaftesbury 14.11.28
The Five O'Clock Girl	1929	Hippodrome 21.3.29
The One Girl	1933	Hippodrome 24.2.33
Me and My Girl	1937	Palace 16.12.37

Many other "Girl" shows toured the Provinces

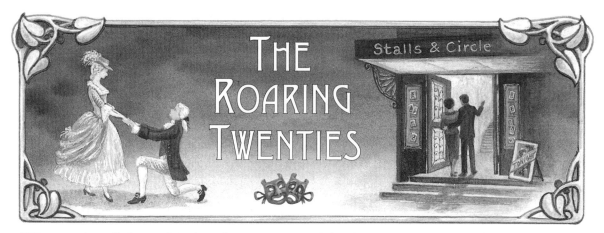

THE ROARING TWENTIES

Despite all the political and economic turmoil, the British public was determined to enjoy itself after the horrors of the 1914-18 War. New syncopated rhythms from America changed the image of the traditional British musical and with new dances now in vogue, The "Roaring Twenties" was aptly named. By the time the Wall Street Crash came in 1929, our popular musical map had been irrevocably altered from strict-tempo to up-tempo.

Three home-grown names came to the fore. Noel Coward was a brilliant composer as well as an actor — likewise Ivor Novello — while the third, Vivian Ellis, had a distinct genius for combining music and lyrics. All three stayed active until well after the Second World War and their careers are covered in separate chapters.

A number of other famous British artistes also came to the fore during the Twenties, including the indomitable husband-and-wife team of Jack Hulbert and Cicely Courtneidge, Gertrude Lawrence, Binnie Hale and Bobby Howes, and the suave and debonair Jack Buchanan who was everyone's epitome of a true English gent, even though he was born in Scotland. Jessie

△ *Florence Mills, the vivacious star of* **Black Birds**, *a 1926 revue staged at the London Pavilion. Sadly, she died young.*

△ *Fred and Adèle Astaire dancing the Oom-pah Trot in* **Stop Flirting** *at the Shaftesbury Theatre in 1923. Ginger Rogers came later.*

△ *Best-remembered for its hit-song "Indian Love Call",* **Rose Marie** *had many other colourful moments, including the "Totem Tom Tom" dance performed here by a swaying chorus of female totem poles.*

△ *This is how the Tiller Girls looked in 1927! The show is* **Lady Luck** *at the Carlton Theatre and the "lucky" man in the picture is Laddie Cliff.*

△ *The crew of "HMS Inscrutable" in full voice during* **Hit the Deck**, *staged at the London Hippodrome, also in 1927.*

Matthews, Beatrice Lillie and Evelyn Laye were all high up in the scholarship class and Anton Dolin's dancing thrilled everyone.

There were many more British stars but the Americans were now very much part of the West End furniture, both on-stage and off it. Brother and sister Fred and Adèle Astaire appeared in London long before Ginger Rogers captured our hearts but it was the appearance of several young American composers who made the biggest impact of all.

The traditional pre-First World War musical was not finished, however, and several more "Girl" shows were produced, including **Little Dutch Girl, The Little Girl in Red, His Girl, The Cabaret Girl, The Girl Friend, The Girl from Cook's, Lucky Girl, That's a Good Girl,** and **The Five O'Clock Girl.**

The only difference now was that several had been written and composed on the other side of the "pond"! George and Ira Gershwin were particularly prolific and had a major hand in **Stop Flirting, The Rainbow, Primrose, Tell Me More, Lady Be Good, Oh, Kay!** and **Funny Face,** and much of their

△ *The Red Shadow (Harry Welchman), woos Margot (Edith Day), in a harem scene from* **The Desert Song** *at Drury Lane in 1927.*

music is still being heard regularly today. Meanwhile, Richard Rodgers and Lorenz Hart were also in full flow and among their productions to successfully transfer across the North Atlantic were **The Girl Friend, Lido Lady, Peggy Ann, Lady Luck, One Dam' Thing After Another** and **A Yankee at the Court of King Arthur.**

Another busy beaver was Oscar Hammerstein II, who wrote the words to several shows including **Sunny** and **Show Boat,** both with music by Jerome Kern, and **The Desert Song** and **The New Moon** in collaboration with Sigmund Romberg. His later partnership with Richard Rodgers came about after the demise of Lorenz Hart. Irving Berlin composed **The Cocoanuts** and another bright young American called Vincent Youmans, had a significant hand in the tuneful music accompanying three shows which made it across the sea to England, namely **No No Nanette, Wildflower** and the naval spectacular **Hit the Deck.**

A most unlikely combination arose when Jerome Kern composed the music to P.G. Wodehouse's **Cabaret Girl** and **Beauty Prize,** while Cole Porter chipped in with **Night Out** (an early collaboration with Melville Gideon), and **Wake Up and Dream**. Further foreign

△ *Composer Rudolf Friml (1879-1972) will forever be associated with his hit-musical* **Rose Marie**, *which was moved from New York to Drury Lane in March, 1925. Its backdrop of Red Indians and Royal Canadian Mounties has remained a popular theme ever since and is still performed by amateur operatic societies.*

△ Richard Dolman and Jessie Matthews sing "My Heart Stood Still" from Richard Rodgers and Lorenz Hart's **One Dam' Thing After Another**. It was staged at the London Pavilion which, like several other famous London theatre names, has since disappeared. Jessie Matthews later starred in "Mrs. Dale's Diary" on BBC radio.

△ Gertrude Lawrence and Harold French together in George Gershwin's **Oh, Kay!** which ran for 214 performances at His Majesty's Theatre.

influence came in Emmerich Kalman's **Gypsy Princess**, while Rudolf Friml captured the public's imagination with his impressive productions of **Rose Marie** and **The Vagabond King**. Another smash hit was Sigmund Romberg's **The Student Prince**.

It must not, however, be assumed that the Americans and Europeans had completely taken over the West End of London, far from it. Several shows were unquestionably true-blue English thoroughbreds, especially those penned by Noel Coward, Ivor Novello and Vivian Ellis but these are covered elsewhere in greater detail because their work was both extensive and hugely influential.

Lesser-known British names of the period included Jack Strachey (1894-1972), whose early collaboration with Rodgers and Hart in **Lady Luck** was followed by much excellent theatrical music. But he will always be better-remembered for his tune *"In Party Mood"* which introduced the long-running BBC radio programme "Housewives Choice". Russian-born but a thoroughly English composer, music publisher and band leader, Herman Darewski (1883-1947), scored dozens of London revues, including **Just Fancy, Oh Julie!, Dover Street to Dixie** and **Saucy Sue**. Another Londoner with a foreign-sounding name, Herman Finck (1872-1939), also wrote several shows and revues, including **Brighter London, Leap Year, Better Days** and **Merely Molly**.

Two more London-born composers and impresarios, Jack Waller (1885-1957) and Joseph Tunbridge (1886-1961), successfully collaborated several times, including **Turned Up, Virginia**, and **Dear Love**, the latter in conjunction with the Yorkshire light-music composer, Haydn Wood (1882-1959). Alfred Reynolds (1884-1969), was another important man of the theatre who, as MD at the Lyric Theatre, Hammersmith, scored **The Duenna** and revived many other shows.

Rather shy Harold Fraser-Simson (1878-1944) followed his hugely successful **Maid of the Mountains** (1916) with **Head Over Heels, Our Nell, The Street Singer**, and **Betty in Mayfair**. Meanwhile, Philip Braham (1882-1934), MD at Wembley Studios in the early days of talkie films, chalked up **Jumble Sale, Battling Butler, Boodle, On With the Dance** and **Up With the Lark**.

A thoroughly English production was **The Co-optimists**, a series of revues initiated by the monocled comedian Davy Burnaby (1881-1949). No fewer than nine different shows were staged between 1921-1935 with most of the music composed and played by Melville Gideon (1884-1933). Many other big names were also involved, including Stanley Holloway, Laddie Cliff and Elsie Randolph. Another successful revue, later repeated during the Thirties, was **Blackbirds**, promoted by the king of pre-war impresarios, C.B. Cochran, more of whom later.

◁ One of the most successful ongoing pre-war revues was **The Co-optimists**, a pierrot-style concert party which ran to nine different editions between 1921-1935. The original cast is shown here at the Royalty Theatre. Up-and-down the trellis, left to right, are Laddie Cliff, Phyllis Monkman, Melville Gideon, Babs Valerie, Stanley Holloway, Davy Burnaby, Elsa Macfarlane, H.B. Hedley, Betty Chester and Gilbert Childs.

such as **The Vagabond King, No No Nanette, The New Moon** and **Hit the Deck** — are unlikely to age much and seem set to continue giving enjoyment and pleasure.

Few of those who take part in today's productions can remember anything about the Twenties, yet the tuneful music still evokes an era when entertainment was relatively simple but hugely successful. Time then was less of a problem than it is now of course, and one cannot help feeling that as the world rushes by at ever-increasing speeds, all those caught up in it are missing something of great value — time to stop and reflect on life itself.

The Roaring Twenties was characterised by glamour, colour and movement. It was part of the heyday of British musicals although many have since dated. Some have stayed the course, however, and are still regularly performed by amateur operatic and dramatic societies.

Set amongst the Mounties and totem poles of rural Canada, **Rose Marie** is a perennial favourite, especially with its famous number, *"Indian Love Call"*; **The Desert Song** still has its sinister character, the Red Shadow, striding around the barren wastes of North Africa; **Show Boat** is based around a 19th century American paddle-steamer; and **The Student Prince** is performed against the backdrop of a thigh-slapping, beer flowing, student-frequented song-singing tavern in the Rhineland. All of these — and other shows

△ In 1926 the London Hippodrome staged **Sunny** by the American trio Otto Harbach, Oscar Hammerstein II and Jerome Kern. From left to right the players are Nancie Lovat, Jack Buchanan, Binnie Hale, Jack Hobbs and Elsie Randolph.

△ Schubert was neglected after his early death in 1828 but was resuscitated in 1922 when **Lilac Time** opened at the Lyric Theatre, later to be revived as **Blossom Time** in 1942. Courtice Pounds is shown here as Schubert with Clara Butterworth as Lili Veit.

△ Three-legged Heather Thatcher and Leslie Henson perform on board ship in **The Beauty Prize** at the Winter Garden in 1923.

△ Phyllis Dare in **The Lady of the Rose**, Daly's Theatre, 1922.

△ Although its composer Victor Jacobi was Hungarian, **Sybil** came to London via America. José Collins was the star of the show.

△ Chorus girls were de rigueur seen here with William Kent in the Gershwin Brothers' **Lady Be Good**, 1926.

THE THEATRICAL THIRTIES

Stalls & Circle

Following the Roaring Twenties came what might aptly be described as the Theatrical Thirties. It was a decade full of false hopes and grim economic reality, but was cleverly disguised by the musical theatre in the form of glamour and optimism which only show business can truly represent. London went on its way regardless of what the rest of the world was up to — at least as far as its theatres were concerned — and attracted all the best artistes from Europe, North America and the Southern Hemisphere.

Dozens of West End shows came and went, some highly successful, others rather less so. The undisputed leading English composers of the period were Vivian Ellis, Ivor Novello and Noel Coward each of whom has a chapter to himself. There were, however, many other characters deserving of serious recognition. Through their talent, professionalism, infectious enthusiasm, words, music and colourful productions they temporarily kept at bay the unpleasant real-ities of world politics and the all-pervading economic depression. Even those less well off, especially in the urban areas of the North, were now able to hear their favourite stars and shows on both radio and 78rpm records.

The Thirties did not exist in isolation, of course, and most of the key players had begun their careers a long time before. One important figure was Paris-born André Charlot (1882-1956), who staged more than 30 shows between 1912 and 1937, after which he moved to Hollywood and devoted the rest of his life to the film industry. Initially the manager of several Parisian theatres, including the Folies Bergères, he crossed the English Channel to become boss of the Alhambra and quickly stamped his mark on the London scene, working with several different theatres and many well-known actors and singers. Among his famous productions were **Keep Smiling** (1913), **Buzz, Buzz** (1918), **A to Z** (1921), **London Calling!** (1923), **Please** (1933), **The Sleeping Beauty**

▷ *Charles Blake Cochran (1872-1951), better-known simply as "CB", was an outstanding impresario and the undisputed king of London revues for three decades. His long theatrical curriculum vitae was unsurpassed. He introduced roller skating to the UK and even found time to manage the Albert Hall. His appropriately titled autobiography, "Cock-a-Doodle-Do" was published in 1941 at the height of the war.*

◁ *André Charlot (1882-1956), an early pioneer of musical revues. Before moving permanently to London, he honed his talents at the Folies Bergères in Paris!*

△ **Rise and Shine** at the Theatre Royal, Drury Lane in 1936 with Syd Walker and Irene Browne enjoying a chat in the semi-fictitious Porchester Hotel. Syd became a fixture in the wartime radio comedy show "Band Waggon" in which he played a dustman who, with government blessing, exhorted the nation to salvage all it could.

△ Musical **Revues** came thick and fast during the Twenties and Thirties. Usually a loosely connected sequence of sketches and songs, they were often used as a vehicle for individual artists to display their talent and for composers to establish and promote popular new tunes. Gitta Alpar (left), Nelson Keys and Binnie Hale are seen here in C.B. Cochran's **Home and Beauty** at the Adelphi Theatre in 1937. **Revues** continued unabated until the Sixties.

SOME MUSICAL STARS OF THE THIRTIES

△ Renée and Billie Houston began their act together by replacing their parents after they became ill.

△ The Carlyle Cousins popped up all over the place but later disappeared without trace.

Tessa Deane

Peggy Cochrane

Diana Churchill

The Two Leslies
(Holmes and Sarony)

△ **Love Laughs!**, a 1935 revue with music written by Noel Gay and played by Billy Mayerl and his band.

and **Shall We Reverse** (both 1935) and **Red, Bright and Blue** (1937).

The undisputed theatrical entrepreneur of the time, however, was Charles Blake Cochran (1872-1951), more affectionately known as "CB" and a veritable giant of London showbiz during the Twenties and Thirties. A larger than life figure, he hailed from Brighton in Sussex and began his career in New York, but by the turn of the 20th century was already established in London where he staged his own revues in the great American tradition. Long lines of high-kicking chorus girls were soon tap dancing and tripping the light fantastic, but he also backed several huge successes involving nearly all the top stage names of the period. Cochran was a name synonymous with success.

Knighted in 1948 for services to the theatre, between 1914 and 1950 he personally supervised no fewer than 128 theatrical productions. In addition he also found time to be manager of the Royal Albert Hall; introduce the British public to both roller skating and the great American escapologist, Houdini; be an active Governor of the Shakespeare Memorial Theatre at Stratford-upon-Avon; stage world championship boxing matches at both the Olympia and Holborn Stadiums; promote the Rodeo at the British Empire Exhibition at Wembley in 1924; be President of the Actors' Benevolent Fund; and in 1950 receive the Legion d'Honneur for services to the French theatre. A truly amazing curriculum vitae.

Down the years, many famous stars emerged from the ranks of "Mr. Cochran's Young Ladies" (as his chorus girls were known) and "CB" must rank right at the forefront of the 20th century British musical theatre. It is impossible to list more than a few of his productions, but memories of the following still live on: **Blackbirds** (1926, 1934, 1936), **This Year of Grace** (1928), **Bitter Sweet** (1929), **Private Lives** (1930), **Nymph Errant** (1933), **Streamline** (1934), **Anything Goes** (1935), **Paganini** (1937) and **Bless the Bride** (1947).

Ralph Reader (1904-1982) is now best-remembered for creating the **Scout Gang Shows** which ran throughout the Thirties and were memorably revived post-war. They had no obvious stars but were skilfully arranged to create a pleasing musical kaleidoscope which the patrons thoroughly enjoyed and have continued to appreciate ever since in amateur Scout productions all over the country. It is unfortunate that their ongoing success has tended to overshadow Reader's talents as a versatile actor, author and producer of other fine shows, especially those of Noel Coward and, so worried was he that the early performances of the **Gang Show** would ruin his West End reputation that he kept his name secret for the first three years of its run. He need not have worried, however, because the official seal of approval came in the form of a Royal Command Performance. Reader never really retired and continued well into his seventies.

Billy Mayerl (1902-1959) was a brilliant pianist with a unique style which he taught via his own musical correspondence school. In addition to his jazz and dance music exploits, he also wrote several musicals including **The Punch Bowl, Nippy, Between Ourselves, Crazy Days, Sporting Love, Over She Goes** and **Runaway Love** which are covered in more detail in a separate chapter.

Ralph Reader presents

NEW SMASH HIT
LIFEBUOY FUN SHOW
FROM LUXEMBOURG
AT SIX O'CLOCK EVERY SUNDAY

The Radio Gang Show!

"I REMEMBER" CORNER

★ ★ ★ ★ ★ ★

BIRDS OF A FEATHER

★ ★ ★ ★ ★ ★

MEXICO

★ ★ ★ ★ ★ ★

GOING HOME

Lifebuoy presents the biggest variety hit for years! The best fun value on the air—every Sunday at six o'clock from Luxembourg! Rollicking choruses, quick-fire jokes and non-stop wit. Compèred by Ralph Reader himself—the brilliant producer who rocketed to new fame with the first Gang Shows. The "plum" numbers from these first smash-hit shows are in the Lifebuoy Radio Gang Show programmes. Don't miss them. Listen in to Lifebuoy every Sunday. Remember it's the original Lifebuoy Soap—on the air for the first time!

We're in it too Mr. Reader!

LIFEBUOY SOAP FOR HEALTH

LUXEMBOURG – SUNDAY from 6 to 6·30. Wavelength 1293 **LIFEBUOY CALLING ALL LISTENERS!**

152-109

A *LEVER* PRODUCT

△ *Ralph Reader's Boy Scout* **Gang Show** *became so popular that in 1938 it appeared on Radio Luxembourg sponsored by Lifebuoy Soap. Reader was a clever but serious writer and was so concerned about his image that he refused to put his name to the show for the first few years. Only when it became taken seriously did he emerge to take any of the credit but he lived long enough to see it become a nationwide tradition, in fact it became a national institution.*

31

△ Perhaps the finest ever British song-writing partnership was that of Michael Carr (playing the piano) and Jimmy Kennedy. Authors of several joint hits, they also wrote many famous songs on their own

△ Davy Burnaby (left) will forever be associated with **The Co-optimists**; while J.H. Squire (right), in addition to running his Celeste Octet was also musical director of six different rival West End theatres — all at the same time!

Continuing a highly successful partnership which began in the Twenties, the two London-born composers and lyricists Jack Waller (1885-1957) and Joseph Tunbridge (1886-1961) progressed from strength to strength during the Thirties. Among their many joint productions were **Silver Wings, For the Love of Mike, Tell Her the Truth, He Wanted Adventure, Mr Whittington, Yes Madam, Please Teacher, Certainly Sir, Big Business** and **Bobby Get Your Gun**. "Bobby" was Bobby Howes assisted by Diana Churchill, while other stars of the multifarious shows included Tessa Deane, Binnie Hale, Harry Welchman, Wylie Watson, Lupino Lane, Syd Walker, Arthur Riscoe, Jack Buchanan, the Carlyle Cousins, Elsie Randolph, Fred Emney and Roma Beaumont.

Guy Bolton (1884-1979) was an extraordinary long-lived and prolific librettist who first trained as an architect, then went to America before teaming up with the humorous author P.G. Wodehouse. Together they wrote a number of witty scripts which were turned into hit musicals including **Oh, Joy!** (1919, music by Jerome Kern), and **Oh, Kay!** (1927, music by George Gershwin). During the Thirties he also collaborated with the composers Martin Broones (1892-1971) in **Give Me a Ring** and **Swingalong**; Vivian Ellis (1904-1996) in **Going Places, Hide and Seek, The Fleet's Lit Up** and **Running Riot**; Al Hoffman (1902-1960) in **Going Greek**; and Eric Maschwitz (1901-1969) and

George Posford (1906-1976) in **Magyar Melody**. Both the latter composers remained active until well after the war and, like their contemporary Richard Addinsell (1904-1977), will be mentioned again later.

Other major foreign offerings in the Thirties included **A Yankee at the Court of King Arthur; Heads Up; Ever Green** and **On Your Toes** (all by Rodgers and Hart); **Music in the Air** and **Three Sisters** (Kern and Hammerstein); **Anything Goes** (Cole Porter); and **Land of Smiles** (Franz Lehar).

Rise and Shine was an unusual joint offering from Americans Fred Astaire (1899-1987) and Vincent Youmans (1898-1946) but also from the Austrian, Robert Stolz (1880-1975). Astaire became a dancing legend during his own lifetime while Youmans was responsible for the music of **No, No, Nanette** (*"Tea for Two"* and *"I Want To Be Happy"*), **Hit the Deck**, and **The One Girl**.

Stolz was initially a conductor closely associated with both Franz Lehar and Richard Tauber, but he also scored several popular musicals of his own, including **The Blue Train, Wild Violets**, and the ever-popular **White Horse Inn** (1931), the latter in conjunction with the Czech composer Ralph Benatzky (1884-1957).

Other big names of the Thirties included the prolific writers Noel Gay (1898-1954), Michael Carr (1904-1968) and Jimmy Kennedy (1902-1984), each of whom contributed to several musicals including **O-Kay for Sound, London Rhapsody** and **The Little**

△ The "Silver Ballet" from **Rise and Shine**, a 1936 American-inspired Drury Lane spectacular which failed to live up to expectations. Its hit song was the appropriately titled "I'm building up to an awful let down"! Although the composers were none other than Fred Astaire, Robert Stolz, Vincent Youmans, Johnny Mercer and Buddy de Sylva the show closed after only 44 performances. The management of this huge theatre moved quickly to stave off bankruptcy and beat a path back to the door of Ivor Novello who effectively saved the day. His **Glamorous Night, Careless Rapture, Crest of the Wave, The Dancing Years, Perchance to Dream** and **King's Rhapsody** were all successful.

Dog Laughed, (all Palladium productions for the Crazy Gang of Flanagan & Allen, Nervo & Knox, and Naughton & Gold). All three are much better-remembered for their songs, however, among the more memorable being Gay's *"Run Rabbit Run"*, *"The King's Horses"*, *"Leaning on a Lamp Post"*, and *"Hey Little Hen"*, Kennedy's *"Red Sails in the Sunset"*, *"Isle of Capri"*, and *"Teddy Bears' Picnic"*, and Carr's *"Dinner for One, Please James"*. Carr and Kennedy jointly penned many classics including *"Ole Faithful"*, *"Why Did She Fall For the Leader of the Band?"*, *"South of the Border"* and the patriotic wartime number *"We're Gonna Hang Out the Washing on the Siegfried Line"* — made famous for posterity by Flanagan and Allen, both singers and song embodying the indomitable British spirit when the country stood alone against Hitler.

Nat Ayer (1887-1952) emigrated to England from America in 1911 and never looked back, scoring among others **The Bing Boys are Here, Houp-La!, The Bing Girls are There, Stop . . . Go!** and **Somewhere in England**. Clifford Grey (1887-1941) wrote the lyrics for many of Ayer's shows but also worked with Vivian Ellis, Rudolf Friml, Youmans, Gay, Kern, Waller and Tunbridge.

Walter Leigh (1905-1942) was a fine musician who was sadly killed in action at Tobruk during the North African Desert campaign. His legacy of the Thirties includes the ironically titled **Pride of the Regiment** and the splendid **Jolly Roger** which starred an ageing George Robey. Had he lived then, Leigh would undoubtedly have added to his other successful West End revues.

In many ways his death signalled the end of an era. Although wartime brought out the best of the British bulldog tradition the home-grown theatre survived only in a much altered form. By 1945 American influence in Europe was at its height and the Oxford-accented British shows of the Thirties suddenly seemed rather tame by comparison. Instead of being allowed to fade away gracefully, however, they were rapidly catapulted into history but — happily for us all — a few musicals (or musical plays as they were referred to then), survived against all the odds and still give great pleasure today when enthusiastically staged by amateurs up and down the country.

THE SECOND WORLD WAR

When Neville Chamberlain suddenly announced the closing of all London theatres and cinemas at the start of the Second World War, he threw thousands of people out of work. Many, like actor and songwriter Hubert Gregg, decided to enlist to earn a crust. Needless to say, when they discovered that the troublesome edict had been quickly rescinded they were highly miffed — because it was then too late to escape their over-hastily acceptance of the King's Shilling.

It was not all gloom, however, because show business carried on and Hubert still found time to write songs and later made major contributions to the shows **Strike a New Note**, **Sweet and Low** and **Strike It Again**. Meanwhile, others who had been less quick to join up, took full advantage of the reopening of London's West End.

Vivian Ellis, Noel Coward, Harry Parr Davies and Ivor Novello are dealt with in separate chapters but there were many other busy British writers and composers during the war. Oxford-born Richard Addinsell (1904-1977) began his career in revues with André Charlot during the Twenties and continued writing both film and show music well into the Sixties, latterly in conjunction with Joyce Grenfell.

Reginald Armitage (1898-1954) was a classically trained organist at the Chapel Royal, St. James, but cleverly changed his name to Noel Gay after spotting a theatre poster advertising Noel Coward and Maisie Gay! He continued his overwhelming success of the Thirties with the music for several wartime revues, including **Lights Up**, **Present Arms** (both with lyrics by Frank Eyton), **Gangway** (with Harry Parr-Davies)

△ Jack Hylton

△ Richard Addinsell

△ Noel Gay

△ Sonnie Hale

FOUR IMPORTANT WARTIME MUSICAL FIGURES

In 1940, Jack Hylton (1892-1965), changed from band leader to theatrical entrepreneur; composer Richard Addinsell (1904-1977), was extremely busy; song writer Noel Gay (1898-1954), wrote the lyrics to several London musicals; and Sonnie Hale (1902-1959), starred in a number of wartime revues.

RADIO PICTORIAL, December 23, 1938. No. 258
Registered at the G.P.O. as a Newspaper

LUXEMBOURG
NORMANDY: LYONS
PARIS : EIREANN
PROGRAMMES
Dec. 25—Dec. 31

CASH
PRIZES
for
LISTENERS
NO ENTRANCE FEE
See Page 37

RADIO PICTORIAL
THE MAGAZINE FOR EVERY LISTENER

3D.

EVERY
FRIDAY

★
S. P. B. MAIS
TALKS
ABOUT
TALKS

CHRISTMAS IN THE
HEART OF BRITAIN
London's Seasonal Cele-
brations to be Broadcast

SECRETS OF A
SCRIPT WRITER

COMEDY
CHRISTMAS
Humorous Article by
Three Famous Comedians

ALL THE WEEK'S
RADIO NEWS,
GOSSIP, HUMOUR
AND PICTURES

GREETINGS FROM
YOUR FAVOURITE STARS

B.B.C.
PROGRAMME
GUIDE

Bebe DANIELS
AND
Ben LYON

Of all the foreign show business stars who performed in Britain during the Second World War, none were as popular as Bebe Daniels and Ben Lyon, who foresook their hugely successful Hollywood careers for battle-scarred London. They eventually settled here and adopted son Richard to complement their daughter Barbara. Together with Vic Oliver (who loved to describe himself as "The Old Vic"), they starred in the live radio comedy show **Hi Gang!** *which had to be moved forward because of the threat of night-time air raids. Also on the show were Jay Wilbur, Sam Browne and the Greene Sisters. This picture dates from Christmas 1938 but* Radio Pictorial *disappeared with the war.*

35

△ *After war broke out, the Theatre Royal, Drury Lane, was commandeered by ENSA and Ivor Novello's* **The Dancing Years** *had to close. Between 1942-4, however, it played 969 times at the Adelphi on the Strand — pictured here during the mid-Eighties.*

Susie, **Meet Me Victoria**, and **La-di-da-di-da** (the latter two with words by Lupino Lane, 1892-1959), and **The Love Racket** in conjunction with Hubert Gregg who was by now broadcasting to the German Forces in their native language!

Music also played an important part in BBC propaganda programmes. **Road to Victory** was planned as a radio show, so it could be heard by more people than could ever be crammed into a single theatre. It required a special production unit together with the closest co-operation with wartime Ministries and all three of the Armed Services. By the time the first episode was broadcast on 21st June, 1940, however, it

had been renamed **Marching On** and included Stephen Potter reporting on Italy and Laurence Gilliam on Dunkirk. The BBC then requisitioned the Monseigneur Restaurant Club, whose main auditorium was below ground level and therefore ideal for recording purposes. The regular production, which was heard right across the country, featured Laidman Browne, Philip Wade, James McKechnie and other members of the BBC Repertory Company. The music was composed by Walter Goehr and each programme began with a rousing theme tune over which the announcer declared:

> "On the Home Front, on the Battle Fronts, behind the frontiers of our enemies, the cause of freedom is ... **Marching On!**"

Despite inevitable bomb damage and the complete destruction of four theatres in 1941 — Kingsway, Gate, Little, and the original Shaftesbury — live London musicals did indeed go marching on, although many were revivals of earlier popular shows including **Rose Marie**, **Chu Chin Chow**, **The Merry Widow**, **White Horse Inn**, **Show Boat**, **The Belle of New York**, **Maid of the Mountains** and **The Desert Song**. As alluded to earlier, most new productions were topical revues but this did not detract from either their vitality or importance at a very difficult time.

△ *Graham Payn and Patricia Burke singing "This Can't Be Love" from* **Up and Doing** *(1940). Other cast members included Binnie Hale, Leslie Henson and Stanley Holloway.*

In October, 1940, a large bomb crashed through the roof of the Theatre Royal, Drury Lane, and exploded among the stalls. The heavy metal nose-cap went even further and came to rest among the night staff asleep in the basement. The explosion did considerable damage and subsequent incendiary devices started a blaze. Determined volunteers, however, managed to extinguish it before any major fire took hold. Remarkably, all those who were in the theatre at the time survived unscathed and are shown here shortly afterwards with their unique trophy of war. Many more incendiaries were later dealt with and the building successfully repaired on each occasion for continued use by **ENSA (Entertainments National Service Association)**.

Max Miller

Four Fine Revue Artistes

Bobby Howes

Hermione Gingold

Jack Buchanan

Other major wartime contributions came notably from George Posford (1906-1976), Eric Maschwitz (1901-1969), Jack Strachey (1894-1972), Billy Mayerl (1902-1959), Douglas Byng (1893-1987) and two Americans, Manning Sherwin (1902-1974) and Phil Charig (1902-1960). The already established partnership of Rodgers and Hart chipped in with words and music for **Up and Doing** and **Funny Side Up**, and Cole Porter exported **Let's Face It**, **Dubarry Was a Lady**, **Panama Hattie** and **Something for the Boys**.

Richard Tauber — by now a naturalised Englishman — teamed up with the Australian, George Clutsam, for yet another Schubert reincarnation in the form of **Blossom Time** and then put on his own show, **Old Chelsea**, which numbered a young Charles Hawtrey among its star cast. Meantime, also in 1943, Irving Berlin headed a touring production called **This is the Army**, staged initially at the Palladium in aid of Service charities. A year later, fellow American, Frank Loesser, presented **Skirts**, which was performed by the US forces at the Cambridge Theatre.

It was obvious by now that the military tide had turned and that the war was entering its final stages. Many American stars therefore took the opportunity to come over and add their considerable clout to the already existing musical fun.

Bing Crosby was already a legend on both sides of the Atlantic, but when a star-struck radio engineer pre-rigged the microphone at the constantly-changing BBC musical for service personnel called **Stage Door Canteen** at the Piccadilly Theatre, he was met with "Hey laddie. I'm not seven feet tall you know!" In reality Bing was little more than 5ft tall, but when the speechless youngster simply stared at his hero, he continued: "Is everything OK?" The 17-year-old eventually managed to say how much he admired the singer's colourful tie, at which point, with typical American generosity it was removed and handed over to the grateful lad, Trevor Hill, who later became a well-known BBC writer and producer.

Another home-grown talent was Alan Melville (1910-1983), an extremely witty writer who was to make a name in broadcasting and television. His wartime revues included **Rise Above It**, **Scoop**, **Sky High**, **Sweet and Low**, **Sweeter and Lower** and, just after the war, **Sweetest and Lowest**. Both the latter productions cleared 800 performances. As much as any wartime show was tuneful or amusing, however, it was the individual personalities which really drove them along. Everyone had their favourites and many became household names.

The **Hi-Gang!** trio of Ben Lyon, Bebe Daniels and Vic Oliver were not English nationals (although Vic married Winston Churchill's daughter, Sarah) but they made their home here and put their heart and soul into the British cause right from the outset. Other outstanding theatrical professionals included Arthur Askey, Richard Hearne, Fred Emney, Leslie Henson, Mary Ellis, Bobby Howes, Jack Buchanan, Jack Hulbert, Cicely Courtneidge and Tommy Trinder.

Behind the scenes a successor to C.B.

△ *An American all-military revue,* **This is the Army** *arrived in England during November, 1943, and began its tour at the London Palladium. The only non-Services actor taking part was its writer and producer, Irving Berlin (1888-1989), seen here sixth from the right. The three hit songs of the show were "This is the Army, Mr. Jones", "My British buddy" and a repeat of the First World War triumph "Oh, how I hate to get up in the morning". Born in Siberia, Russia, Irving Berlin had an extraordinarily long and successful career. Still active in his eighth decade this adopted American icon of show business died in New York, four months after his 100th birthday!*

Cochran was emerging in the shape of former band leader turned entrepreneur, Jack Hylton. From 1940 onwards he busily beavered away creating what the public desperately craved for in those dark days of conflict — escapism from the grim reality of a war which had sucked in all five continents. His best-remembered productions are probably the repeated madcap antics of the Crazy Gang who excelled initially at the Palladium and later at the Victoria Palace. Their slapstick and practical joke style of humour had been comprehensively established during the Thirties and everyone loved the unpredictable nature of their shows which were ideal for raising morale. With Bud Flanagan usually in the lead, the gang was never short of a trick and commonly scaled ladders into private boxes or marched through the audience dispensing comic colour at the expense of anyone who was unfortunate enough to get in the way. They were just the same off-stage. Meanwhile, at the Prince of Wales, Harry Korris, Robbie Vincent and Cecil Frederick, ("We three!") played Mr. Lovejoy, Enoch and Ramsbottom, in the fictitious **Happidrome** theatre.

It is to the very great credit of the theatre-going British public that musicals kept going at all between 1939-1945. It is not possible to list all the people who trod the wartime theatrical boards — not even those who appeared just in the Metropolis — but other significant favourites included Jessie Matthews, Roma Beaumont, Zena Dare, Sybil Thorndike, Beatrice Lillie, Florence Desmond, Elisabeth Welch, Frances Day, Pat Kirkwood, Sonnie and Binnie Hale, Peter Graves, Arthur Riscoe, Stanley Lupino, Anne Ziegler, Webster Booth, Hermione Gingold, Leslie Hutchinson (Hutch), Max Wall, Elsie Randolph, Doris Hare, James Hayter, Evelyn Laye, Patricia Burke, Noele Gordon, Claude Hulbert, Hermione Baddeley, Wylie Watson, Evelyn Dall, Ronald Shiner, Jerry Desmonde, Sid Field and Stanley Holloway.

Many of these stars also toured abroad with **ENSA** and the Army equivalent, **Stars in Battledress** so, come the end of hostilities, they might have been forgiven for expecting a more comfortable niche back home but it was not to be.

First, Clement Attlee surprisingly ousted Churchill as Prime Minister in 1945, and then perhaps the biggest wartime stars of them all, George Formby and Gracie Fields, suddenly found themselves out in the cold. The traditional British musical — seemingly well-entrenched and economically viable — was also in for a big shake-up.

POST-WAR

War was over and the Yanks were here in large numbers, both in uniform and in "civvy street". Change was inevitable and between 1945 and 1950 there was a remarkable juxtaposition of new shows from across the Atlantic running alongside traditional home-grown British musicals. It was an uneasy alliance.

Ivor Novello had big hits with both **Perchance to Dream** at the Hippodrome and **King's Rhapsody** at the Palace, while Vivian Ellis filled the Adelphi with **Bless the Bride**. Noel Coward had rather less success but still remained an influential figure in the London theatre.

Other exciting British talent also flowered at this time, including lyricists Frank Eyton, Harold Purcell, Robert Nesbitt, Joyce Grenfell, Eric Maschwitz, Alan Melville, Max Kester, A.P. Herbert, Douglas Byng, James Dyrenforth and Douglas Furber. Putting their words to music were Noel Gay, Jack Strachey, Kenneth Leslie-Smith, George Posford, Eve Lynd, Richard Addinsell, Charles Zwar and Harry Parr-Davies.

Foreign composers Hans May and Manning Sherwin also made notable contributions working with British writers, while the Crazy Gang, led by cheeky and irrepressible Bud Flanagan, combined their outrageous antics

△ Henry Kendall and Hermione Gingold in **Sweetest and Lowest** (1947), the last in a successful trilogy of revues by Charles Zwar and Alan Melville, which ran for 791 performances at the Ambassadors. Theatre.

△ Silvia Ashmole and Denis Martin in **Oranges and Lemons**, a 1948 revue at the Lyric Theatre, Hammersmith. Richard Addinsell, Joyce Grenfell, Michael Flanders, Donald Swann and Sandy Wilson also took part.

△**Oklahoma!** *arrived at Drury Lane in April 1947, immediately after one of the worst winters in living memory. Its colourful impact was massive and did much to dispel the drab gloom of post-war austerity. Handsome Howard Keel played opposite Betty Jane Watson and they are seen here together with the rest of the cast, plus the famous "Surrey With the Fringe On Top".*

more than 1,500 times in the revue **Together Again** at the Victoria Palace. Also making their first appearances in musical form were three young men who were destined to flourish during the following decade — Michael Flanders, Donald Swann and Sandy Wilson.

During the war years there had been several musical collages plus repeats of popular shows from earlier years. Included in these was yet another revival of Schubert in **Blossom Time**, while in 1945 came **Gay Rosalinda**. Based on the music of Johann Strauss, one of its main participants was the world-famous tenor — but now a fully-naturalised British citizen — Richard Tauber. A year later **Song of Norway** provided a successful synopsis of the life and music of Edvard Grieg and ran for 526 performances at the Palace Theatre.

Clearly there was still enough room for nostalgia and traditional music but it was the new shows imported from America which really set the tone of the post-war era. An expectant public was ready and eager for something new.

First off the mark was Phil Charig's **Follow the Girls** which opened at His Majesty's Theatre in October, 1945. With arch-comedian Arthur Askey taking the lead, ably supported by Evelyn Dall (an impressive American singer who made a big impact over here during the Thirties as "The Blonde Bombshell"), the show ran for a remarkable 572 performances.

But the best was yet to come and in 1947 it arrived in double-spectacular fashion. First, **Oklahoma!** exploded on to the scene at Drury Lane where it succeeded Noel Coward's disappointing **Pacific 1860**. At the time the country was emerging from the worst winter in living memory, with rationing, fuel shortages, austerity biting hard and the government insisting that theatres should not be heated! The contrast could not have been greater and the song *"Oh, What a Beautiful Morning"* sparked off a show full of

41

sunshine and vigour. London was never the same again.

Howard Keel led the British version of this tour de force put together by Richard Rodgers and his new partner Oscar Hammerstein II — Lorenz Hart having died prematurely in 1943. The hit songs were, and still are, extremely popular, with the show continuing to run successfully all over the country in amateur productions. Among the other well-known numbers are *"The Farmer and the Cowman"; "People Will Say We're in Love"; "I Can't Say No"; "Surrey With the Fringe on Top"; "Out of my Dreams"* and the show-stopper, *"Oklahoma!"*.

Set in the American Mid-West during the heyday of 19th-century colonisation of virgin territory for cattle ranching, the colourful cowboys and their equally colourful young ladies danced and sang their way round the wide-open spaces with great aplomb. It is hard to appreciate today just how drab the immediate post-war period had become, with khaki still a predominant colour in the landscape. If the dramatic final seconds of the show still send a shiver down your spine, then imagine what it must have been like for those experiencing the sensation for the very first time in 1947. **Oklahoma!** (with an exclamation mark) was exactly right and still is.

△ *Irving Berlin's* **Annie Get Your Gun** *ran for more than 1,300 performances at the Coliseum. Dolores Gray played Annie Oakley with Bill Johnson as Frank Butler.*

Hard on its heels came another 19th-century American western called **Annie Get Your Gun**. Loosely based on the exploits of legendary gun-slinging Annie Oakley, the Broadway version starred the foghorn voice of Ethel Merman but transferred naturally to London's West End with Dolores Gray in the title role at the Coliseum. Famous songs included *"You Can't Get a Man With a Gun"; "The Girl That I Marry"; "Anything You Can Do, I Can Do Better"; "Doin' What Comes Natur'lly"* and *"There's No Business Like Show Business"*. The composer was, of course, Irving Berlin.

The other big American success of the late-Forties was Alan Jay Lerner and Frederick Loewe's Scottish fantasy, **Brigadoon**, which took root at His Majesty's Theatre in 1949. It was based on romantic love and a Scottish village which appears out of the mist every 100 years. With Bruce Trent in the lead, it charmed its way to 685 performances.

◁ *Cicely Courtneidge and Thorley Walters in* **Under the Counter**, *a successful 1945 production at the Phoenix Theatre. It was produced by Cicely's husband and long-term acting partner, Jack Hulbert.*

△ *It is easy to see why* **Annie Get Your Gun** *was so popular with post-war British audiences. Despite arriving at almost exactly the same time as* **Oklahoma!***, the two shows ran successfully in tandem and together notched up almost 3,000 performances.*

In between the extended runs of **Oklahoma!** (1,543 performances) and **Annie Get Your Gun** (1,304) came a somewhat surprising failure. **Finian's Rainbow** had done well on Broadway but a leprechaun seeking a crock of gold at the end of a rainbow somehow did not appeal to the English. However — and this is the interesting point — it was later successfully revived and has since become staple fare for amateur operatic societies. The critics and public somehow misjudged the original.

Apart from Ivor Novello, Vivian Ellis and the Crazy Gang, there were four other major British shows which enjoyed long runs during this period. The first was **Under the Counter** which took off in 1945, based mainly around established and seasoned professional Cicely Courtneidge (later replaced by Florence Desmond). Produced by Cicely's husband, Jack Hulbert, it also included a young Irene Handl. After 665 performances at the Phoenix, it was taken to Broadway but turned out to be a case of "Coals to Newcastle" and flopped. Undeterred, indefatigable Cicely took it to Australia instead.

A year later came Dick Hurran and Phil Park's **Piccadilly Hayride** which ran for 778 performances at the Prince of Wales. It was a foil for the talents of comedian Sid Field and his stooge Jerry Desmonde, ably abetted by upper-class twit, Terry-Thomas. Ironically, it was Desmonde who went on to become a major television and film star while Fields, at the time a national comic institution, died young and is now largely a forgotten figure.

1947 also saw Eric Maschwitz and George Melachrino's **Starlight Roof** staged at the London Hippodrome. Prominent among the cast was a young Julie Andrews, holding her own with stalwart comedians Vic Oliver and Fred Emney, together with Pat Kirkwood. A run of 649 was highly commendable although all that is remembered from the show today is Melachrino's beautiful *"Starlight Roof Waltz"*.

The fourth long run was Hans May and Eric Maschwitz's 1948 **Carissima**. The critics

43

△ Lerner and Loewe's **Brigadoon** was set in the wilds of a Scottish glen where a mysterious village appears once a century. With 685 appearances at His Majesty's Theatre, alongside **Oklahoma!** and **Annie Get Your Gun** it completed a trio of post-war American hits.

Shows and Revues of
RICHARD ADDINSELL

Charlot Show of 1926	1926
RSVP	1926
Jumbles	1927
Adam's Opera	1928
Good Companions	1931
Come of Age	1933
Moonlight is Silver	1934
Happy Hypocrite	1936
Taming of the Shrew	1937
Alice in Wonderland &	
Through the Looking Glass	1943
Trespass	1947
Ring Round the Moon	1950
Penny Plain	1951
Airs on a Shoestring	1953
Joyce Grenfell Requests the Pleasure	
of Your Company	1954
Living for Pleasure	1958
Re:Joyce	1988

Addinsell also wrote the the music for many films including "Dangerous Moonlight", Goodbye Mr. Chips" and "Tom Brown's Schooldays".

did not like it but the public did, as testified by 488 performances at the Palace. Specially imported from grand opera were Lester Ferguson and Elisabeth Theilmann who, engaged in romantic and operatic entanglements, flitted back and forth between Venice and New York before finally tying the lover's knot. It was a good show but is rarely heard today.

Other productions of note included **Big Ben, Sweetheart Mine, Bob's Your Uncle, Cage Me a Peacock, Her Excellency, Here Come the Boys, High Button Shoes, The Kid From Stratford, Belinda Fair** and **Tough at the Top**. Successful revues included **Folies Bergère** (881 performances), **Sweetest and Lowest** (791), **The Night and the Music** (686), **Fine Feathers** (578), **High Time** (570), **Latin Quarter** (455), **For Crying Out Loud, Sauce Tartare, À La Carte, Oranges and Lemons, One Two Three, Four Five Six,** and **Tuppence Coloured**.

Within the short space of just five years, post-war Broadway had come to London ... seen it ... and comprehensively

△ After the huge success of **Bless the Bride** (1947), Vivian Ellis had a hard act to follow. Although **Tough at the Top** (1949) starred Brian Reece (soon to be everyone's favourite radio hero as the eponymous P.C. 49), it never quite caught on and contrasting this picture with **Annie Get Your Gun** probably explains why. Reece is seen (second right) as Count Victor of Plusch in what can only be described as a very middle-class English late-Victorian scene. The show was also poignant in that it proved to be the West End swan-song of probably the greatest ever British theatrical entrepreneur, C.B. Cochran, known to everyone as "CB" or "Cocky".

conquered the West End. A new era had arrived. **Oklahoma!**, **Annie Get Your Gun** and **Brigadoon** were the extravagant precursors of a new style of show which had many more tricks to teach us. Even greater musicals would soon visit these shores.

SELECTIONS OF POST-WAR SHOWS

1945
Fine Feathers *(Parr Davies)*
Follow the Girls *(Charig)*
Gay Rosalinda *(Strauss)*
Perchance to Dream *(Novello)*
Sigh No More *(Noel Coward)*
The Night and the Music *(Nesbitt)*
Under the Counter *(Purcell/Sherwin)*

1946
Big Ben *(Herbert/Ellis)*
Here Come the Boys *(Kester/Purcell/Sherwin)*
High Time *(Nesbitt)*
Pacific 1860 *(Noel Coward)*
Piccadilly Hayride *(Hurran/Park)*
Song of Norway *(Grieg)*
Sweetest & Lowest *(Melville)*
Sweetheart Mine *(Lane/Eyton/Gay)*

1947
Annie Get Your Gun *(Irving Berlin)*
Bless the Bride *(Herbert/Ellis)*
Oklahoma! *(Rodgers/Hammerstein)*
Starlight Roof *(Maschwitz/Melachrino)*
Together Again *(Crazy Gang)*

1948
Bob's Your Uncle *(Eyton/Gay)*
Cage Me a Peacock *(Lynd/Leslie/Langley)*
Carissima *(Maschwitz/May)*
High Button Shoes *(Styne/Cahn)*
The Kid from Stratford *(Sherwin)*

1949
Brigadoon *(Lerner/Loewe)*
Folies Bergère *(Hurran/Derval)*
Her Excellency *(Sherwin/Parr Davies)*
King's Rhapsody *(Novello)*
Latin Quarter *(Nesbitt)*
Sauce Tartare *(Parsons/Fase)*
Tough at the Top *(Herbert/Ellis)*

IVOR NOVELLO

Although Ivor Novello was not quite as prolific a writer as Noel Coward or Vivian Ellis, he nevertheless exerted just as much influence on the London stage. He also made several films and was something of a heart-throb during the days of silent movies. Ivor abruptly ended his film career in 1934, however, to concentrate — extremely successfully — on full-time musicals.

David Ivor Davies was born in Cardiff in 1893. Encouraged by his father and mother, the latter a full-time music teacher, he often visited London where he lapped up everything associated with the theatre.

His early tuition in Wales was followed by the award of a scholarship to Magdalen College School in Oxford, where he was given a free education in return for singing in the prestigious choir. An outstanding soloist, he continued performing until his voice broke at the age of 16, an event which reduced him to tears. His initial thought was that he would never be able to sing professionally again — and he was right!

He soon began composing songs, however, and as early as 1914 wrote the classic wartime ballad *"Keep the Home Fires Burning"*, a tune which netted him huge royalties and provided insurance

◁ Ivor Novello in 1894 with his proud parents, David and Clara Novello Davies. He later adopted his mother's maiden name. The music publishing firm of Novello, however, was not connected to him.

▷ By the age of four, Ivor was already looking self-assured and after winning a choral scholarship to Magdalen College School, Oxford, he maintained his fine treble voice until he was 16. This was not unusual for the times but after it broke he was never able to sing professionally again.

△ *The first Drury Lane theatre was burnt down in 1672. The second (illustrated left and reputedly built by Sir Christopher Wren) was demolished in 1791 because it was regarded as too small.*

△ *The Theatre Royal, Drury Lane, as it appears to day (right). Without the help of Ivor Novello, however, then it would almost certainly have closed its doors during the Thirties when the economic depression was at its height.*

◁ *The 1809 fire (seen here from Westminster Bridge), cost the third theatre's famous owner, playwright Richard Brinsley Sheridan, almost half a million pounds!*

▽ *Three of the shows which ensured the survival of Drury Lane:* **Glamorous Night** *(1935);* **Careless Rapture** *(1936); and* **The Dancing Years** *(1939). The war forced the closure of the theatre but the latter show later returned to the Adelphi for another long run.*

△**Careless Rapture** *(1936) followed hard on the heels of* **Glamorous Night**. *It was an equally lavish and lush production and broke new ground with a massive earthquake scene. This show was then itself succeeded in 1937 by* **Crest of the Wave**. *Ivor Novello was then at his peak and his leading ladies of the time included Mary Ellis, Roma Beaumont, and Dorothy Dickson. This all-white finale was known as "The Bridge of the Lovers".*

against any future failures. A patriotic and nostalgic success it was a welcome boost for an aspiring young musician and he never looked back.

By the end of hostilities he had contributed to five different London revues, an extraordinary feat for one so young and inexperienced. His theatrical reputation was caused partly by his failure to become a pilot, because instead of chasing German air aces around the skies he ended up with a desk job, thus allowing him more time to compose. In between silent movies he produced more and more music, including the lion's share of **Who's Hooper?** (1919) with Howard Talbot, and **A Southern Maid** (1920) with Harold Fraser-Simson, both highly-respected establishment figures.

In October 1921 Ivor had two London musicals running at the same time. While Jack Buchanan was starring in André Charlot's revue **A to Z** at the Prince of Wales, resident comedian W.H. Berry was pulling in the crowds at the Adelphi with **The Golden Moth**. Both shows enjoyed great success and the dashing young composer could do no wrong. But he was still inextricably bound up with filming and also his personal stage career which, following the demise of his fine boy soprano voice, had been reduced to acting without singing, a fact he never really came to terms with.

Films and plays kept him fully occupied for the next ten years and it was not until 1935 that he produced another full-length musical. During the interim, however, he still found time to compose for both **Puppets** (another André Charlot revue from 1924) and the 1929 aptly-named joint Jack Hulbert and Cicely Courtneidge romp, **The House That Jack Built**.

In 1934 Ivor's final film, "Autumn Crocus", signalled the start of a brilliant new era and the late-Thirties saw him at his peak. The four musicals he staged at Drury Lane were not only a landmark in British musical theatre but also saved the Theatre Royal from financial catastrophe. **Glamorous Night**

△*Ivor Novello and Mary Ellis (1897-2003) in* **The Dancing Years** *(1939). Mary settled over here from America and became a celebrated centenarian in London's Belgravia, dying at the age of 105.*

△**Crest of the Wave** *used many clever scenic effects including this ghostly ensemble singing the patriotic song "Rose of England" which is, perhaps surprisingly, the only song which is now remembered from the show.*

(1935), **Careless Rapture** (1936), **Crest of the Wave** (1937) and **The Dancing Years** (1939) were perfect for both time and place.

Ivor was given carte blanche to do as he liked by the theatre management because they knew that only he could rescue this most historic of venues from being turned into a cinema. Aided by his youthful librettist, Christopher Hassall, plus many other loyal artistes, some of whom were poorly paid because of the high cost of extravagant sets, the turnaround was completed within four years.

Members of the public who could still afford it, regularly dressed up for the theatre with smart gentlemen in dinner jackets (or even white tie and tails), accompanied by jewelled ladies in evening gowns. **Glamorous Night** was an apt title and included Ivor playing opposite the recently-domiciled big American star, Mary Ellis, with Trefor Jones and Olive Gilbert in support.

Although the show was a sell-out, behind the scenes the Theatre Royal had craftily failed to put all its eggs into this one Novellian theatrical basket and hedged its bets by secretly booking a Christmas pantomime. **Glamorous Night** would certainly have made everyone's fortune in London but after 243 performances it was forced to move out and tour the provinces instead. Understandably, Ivor was not amused!

△*American actress Dorothy Dickson starred in* **Careless Rapture** *and* **Crest of the Wave**. *Like Mary Ellis, she loved England and settled down in London.*

49

△ *It is easy to see why Ivor Novello had so many admirers. Seen here as Sir Graham Rodney in* **Perchance to Dream** *(1945), he still set hearts throbbing even in middle age.*

A year later in 1936, **Careless Rapture**, co-starring Dorothy Dickson and Zena Dare, switched from the make-believe world of Ruritania to more contemporary times. Although the singing was left to others, this did not stop Novello from humming along to his own tunes while playing the piano, much to the annoyance of the orchestra.

In 1937, based on a train crash and featuring a naval backdrop with spectacular scenery and sound effects, **Crest of the Wave** completed a notable hat-trick. It did not make quite the impact of its predecessors, however, and the patriotic song *"Rose of England"* is all that is remembered today. Sung by the ghosts of mediaeval knights, it remains a timeless offering, perfectly summarising our country's great heritage.

By now it was all too obvious what was happening in Europe, and in 1939 **The Dancing Years** was Ivor Novello's controversial musical attempt to portray his loathing of politics and what it was doing to the arts.

Mary Ellis returned to play opposite Ivor's downtrodden young Austrian Jewish composer but the show was forced out of the theatre when ENSA moved in at the outbreak of war. Following a provincial tour, however, in 1942 it returned in triumph to the Adelphi, where it ran for a further 969 performances. Revived in 1947 and 1968, it was also turned into a film in 1950, staged as an ice show in the Empire Pool at Wembley in 1954, and made into a television programme in 1981.

But not everyone liked Ivor Novello, and during the war he was sent to prison for allegedly misusing petrol coupons. He had certainly broken the law, but entirely through his own naivety and misplaced trust in a third party who turned out to have bogus credentials. Four weeks in Wormwood Scrubs was a harsh sentence and had a profound effect on him, but not, it seems, on his adoring public. On release, instead of travelling in his Rolls-Royce to **The Dancing Years**, he decided to walk instead. Although understandably nervous he was quickly spotted by passers-by, all of whom gave him the thumbs-up. When he arrived on stage he received a rapturous ovation.

For another of his wartime musicals, **Arc de Triomphe** (1943), he successfully tempted Mary Ellis away from her self-imposed nursing duties in Scotland and based the whole show around her. It ran for 222 performances at the Phoenix Theatre but, some-

London shows and revues involving the words & music of **IVOR NOVELLO**	
The Bing Boys Are Here	1916
See-Saw	1916
Theodore & Co.	1916
Arlette	1917
Tabs	1918
Who's Hooper?	1919
A Southern Maid	1920
A to Z	1921
The Golden Moth	1921
Puppets	1924
The House That Jack Built	1929
Glamorous Night	1935
Careless Rapture	1936
Crest of the Wave	1937
The Dancing Years	1939
Arc de Triomphe	1943
Perchance to Dream	1945
King's Rhapsody	1949
Gay's the Word	1951

what surprisingly, was regarded by many as a failure. When measured against **The Dancing Years** and his next show, maybe it was, but everything is relative and most producers would have been delighted to own it.

By now the war was coming to an end which was perfect timing for **Perchance to Dream** which opened at the London Hippodrome in April 1945. Set in a large country house, it told the story of continued love through three generations, with its show-stopper *"We'll Gather Lilacs"* causing moist eyes each night. Roma Beaumont was again in the cast, and so too was the delightfully eccentric Margaret Rutherford.

It was a fine and typically English production in both mode and fashion — especially the charming Regency period — but the alarm bells of changing times, witnessed by **Oklahoma** and other new American musicals, were beginning to ring loudly. They fell on deaf Novellian ears, however, and the new foreign interlopers were deliberately ignored.

Ivor was resolutely determined to go one better and, quite remarkably, he did! **King's Rhapsody** was arguably his best show ever, with Vanessa Lee bringing the house down each night with *"Some Day My Heart Will Awake"*. Other stars included stalwarts Zena and Phyllis Dare. It opened at the Palace Theatre and ran to great acclaim, notwithstanding the close attention of its American rivals which were also doing rather well.

Meanwhile, Ivor found time to write **Gay's the Word** for fellow trouper Cicely Courtneidge which opened at the Palace Theatre, Manchester, before going on tour. When it reached London's Saville Theatre in February 1951, the Press responded by asking "How long can Ivor Novello go on turning out successful new hit songs?" Sadly, their question was to be answered all too soon.

On 5th March, 1951, back in his flat after yet another successful performance of **King's Rhapsody**, Ivor suddenly found himself too weak to uncork his favourite champagne. As usual, he made a joke out of infirmity and tried to knock the neck off the bottle on a table. Unfortunately, it shattered all over the floor and impresario Tom Arnold, who had overseen many of his friend's shows, was forced to open another one.

Following a light meal, Ivor retired early to bed but became increasingly unwell and a doctor was hurriedly called.

△ The composer's last great musical was **King's Rhapsody**, in which he introduced Vanessa Lee as his leading lady. Sadly, he died just a few hours after a performance of the show in March 1951, aged 58.

Long-standing friend and supporter, Olive Gilbert — who played in more Novello musicals than anyone apart from Ivor himself — was also summoned from her downstairs flat. It was clear the situation was serious and even Ivor himself realised the end was near. With a final sigh, he died from a coronary thrombosis, aged just 58. **King's Rhapsody** soldiered on in his wake until 6th October, when it too expired after an outstanding run of 881 performances.

The nation was shocked but — like his popular contemporary fellow composers, Vivian Ellis and Noel Coward — Ivor Novello's memory lives on in musical form. Together they will go down as the undisputed top trio of 20th-century British musical theatre.

MARY ELLIS

This remarkable lady, who died in January 2003, aged 105, enjoyed an amazing career which encompassed almost the whole of the 20th century.

Born in New York to European immigrant parents, her original surname was "Elsas" but even that had been hastily adopted by a Spanish ancestor living near the River Rhine in the volatile borderland of Alsace and Lorraine during the Franco-Prussian War. She became Mary Ellis at the end of the First World War when she was offered a contract by the Metropolitan Opera House who insisted that her name should sound less German! By then, however, she was already an accomplished artiste with great experience.

Her mother was keen on the arts and with her father making a great deal of money in the timber industry, it had been possible for her to take part in regular educational visits to mainland Europe where she soaked up the atmosphere. She had a narrow squeak when stranded in Paris at the outbreak of war in 1914, however, only escaping via a cattle train to Marseilles and a crowded boat back home across the Atlantic to New York. She was very fortunate!

Nevertheless, a bout of laryngitis shortly before her audition at the "Met" very nearly ruined everything, but fortunately she recovered just in time and enjoyed a relatively brief but extremely colourful operatic career, performing with all the top singers, composers and conductors of the time. She could have become a great operatic star but her destiny lay elsewhere.

Mary Ellis appeared several times at the Theatre Royal, Drury Lane, notably with Ivor Novello. Its chequered and regal history has no parallel and this illustration shows the third building which was opened in 1794, housing no fewer than 3,600 people. Supposedly fire-proof, it burned down in 1809, leaving the theatre manager, Richard Brinsley Sheridan, out of pocket to the tune of nearly £500,000, a simply astronomical sum in those days. He watched the conflagration from a nearby tavern saying: "Leave me, 'tis a pity a man cannot take a glass of wine by his own fireside!"

After three years she moved into straight theatre from which she was head-hunted by Rudolf Friml and Oscar Hammerstein to play the title role in their 1924 musical, **Rose Marie**. It was the beginning of a new career but when she asked to leave the show after her voice became severely strained, Hammerstein persuaded her to sign a contract agreeing never to perform in musicals for anyone else. It meant she never sang in the USA again, although she acted in various plays and regularly met up with George Gershwin, Fred and Adele Astaire, Yascha Heifetz and Harpo Marx.

During the Thirties she moved to London and took out British citizenship in 1946. Meanwhile she played in C.B. Cochran's **Music in the Air** (1933), and both Ivor Novello's **Glamorous Night** (1935) and **The Dancing Years** (1939). She also appeared in the films "Paris Love Song" and "All the King's Horses".

Wartime saw her determined to help out on the welfare front rather than with ENSA,

who wanted her to go on tour. After sterling voluntary service in the Hebrides, she completed a valuable stint at a hospital in the Scottish borders near Peebles.

She then returned to the London stage and starred in **Arc de Triomphe** (1943) at a time when bombs and rockets were falling all around. After hostilities ceased she performed in several successful stage plays, notably *The Browning Version*, *The Man in the Raincoat*, *Coriolanus* and *Mourning Becomes Electra*. She also memorably starred with Vanessa Lee in Noel Coward's **After the Ball** (1954).

Unlucky in love more than once, Mary Ellis bounced back many times from adversity and at the end of her first volume of autobiography, *Those Dancing Years* (1982), explained how reluctant she was to finish it — because she always felt there was something else around the corner! She did finish a second volume called *Moments of Truth* (1986) and stayed active till the last in her flat at Eaton Square in Belgravia.

NOEL COWARD

W as there anyone more English than Noel Coward? Playwright, producer, composer, film star, actor, singer, "The Master" was them all.

History will remember him visually as the fiercely patriotic captain of the ill-fated destroyer *HMS Torrin* in the epic 1942 wartime film **In Which We Serve** (which he also co-directed), and as the mastermind behind **The Italian Job**, a 1969 movie thriller about a daring robbery involving Austin-Morris mini

△ *Noel pictured in the wartime film* **In Which We Serve**.

cars leaping high across the roofs of Rome. But he really ought to be remembered more for his major part in the evolution of the 20th-century British stage over which he exerted a profound influence.

Although this chapter concentrates on Noel Coward's musicals it must also be remembered that he wrote a ballet, **London Morning** (1959), and several plays, all typifying the era in which they were set. Knighted in 1970, he was indeed a thespian in shining armour.

△ *The young Noel Coward, aged 8.*

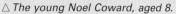

▷ *Noel Coward and Gertrude Lawrence first met as teenagers at the Italia Conti Stage School in London and remained firm friends for life. They are seen here together in the musical play* **Private Lives** *(1930).*

△ *24-year-old Noel Coward and chorus singing "Other Girls" from his first revue,* **London Calling** *(1923).*

Born of keen amateur operatic singers at Teddington, Middlesex, in 1899, young Noel received no formal musical education but his interest in rhythm was soon evident. At a very early age he took umbrage at being restrained from dancing in the church aisle to the sound of the organ but after he enrolled as a teenager at the Italia Conti Stage School he was finally able to indulge his passion for acting and singing. He also met a girl six months older who became his favourite leading lady — Gertrude Lawrence.

Having cut his professional teeth in the provinces, in 1916 he appeared in Robert Courtneidge's West End musical **The Light Blues** but, despite everyone's high hopes, it closed after only 20 performances. Noel was not dismayed, however, and soon bounced back, even having the temerity to try his luck in New York. In conjunction with Philip "Pa" Braham, in 1923 he wrote **London Calling** and the following year penned much of the material for what turned out to be the first of seven revues for the impresario, André

△ *Romney Brent, as Rev. Inigo Banks, sings* "Mad Dogs and Englishmen" *from the 1932 revue* **Words and Music** *staged at the Adelphi Theatre. Noel Coward's own recording of the song is still popular.*

△ **On With the Dance** was a Noel Coward revue sponsored by C.B. Cochran, in 1925 and caused the London Pavilion to feel important and confident enough to describe itself as "the centre of the world". Coward allegedly said "Oh, Cocky. I've just seen my name in lights." Like many other theatres, however, the London Pavilion eventually closed its doors.

Charlot. His name was now in lights and would remain so for the next 50 years.

In 1925 **On With the Dance** opened at the London Pavilion starring Alice Delysia, yet strange to relate, the hit song *"Poor Little Rich Girl"* was nearly removed by its financial backer, C.B. Cochran, only fierce remonstration by Alice and Noel saving the day. Coward's next revue, **This Year of Grace,** (which included the songs *"Dance Little Lady"* and *"A Room With a View"*) opened four years later, also at the Pavilion, a building still visible today behind Eros's outstretched bow in Leicester Square but alas no longer a theatre. In his autobiography Noel pointed out how he was able to watch the first 45 minutes before rushing off to appear in **The Second Man** at the Playhouse Theatre on the nearby Embankment. One night he even persuaded the other three members of the play, Ursula Jeans, Raymond Massey and Zena Dare, to race through the final act in double-quick time so they could all dash back across Trafalgar Square and watch the finale at the Pavilion!

Bitter Sweet opened in 1929 at His Majesty's Theatre but the hit song *"I'll See You Again"* was rather inappropriate because the show had been written specially for Gertrude Lawrence who was contracted elsewhere and therefore unable to appear. She and Noel did get together again in **Private Lives** the following year, however.

The inspiration for **Bitter Sweet** had come during a return trip from America aboard the large Cunard liner *Berengaria* when, against their wishes, Coward and C.B. Cochran were forced to share a cabin because of severe overcrowding. Fortunately, neither of them snored and when Coward revealed his idea for the show Cochran immediately backed it! He was a shrewd judge because it ran for nearly 700 performances at the Palace Theatre.

Private Lives was a play with music which ran for a fixed run of only three months at the new Phoenix Theatre. Sold out during the first week, it now seems rather dated but the song *"Someday I'll Find You"* has managed to withstand the test of time.

Cavalcade (1931) utilised the large Drury Lane stage to great effect, although the first night was delayed because the weight of the chorus prevented the raising of a stage lift. This memorable anti-war pageant covered the first three decades of the 20th century, including the relief of Mafeking, the funeral of Queen Victoria and a spectacular sinking of the *Titanic*.

Words and Music (1932) contained one of Coward's best songs, *"Mad Dogs and Englishmen"* while two years later **Conversation Piece** was set in Regency Brighton. Both enjoyed respectable runs.

▷ *Graham Payn singing "Matelot" from the 1945 revue* **Sigh No More**. *Originally from South Africa, Payn came to this country during the Thirties and enjoyed a distinguished career as a boy soprano, or "treble" as it was called in those days. Over 50 years later he presented a bronze statue of his mentor to the Theatre Royal, Drury Lane.*

△**Words and Music** *contained a sketch called* Children's Hour *featuring Steffy Duna (left), Doris Hare and John Mills as Lilli, Jane and Bobbi, singing the song "Let's Live Dangerously".*

Tonight at 8.30 (1936) consisted of nine separate plays, three of which were musicals with *"Has Anybody Seen Our Ship?"* being the one song to last the course. **Operette** was a modest success in 1938 before war put a stop to any new plans. By now, however, Noel Coward was a huge international celebrity and ranked alongside the best of British on both Broadway and the West End.

His war effort was greatly valued but even his reputation and the film **In Which We Serve** — where he based his role as sea captain on his friend Lord Mountbatten — could not save his post-war efforts from relative obscurity. **Sigh No More** (1945) sent up the last remnants of the British Raj while **Pacific 1860** (1946) was a huge disappointment, with American actress, Mary Martin, miscast in the main role. To add insult to injury it was chosen to reopen London's greatest musical theatre, Drury Lane, which had been renovated after bomb damage. It ran for only 129 performances, far fewer than expected.

In 1950, like many of his plays and musicals, **Ace of Clubs** was first tried out in the provinces at Manchester's Palace Theatre before moving to the Cambridge in London. Set in a contemporary Soho nightclub it starred Pat Kirkwood and Coward's young protégé, Graham Payn. Later musicals included the **Lyric Revue** (1951), **Globe Revue** (1952) and **After the Ball** (1954), the latter based on Oscar Wilde's play Lady Windermere's Fan.

Eight years later **Sail Away**, starring Elaine Stritch, docked at the Savoy via New York, and although not deemed a success by its critics, ran for a highly creditable 252 performances. The **Girl Who Came to Supper** (1963), the Mermaid revue **Cowardy Custard** (1972) and finally the posthumous **Noel and Gertie** (1986), written by Robert Morley's elder son, Sheridan, rang down the musical curtain on an extraordinary person who had enjoyed many brilliant successes but also survived numerous failures and the multitudinous slings and arrows of constant change.

Noel Coward's personal accounts of his life were eventually put together as an autobiography containing many fascinating anecdotes. He died in Jamaica in 1973 and it is a great pity he never completed the full story in print. What he left behind on stage and screen, however, leaves us in no doubt as to his creative talent and genius. In 1998 a bronze statue of him was unveiled in the foyer of the Theatre Royal, Drury Lane, by the Queen Mother.

NOEL COWARD SHOWS

London Calling	**1923**
Charlot's Revues	**(1924-1937)**
On With the Dance	**1925**
This Year of Grace	**1928**
Bitter Sweet	**1929**
Private Lives	**1930**
Cavalcade	**1931**
Cochran's Revue	**1931**
Words & Music	**1932**
Conversation Piece	**1934**
Tonight at 8.30	**1936**
Operette	**1938**
Sigh No More	**1945**
Pacific 1860	**1946**
Ace of Clubs	**1950**
Lyric Revue	**1951**
Globe Revue	**1952**
After the Ball	**1954**
Sail Away	**1962**
The Girl Who Came to Supper	**1963**
High Spirits	**1964**
Mr. & Mrs.	**1968**
Cowardy Custard	**1972**
Noel & Gertie	**1986**

GERTRUDE LAWRENCE

I n 1968 a film was released entitled simply — **Star!** It was an entirely appropriate appellation because it featured Julie Andrews acting the title role of probably the most successful English woman ever to appear on Broadway — Gertrude Lawrence.

She was born Gertrud (minus the "e") Alexandra Dagmar Lawrence Klasen on 4th July, 1898, near the Oval cricket ground in south London. Her father was a Danish musical hall singer and her mother, Alice Louise Banks, was a part-time actress. But they divorced while little Gertrud was only two and her formative years were spent with her mother and second husband in a series of moonlight flits avoiding irate landlords chasing their unpaid rent. Her education at the Sacred Heart Convent, Streatham, suffered and she later ran away to live with her father.

The hopeful young actress made her first stage appearance as a juvenile ballet dancer in the pantomime **Babes in the Wood** at Brixton in 1910. After joining Italia Conti's theatrical school she met a young Noel Coward and an even smaller boy from Sussex called Patrick Healey-Kay, later to become the famous dancer Anton Dolin. At the age of only 14 she travelled by train with Noel to Liverpool, where they appeared as a pair of angels in a local production.

In his memoirs he noted that she wore a black satin coat matched by a black velvet military hat, and carried a handbag from which she frequently powdered her nose.

She also insisted on being called "Gert" and, smitten by her natural charm, thereafter became his most popular leading lady

Touring was a vital part of her apprenticeship but not always successful. On one occasion, in order to pay her board and lodgings, she ended up working as a barmaid at the Red Lion hotel in Shrewsbury — because the theatre manager had run off with the company's takings! Nevertheless, her professionalism continued to shine through and, with her original Cockney accent supplanted but still bubbling underneath the surface, she never looked back.

While still in her late teens she was invited to appear in London's West End where she understudied both Beatrice Lillie and Phyllis Dare. But her name was made when she played opposite Jack Buchanan in André Charlot's 1921 revue **A to Z**, following which she was forever in demand both at home and abroad. Despite the fact that transatlantic journeys took several days, she alternated between England and America for the rest of her life, being fêted each time she stepped aboard one of the giant ocean liners crossing between Southampton and New York.

Among her many memorable performances of the Twenties were Noel Coward's **London Calling** (1923), and the title role in **Oh, Kay** (1926). By now acknowledged as an equally brilliant and versatile dancer, singer and straight actress, Gertrude Lawrence had emerged as a super-star.

△ *Gertrude Lawrence and Noel Coward's lifelong friendship began when they met as children at the Italia Conti stage school in London. They toured together as teenagers and became lifelong friends..*

In 1929 Noel Coward wrote the musical **Bitter Sweet** specially for her but contractual obligations unfortunately prevented her from performing in it. In 1930, however, they came together in **Private Lives** which also featured Laurence Olivier. The very epitome of upper-middle class romance, after 101 performances at the newly opened Phoenix Theatre in Charing Cross Road, London, it transferred to the Times Square, New York. The world was now Gertrude's oyster.

Among her Thirties smash hits were Evangeline in **Knight Errant** and a cameo of roles in Noel Coward's touring success **Tonight at 7.30**. Consisting of nine one-act plays (three per night), after the Provinces it ended up in the West End, again at the Phoenix. One critic penned her performances with the words: "She has extraordinary variety of expression and the supreme gift of the artist in comedy, that of thinking with her features so that you know exactly the significance of every sentence."

Wartime found her in America where she discovered happiness by marrying Richard Aldrich — an earlier teenage wedding to Francis Gordon-Howley having resulted in a daughter but also a divorce. She twice starred in the Kurt Weill musical **Lady in the Dark** before returning to Europe in 1944 to entertain the troops in Britain, Belgium and France. As President of the American equivalent of ENSA, in 1945 she also toured the Pacific theatre of conflict and appeared in Hawaii as Elvira in Noel Coward's **Blithe Spirit**. Back in New York, after hostilities ceased she played Eliza Dolittle in George Bernard Shaw's play **Pygmalion** and then took it successfully on tour throughout the United States and Canada.

Popular wherever she went, Gertrude Lawrence was equally active outside the theatre. A keen gardener and swimmer, she also found time to be Director of the British Actors' Orphanage and, in 1945, published her memoirs in *A Star Danced*. Her undoubted elegance and charisma, however, were best described in Noel Coward's two books *Present Indicative* (1937) and *Future Indefinite* (1954) but, by the time of the latter's publication, tragedy had already overtaken her.

Performing across a time-span of five decades she appeared in more than a dozen films but it was live theatre where she was at her happiest and most beguiling. Her effect on audiences was spell-binding and she played to packed houses wherever she went. The final chapter of her glittering career, however, came suddenly and prematurely.

While playing the title role of Anna in **The King and I** in New York, she collapsed and died on 6th September, 1952. Aged only 54, she had lost a private battle against cancer and the whole world of show business was shocked by her demise. When she was laid to rest, all the lights of New York's Broadway and London's West End theatres were dimmed for three minutes in her memory. It was an appropriate tribute to a great international star taken well before her time.

△ *Phyllis Dare (1890-1975), younger sister of Zena, was a top star whom Gertrude Lawrence understudied during the Twenties.*

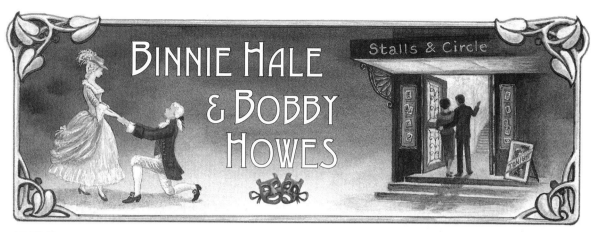

BINNIE HALE & BOBBY HOWES

There were many famous stage partnerships between the wars, but few bigger than Binnie Hale and Bobby Howes who were universally acclaimed for their lively personalities and sparkling performances. Although always closely linked, however, they actually appeared jointly in only three main theatrical productions, but so great was their charm that many people assumed they had always been together.

Born at Liverpool in May 1899, Binnie's real name was Beatrice Mary Hale-Monro. She first emerged as a 16-year-old chorus girl in a London production of **Follow the Crowd** but, not wishing to be compared with her father, Robert Hale, who was a star of the show, she briefly changed her name to May Binnie. Despite the 70 steps up to her dressing room on the top floor and 14 costume changes, she decided that the theatre was to be the life for her. Several more acting roles followed until, in 1925, she established her reputation as a solo artiste in **No, No, Nanette** famous for its hit songs *"Tea For Two"* and *"I Want to be Happy"*. In 1926 she appeared with Jack Buchanan, Claude Hulbert and Elsie Randolph in **Sunny**, the romantic story of a female English circus performer.

Bobby Howes was born at Battersea, in August 1895 and began his career at the local Palace Theatre. Often playing the part of an upper-class numskull, complete with an affected accent, he took part in many musicals, including the 1927 London production of **The Blue Train** ("I say chaps, anyone for tennis?"). Other shows included **The Punch Bowl**, **Vaudeville Vanities** and **The Yellow Mask**. Married to Patricia Malone, he had two children, Peter and Sally Ann. By the end of the Twenties, like Binnie Hale, he was a star.

In 1929, a young composer called Vivian Ellis wrote the music for a new London show called **Mr. Cinders**, which became the perfect vehicle for their combined talents. Bobbie played the title role, the masculine equivalent of Cinderella, and Binnie his sweetheart. Opening at the Adelphi Theatre in February, it ran for 528 performances. Their rendering of the hit song *"Spread a Little Happiness"* has remained a firm favourite ever since. In 1930 the show was staged in Berlin under the title **Jim und Jill** and, in 1934,

was turned into a film starring the Western Brothers.

Binnie, who was married to Jack Raine, recorded two well-known songs in the Thirties, *"Dancing in the Dark"* and *"As Time Goes By"*, the latter melody eventually becoming an integral part of the classic Humphrey Bogart and Ingrid Bergman wartime film, "Casablanca". In 1932 Binnie teamed up with her father in the stage show **Bow Bells** in which she sang *"You're Blasé"* and, in 1935, starred with Eric Portman and Gordon Harker in the film "Hyde Park Corner". In 1937 she sang *"A Nice Cup of Tea"* in C.B. Cochran's review **Home and Beauty**, a hurriedly conceived title after Edward VIII's sudden Abdication rendered the originally planned grandiose **Coronation Revue** totally obsolete!

During the war she entertained the troops in **Flying Colours** and also in **Up and Doing**, featuring Noel Coward's famous song *"London Pride"*. In addition she sang *"Room 504"* and *"It's a Lovely Day Tomorrow"*, the latter being a world première tribute to Britain from Irving Berlin. On the radio she co-starred with her famous brother Sonnie Hale in the cleverly named production "All Hale", in which they played the part of all the characters. The programme ran for three series and so good were their impersonations that many people remained blissfully unaware they were not actually listening to the real "guests" in person.

Following the success of **Mr. Cinders** the career of Bobby Howes also went from strength to strength. A keen golfer and motorist, he appeared in several more London shows before the war, including **For the Love of Mike** featuring the songs *"Got a Date with an Angel"* and *"Who Do You Love?"*, **Hide and Seek**, including *"She's My Lovely"*; and **All Clear** with Fred Emney, and Beatrice Lillie which was optimistically staged in December 1939!

△ **Mr. Cinders** *(1929) was Cinderella in reverse. Binnie Hale played the rich man's daughter who, dressed as a maid, falls for the manservant. All ends happily with her singing "I'm a one-man girl who's looking for a one-girl man". Needless to say Bobby Howes responds with vice versa!*

It may seem surprising that the public linked the two stars so closely together until one remembers they both appeared in the 1934 London Hippodrome production of **Yes Madam?** Coming five years after **Mr. Cinders** it was just the right timing to keep their alliance intact. No doubt they would have got together again if war had not intervened but it was a further 14 years before they joined forces for the third and final time, at the Duke of York's Theatre in the 1948 revue **Four, Five, Six**, which immediately followed Binnie's 1947 success in **One, Two, Three**.

Thereafter, Binnie, by now a grandmother, made several appearances as a straight actress before her death in 1984. Bobby, meanwhile teamed up with his vivacious daughter, Sally Ann Howes, in the 1953 stage production of **Paint Your Wagon**, with the song *"Wand'rin Star"*, later famously rendered by Lee Marvin's husky voice in the 1969 film version. Latterly, Bobby appeared on television and also in the Broadway production of **Finian's Rainbow**. He died in 1972, aged 76.

VIVIAN ELLIS

Stalls & Circle

Almost everybody has enjoyed the music of Vivian Ellis who created more than 60 English stage musicals and was behind many of the popular songs which thrilled listeners before and after the last war. Close your eyes and think back to the exciting tune that introduced the BBC Radio "Paul Temple" murder mysteries.

Can you remember the title? It was Vivian Ellis's *"Coronation Scot"* named after the famous express train and inspired by the clickety-clack of the rails as the composer made regular trips from his home up to London. But it was only a small part of his musical repertoire, indeed his well-known song *"Spread a Little Happiness"* even made the pop charts in a recent recording, more than 60 years after it was first heard.

Born at Hampstead, London, in 1903, Vivian Ellis was educated at Cheltenham College and initially trained as a classical pianist under Dame Myra Hess. But before he was out of his teens he contributed to a 1922 London revue called **The Curate's Egg** and so much enjoyed the experience that from henceforth he was completely hooked on the stage, his subsequent career comparing more than favourably with anybody else in the profession. All told he featured prominently in nearly 70 West End shows in 36 years — almost two a year and with World War Two putting things on hold in the middle!

While still only 25 he produced a smash hit musical which established him at the forefront of popular composers. **Mr. Cinders**

▷ *Bobby Howes and Binnie Hale in a scene from* **Mr. Cinders** *in 1929. The show was a great success with some fine numbers, in particular the songs "On the Amazon"; "Every little moment" and, best of all, "Spread a little happiness" which has since become a standard.*

▷ *Julian Wylie was originally producer at the London Hippodrome but fell from grace and* **Mr. Cinders** *went instead to the Adelphi. However, he later returned from exile to lead it to more than 500 performances.*

SOME FAMOUS STARS WHO APPEARED IN VIVIAN ELLIS MUSICALS

| Elsie Randolph | Florence Desmond | Hermione Baddeley | Beatrice Lillie | Anna Neagle |

was a modern Cinderella with the roles reversed and brought together a partnership which is still remembered with affection. The songs *"Spread a Little Happiness"*, *"I'm a One Man Girl"*, and the brilliantly witty *"On the Amazon"* were performed by Binnie Hale and Bobby Howes, the two main stars of a show which ran for 528 performances at the Adelphi Theatre.

The brains behind the production was Julian Wylie who, after touring successfully with it in the provinces, hoped to persuade his former home, the London Hippodrome, to stage it in the West End. They refused and he was forced to sell it to a company who asked someone else to direct it instead. Wylie was both outraged and embittered but the tables suddenly turned when J.A. Malone's alterations failed to impress the public and he was invited back. Malone responded with the classic phrase "Over my dead body" — and promptly expired! Wylie's magic did the rest and the show became a classic.

△ *In 1938 the Gaiety Theatre staged Vivian Ellis's* **Running Riot**. *This scene shows three classic clowns of comedy — Richard Hearne (in the back), Leslie Henson (driving) and Fred Emney, all being booked by village constable John E. Coyle. The second-hand Austin car in the show cost the producers only £2 to buy. Richard Hearne later became famous as Mr. Pastry, a hugely popular children's entertainer of the Fifties, who always came to grief and ended up in a tangle. Thanks to his professional circus background, he did all his own stunts and continued performing well into old age.*

During the Thirties, there was nearly always at least one Ellis production running somewhere in the West End and their popularity can be gauged by the leading stars who performed in them — Jack and Claude Hulbert, Hermione Baddeley, Cicely Courtneidge, Richard Murdoch, Anna Neagle, Jack Buchanan, Florence Desmond, Elsie Randolph, Beatrice Lillie, Naunton Wayne, John Mills, Patricia Burke, Ralph Reader, and a great many more.

In addition, Ellis's musical directors included Ray Noble, Lew Stone, Carroll Gibbons and Geraldo, with all the other top band leaders of the period recording his entertaining music at every opportunity. Not even Noel Coward or Ivor Novello could match that!

Four of the shows from this time were scripted by the prolific librettist Guy Bolton (1884-1979) but probably the most famous productions were **Running Riot** (207 performances at the Gaiety Theatre), **Jill Darling** (242 at the Saville), and **Under Your Hat** (512 at the Palace).

War then intervened during which Ellis served as a Lt.-Commander in the RNVR. Happily, he emerged relatively unscathed and in 1946 staged **Big Ben**. But by now British musicals were beginning to change from the cut-glass Oxford accent of the Thirties and were moving inexorably towards the imported American showbiz creations epitomised by **Annie Get Your Gun** and **Oklahoma** both of which coincided in 1947 with what was arguably Ellis's greatest ever success.

Bless the Bride was a full-blown British musical in the best traditions and is still a great favourite with amateur dramatic societies. The original production paired the French film star Georges Guétary opposite Lizbeth Webb, and the immortal songs *"Ma Belle Marguerite"* and *"This Is My Lovely Day"* became immediate hits. Other members of the cast included Brian Reece (soon to become famous as BBC Radio's "PC 49"), Anona Winn and Betty Paul. The librettist was the redoubtable A.P. Herbert (1890-1971), parliamentarian, novelist and editor of *Punch* with whom Ellis also collaborated on **Streamline**, **Big Ben**, **Tough at the Top** (1949) and **The Water Gypsies** (1954). This latter delightful production took place at the Prince's Theatre and was

Shows and Revues of VIVIAN ELLIS

1922	The Curate's Egg
	Radios
	Crystals
1923	Mirrors
1924	Little Revue
	The Punch Bowl
	Yoicks!
1925	Records
	Notions
	Headlights
	Designs
	Mercenary Mary
	Still Dancing
	By the Way
1926	Just a Kiss
	The Street Show
	The Glad News
	Kid Boots
	Merely Molly
	My Son John
	Palladium Pleasures
	The Other Girl
	Cochran's Revue
1927	Blue Skies
	Clowns in Clover
	The Grass Widow
	The Call of the Legion
	The Girl Friend
1928	Will o' the Whispers
	Peg o' Mine
	Charlot's Revue
	Vogues and Vanities
1929	Yankee at King Arthur's Court
	The House that Jack Built
	Mr. Cinders
1930	Follow a Star
	Cochran's Revue
	Little Tommy Tucker
1931	Blue Roses
	Folly to be Wise
	The Song of the Drum
	Stand Up and Sing
1932	Out of the Bottle
	Over the Page
1933	Please
1934	Jill Darling
	Streamline
1936	Going Places
	The Town Talks
1937	Floodlight
	Hide and Seek
1938	The Fleet's Lit Up
	Running Riot
	Under Your Hat
1943	It's Foolish but It's Fun
1945	Henson's Gaieties
	Fine Feathers
1946	Big Ben
1947	Bless the Bride
1949	Tough at the Top
1951	And so to Bed
1953	Over the Moon
1955	The Water Gypsies
	Listen to the Wind
1958	Half in Earnest

△ *Composer, Vivian Ellis (left), librettist, A.P. Herbert (at the piano), and theatrical entrepreneur, C.B. Cochran, trying out a melody from the 1946 production of* **Big Ben**, *a parliamentary satire written by Herbert who at the time was an Independent MP. Carol Lynne (right) was the star of the show.*

set in the contemporary new reign of Elizabeth II. It starred Dora Bryan, Roy Godfrey, Pamela Charles, Peter Graves and Doris Hare but, like so many other musicals down the years, never quite achieved the success which it initially promised or deserved.

From the Sixties onwards, Ellis faded a little from the public eye but remained a prolific composer and in later years became great friends with a man who was perhaps his natural successor. Like Ellis, whose grandmother was the composer Julia Woolf, Andrew Lloyd-Webber came from proven classical music stock, his composer father, William, having been Director of the London College of Music. Lloyd-Webber was a person whom Ellis acknowledged as a similar master of tuneful melody which the public enjoyed and one wonders how much of his success during the last quarter of the 20th century was down to the influence of the older man?

A confirmed bachelor, Ellis lived much of his life with sister Hermione near Minehead in Somerset, where he particularly enjoyed gardening. He was nevertheless well-travelled and during the Thirties worked with George Gershwin in Hollywood when he claimed to have been the first person to hear the Variations on *"I Got Rhythm"*. He also wrote an interesting account of his experiences there which he cleverly titled "Ellis in Wonderland".

A grateful Performing Rights Society, of which he was a dedicated President, established an annual Vivian Ellis Prize for stage musical writers. His acerbic but amusing wit endeared him to all and in addition to his vast musical output he also wrote a number of humorous books. His only sadness was that his songs tended to be more associated with their original performers than with him — but then that is true of nearly all the established standard repertoire.

Vivian Ellis died on 19th June 1996, a true blue-blooded Englishman who left behind much for which we should be thankful, not just songs but also a substantial amount of light music. His epitaph is perhaps best summed up by actress Ruth Madoc who described him as "A gentleman who wrote some of the most beautiful tunes in the whole of British theatre history."

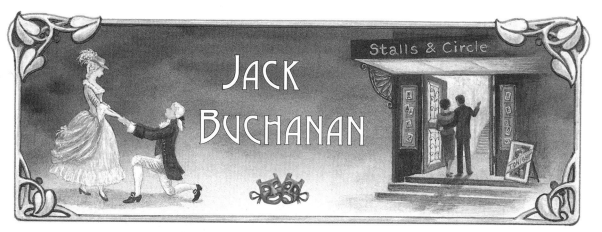

JACK BUCHANAN

Although a Scot, Jack Buchanan was the epitome of a genuine English gentleman. Often described as being "elegant", "suave", "smooth" and "debonair", he had many parallels with the popular American dancing star, Fred Astaire.

Born at Helensburgh, near Glasgow, in April 1890, Walter John Buchanan always wanted to act and, after a brief spell as an auctioneer and a comedian, came south to London as understudy to the revue artist Vernon Watson. Better-known as "Nosmo King", Watson vowed he would eventually have his name up in lights in every theatre — hence "No Smoking" with the letters cunningly rearranged!

When the Great War broke out Jack was rejected for active service, ill health dogging much of his career but it proved a stepping stone to success. Before long he was acting with Ivor Novello and George Grossmith Jr. and when Jack Hulbert was called up, Buchanan replaced him in the revue **Bubbly** at the Comedy Theatre. Before the war was over he had also appeared in **Round the Map** at the Alhambra, then returned to the Comedy in **Tails Up**.

"Tails" was an appropriate word, because the seemingly casual, well-bred and courtly young man was hence always to be associated with a white tie, top hat and tails. In reality, he never lost his Scottish business acumen but his professional performance, both on and offstage, was never less than first class. His leading ladies always spoke very highly of him. By 1920, his talent and reputation made him an integral and important part of the London theatre.

In addition to many solo songs, he also shared duets with Elsie Randolph with whom he appeared in **Boodle** (1925), **Sunny** (1926), **That's a Good Girl** (1928), **Stand Up and Sing** (1931), **Mr. Whittington** (1934) and **This'll Make You Whistle** (1935). They also performed together in three popular films — the screen version of "That's a Good Girl" and "Yes, Mr. Brown", both of which were co-directed by Jack in 1932 — and "Smash and Grab" five years later in 1937.

Jack also starred in more than 30 other films. The first, "Auld Lang Syne", one of several silents, was shot as early as 1917 and the last, "The Diary of Major Thompson", a year before his death in 1957. He is probably best-remembered, however, for "A Man of Mayfair", "Monte Carlo", "Goodnight Vienna" (opposite the impressive Anna Neagle), "Brewster's Millions", and "When Knights Were Bold", all from the early-Thirties.

Other Buchanan leading ladies included Fay Wray, Beatrice Lillie, Lili Damita, Joan Barry, Fay Compton, Nancy O'Neil, Ellaline Terriss, Lilian Braithwaite, Gertrude Lawrence, Greta Gynt, Jessie Matthews, June Knight, and Jeanette McDonald.

What made Jack Buchanan so special? It was not so much his singing and possibly not even his acting or dancing ability, but a combination of creative talents and a charming personality which together produced the perfect chemistry for a superstar.

Among his most famous songs were. *"Fancy Our Meeting"* which came from **That's a Good Girl** staged at the London Hippodrome, while an earlier song *"And Her Mother Came Too"* still brings a wry smile to all young couples who hear it. Actually an Ivor Novello number, it was first heard in the revue **A to Z**, an André Charlot inspiration staged at the Prince of Wales in 1921.

"Who (Stole My Heart Away?)" was from Jerome Kern's **Sunny** (1926), while *"Goodnight Vienna"* and *"Everything Stops For Tea"* came from the silver screen, the former from a film of the same name in 1932, the latter two years later from "Come Out of the Pantry". In fact Jack was so busy in films that it is remarkable how he managed to fit in all his other commitments. A measure of his fame during the silent era was his title role of the dashing airman in "Bulldog Drummond's Third Round", one of four films he made in 1925.

In 1915 Jack had been married briefly but mysteriously to a Bulgarian opera singer called Drageva (real name Saffo Arnau). Whatever the reason for the marriage — it may have been simply to prevent her from being interned as an alien — it quickly failed and Jack always pretended it had never taken place. He preferred instead to be known as the eternal bachelor but later discovered great happiness with an American, Susan Bassett, whom he married in 1949 — much to the astonishment of his close friends who had never met her.

During the mid-Twenties he moved into real estate, founded his own company and built a short-lived theatre in Leicester Square. He also sponsored his old Scottish friend, John Logie Baird, in the development of early television.

By 1930 he had already performed in four New York productions and 50 later visits were equally successful. Wartime saw no diminution of effort and in 1940 Jack played another cinema airman called "Bulldog", not the early biplane ace this time but a contemporary test pilot involved in tracking down enemy agents. "Bulldog Sees It Through" was a typically patriotic film involving Jack frustrating efforts to blow up the Houses of Parliament after a desperate air battle over the River Thames.

When real action destroyed his penthouse flat during the Blitz, however, he bounced

△ *Jack Buchanan and Elsie Randolph dancing in* **Mr. Whittington** (1934).

back with the appropriately-titled Winter Garden show **It's Time to Dance**. Later, when the Lyons Corner House on Piccadilly was converted for the wartime Services show **Stage Door Canteen**, Jack was a sensation. On the opening night he stopped the huge audience in its tracks and when he ad-libbed an unexpected and totally unscripted 30 minute joke session with Bing Crosby — who just happened to be passing through — they went positively wild.

In 1953 he co-starred with Fred Astaire in a memorable MGM film called "The Band Wagon". It was possibly the pinnacle of his career because he more than held his own among the exalted company which also included Cyd Charisse and Nanette Fabray.

But his final years were painful — although he never complained — spinal arthritis being the real cause not the tuberculosis which popular rumour suggested. After many years of suffering he died on October 21st, 1957, when his career was perfectly summed up by his most famous partner, Elsie Randolph:

"He was not only immaculate in dress but also in behaviour. His was a completely unselfish dedication to the theatre. Nothing was too much trouble for the good of the show. That is what made Johnny B. so great."

In the words of his 1931 film, Jack had truly become "The Man of Mayfair".

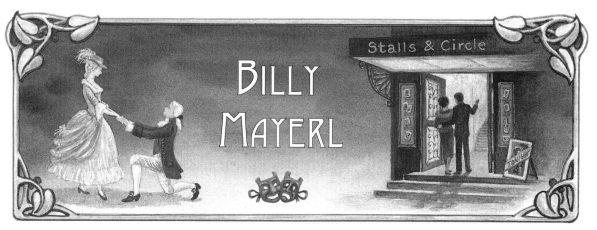

BILLY MAYERL

Born in Tottenham Court Road on 31st May, 1902, a stone's throw from London's West End theatreland, pianist Billy Mayerl won a scholarship to nearby Trinity College while still only a small boy. Before long he publicly performed Grieg's *"Piano Concerto"* at the Queen's Hall and by his early teens was playing in dance bands and accompanying silent films in a variety of cinemas. Before he reached his majority he became solo pianist with the prestigious Savoy Havana Band at London's top hotel on the Strand.

Numerous recordings and broadcasts quickly brought Billy's name to the fore and in 1923 he married his childhood sweet-heart, Jill Bernini. Two years later he gave the first British concert per-formance of Gershwin's *"Rhapsody in Blue"* and his "lightning fingers" were filmed by a slow-motion camera. Then, in 1926, he launched out into the total-ly unknown and unpre-dictable with his "Cor-respondence Course in Modern Syncopation" from rented premises in Oxford Street.

By the late-Thirties he had a staff of more than 100, with 117 branches world-wide and a clientele in excess of 30,000 students. It was not to last, however, and although he tried to revive it after the war, this proved ineffective and the Billy Mayerl School finally closed down in 1957. It was a sad end to a brilliant career and within two more years, the "nimble-fin-gered gentleman" himself had expired early from a heart condition, probably exacerbated by a punishing schedule of concerts and composition.

Throughout the Twenties, Billy made many appear-ances in Metropolitan and provincial variety theatres and also contributed songs for a host of London revues. By 1930 he was performing with the **Co-Optimists** and was ready for full musical scores, the first of which was

△ *In common with all famous wartime stars, Billy Mayerl did his stint entertaining the troops and is seen here enjoying himself with members from all three Armed Services. Cockney comedian Tommy Trinder is seated at the piano immediately to Billy's right.*

Nippy, followed by **The Millionaire Kid**, **Sporting Love**, **Twenty to One**, **Over She Goes**, **Crazy Days**, and **Runaway Love**, many with horse-racing as the main theme. Although none of the musicals was a spectacular success, each had a healthy run in a large theatre.

Billy was now a household name and performed regularly on both Radio Luxembourg and the BBC. His records sold in their thousands and all around the country budding pianists were wrestling with the intricacies of his vast array of piano compositions, of which the most famous was his unofficial signature tune *"Marigold"*, one of a whole variety of horticultural pieces, gardening being one of his many hobbies.

△ *This photo of Billy Mayerl shows him with a sheet music copy of his popular but unofficial signature tune, "Marigold".*

In 1940 he took part in a Royal Command Performance and led his own band in the popular radio programme "Music While You Work", conceived to encourage wartime factory workers but which outlasted hostilities by 20 years. His first small musical group dated from the Twenties but by the mid-Thirties he was running a 26-piece orchestra to accompany his musicals at the Gaiety and other theatres. His Grosvenor House Orchestra dated from 1941 and he continued band leading into the Fifties.

It was a hectic pace while it lasted and had the war not intervened then it is difficult to surmise where the maestro might have ended up in public affection. He did his bit for the Services but post-war entertainment changed and in 1958 he made what turned out to be his last broadcast when he was chosen by Roy Plomley to appear on "Desert Island Discs". He signed off with his characteristic "Goodbye chaps, and chapesses" but this time he really seemed to mean it. It was almost as though he knew the end was near and he died 10 months later at Beaconsfield, on 25th March 1959.

Most people today remember Billy for his eccentric but highly-pleasurable piano pieces which for the amateur are difficult to play. Even the professional has trouble staying the course but a reappraisal of his music in recent years has given a new generation the chance to enjoy the music which made him such a great pre-war favourite.

Shows and Revues involving the music of **BILLY MAYERL**	
The Punch Bowl	1924
The London Revue	1925
White Birds	1927
So Long Letty	1928
Change Over	1929
Love Lies	1929
The Love Race	1930
Silver Wings	1930
Darling I Love You	1930
Nippy	1930
The Millionaire Kid	1931
Between Ourselves	1932
Sporting Love	1934
Love Laughs	1935
Twenty to One	1935
Over She Goes	1936
Crazy Days	1937
Runaway Love	1939
Happy Birthday	1940
Kiki	1942
Six Pairs of Shoes	1944

HARRY PARR DAVIES

Born at Briton Ferry in South Wales, while still only 17 years old, Harry Parr Davies bought a day-return rail ticket from Neath to London and, clutching a song he had just written, managed to evade the stage door keeper at the Winter Garden theatre and hand it to Gracie Fields who was starring in the musical revue **Walk This Way**. She was impressed and despite it being called *"I Hate You"*, Harry quickly became her full-time accompanist and travelling companion around the world.

Throughout the Thirties, in addition to several other hit tunes, he wrote a string of songs for Gracie, the most famous being *"Sing as We Go"* from the 1934 movie of the same name. Her other films of the period all owed much to Harry's music and lyrics. By the time war arrived in 1939 he was heavily involved with musicals, and his songs appeared in 13 different wartime shows, four of which were entirely his own work.

Black Velvet opened shortly after the war began and included the famous blackout song *"Crash, Bang, I Want to Go Home"*. It was staged at Harry's favourite venue, the popular London Hippodrome and the stars were Roma Beaumont, Pat Kirkwood, Carol Lynne (later Lady Delfont), and Vic Oliver. The show ran for 620 performances and established Harry among the popular musical elite.

Haw-Haw was a revue featuring the "Cheeky Chappie", Max Miller, and the adopted American husband-and-wife team of Bebe Daniels and Ben Lyon. **Come Out To Play** featured Sonnie Hale and Jessie Matthews, while **Top of the World** included the antics of the Crazy Gang and Tommy Trinder, a sure recipe for success. Like the latter, **Gangway** and **Best Bib and Tucker** were staged at the 2,500-seat London Palladium, the biggest major theatre

▷ *Harry accompanied Gracie Fields not just on the piano but all over Africa and North America, including a trip to Hollywood where they met both George Gershwin and Charlie Chaplin.*

◁ *Patricia Burke was the heroine of **The Lisbon Story** (1943), a musical which told the intriguing story of a Parisian theatre girl trying to outwit the German Gestapo.*

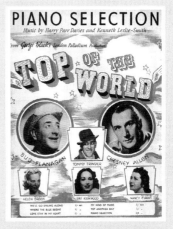

Wartime revues were invariably topical, and none more so than **Black Velvet**, **Haw-Haw**, **Top of the World** and **Fine Feathers**. The music came largely from the pen of Harry Parr Davies and delighted the London theatregoing public who were determined that the nightly bombing raids by Hitler's planes and rockets were not going to stop them from going out and enjoying life.

**SOME SHOWS FROM
THE PEN OF
HARRY PARR DAVIES**

Dear Miss Phoebe revolved around Peter Graves and Carol Raye; **Blue for a Boy** around the rotund figure of comedian Fred Emney; **Her Excellency** around the experienced and popular Cicely Courtneidge; and **The Glorious Days** around the impressive Anna Neagle.

The Shephard Show was staged at the Prince's Theatre in 1946. With Richard Hearne ("Mr. Pastry"), Douglas Byng, Arthur Riscoe, Marie Burke and "Monsewer" Eddie Gray in the cast it must have been an exhilarating experience for all its post-war audiences.

71

PIANO SELECTION

BRITISH NATIONAL FILMS LTD
present

PATRICIA BURKE
DAVID FARRAR
WALTER RILLA

in

The Lisbon Story

with

LAWRENCE O'MADDEN
AUSTIN TREVOR · PAUL BONIFAS
and

RICHARD TAUBER

LYRICS BY
HAROLD PURCELL
MUSIC COMPOSED BY
HARRY PARR DAVIES

CHAPPELL

△ **The Lisbon Story** (1943) broke new ground because the heroine — Patricia Burke, playing Gabrielle, a Parisian theatre star trying to outwit the Gestapo — gets shot during the final scene in Portugal. The press were outraged but the public flocked to see it.

in the Metropolis. Harry also contributed lyrics to the stage version of the radio comedy show **Happidrome** starring Harry Korris as the theatre proprietor, Mr. Lovejoy; Cecil Frederick as his stage manager, Ramsbottom; and Robbie Vincent as the gormlesss call-boy, Enoch. Other stars of the show included Leslie Hutchinson (Hutch) and "Two Ton" Tessie O'Shea.

Big Top opened shortly afterwards at His Majesty's Theatre with Patricia Burke alongside Beatrice Lillie and Fred Emney. "Bea" was the widow of band leader Sir Robert Peel, who had died young in 1934, but she liked being called Lady Peel. Sadly, the title disappeared with the death of their son Robert who was killed during the war.

By now it was 1942 and hostilities were at their height. Harry was determined to do his bit for the Home Front and, with the help of George Posford, put together a show called **Full Swing** which opened at the imposing Palace Theatre. The stars were husband-and-wife team Jack Hulbert and Cicely Courtneidge, involved in a clandestine mission to track down state secrets on behalf of the War Office.

In 1943, **The Knight was Bold** had Sonnie Hale as the titled aristocrat dreaming he was back in the Middle Ages, but after successfully touring the provinces under the title **Kiss the Girls**, it became a West End flop and left the Piccadilly Theatre after only 10 performances. Few people noticed, however, because unfolding at the Hippodrome was a smash hit which everyone wanted to see.

Set amidst Second World War intrigue **The Lisbon Story** ran from June 1943 until July 1944 when heavy bombing forced the temporary closure of more than half of London's theatres. It notched up 492 performances with Patricia Burke (later to become Jimmy Clitheroe's mother in the radio comedy series "The Clitheroe Kid"), in the star role of Gabrielle, a theatrical star who escapes from the Nazis in Paris, only to be executed during the final scene in Portugal. Press reactions were mixed, however, "The heroine is shot at the end!" gasped the *Manchester Evening News* while the *Daily Mail* described it as "The Gestapo set to Music!" The public had no such qualms, though. With Vincent Tildsley and his Mastersingers colourfully dressed as Portuguese sailors merrily whistling their way through the hit song *"Pedro the Fisherman"*, the show would have run longer had the Luftwaffe allowed. It was later turned into a film with Patricia Burke, fresh from duty with **ENSA**, joined by the redoubtable Richard Tauber (now a British citizen), singing *"Pedro"*.

Jenny Jones ran for 153 performances and was about a Welsh miner with 18 children who wanted to make it 21! The stars were

Shows and revues of **HARRY PARR DAVIES**	
Black Velvet	1939
Haw-Haw	1939
Come Out To Play	1940
Top of the World	1940
Gangway	1941
Big Top	1942
Best Bib & Tucker	1942
Happidrome	1942
Full Swing	1942
The Knight was Bold	1943
The Lisbon Story	1943
Jenny Jones	1944
Fine Feathers	1945
The Shephard Show	1946
Her Excellency	1949
Dear Miss Phoebe	1950
Blue for a Boy	1950
The Glorious Days	1953

comedian Jimmy James and Carol Lynne but it was cherub-faced Welsh choirboy soprano, Malcolm Thomas, who captivated the audience each evening.

Fine Feathers (1945), starred Jack Buchanan at the Prince of Wales and was followed a year later by **The Shephard Show** at the Prince's Theatre. Produced by the impresario Firth Shephard, it starred Douglas Byng, Marie Burke, Richard Hearne (Mr. Pastry), Eddie Gray and Arthur Riscoe.

Amazingly, while still writing music, Harry enlisted in the Irish Guards, but when Gracie Fields was asked to join **ENSA** she said it would be impossible without her accompanist. He was therefore extradited specially for the job but then, even more surprisingly, joined the Lifeguards based in Knightsbridge. At least he was close to the West End.

In 1949 Harry teamed up with Manning Sherwin to compose **Her Excellency**. Produced by Jack Hulbert, it starred his wife Cicely Courtneidge playing the role of an upper crust British ambassador in South America. Another Hippodrome success, it ran for 252 performances. **Dear Miss Phoebe** followed at the Phoenix in October 1950 with lyrics by Christopher Hassall who had served Ivor Novello so well. An adaptation of J.M. Barrie's book "Quality Street", it told the tragic story of a Napoleonic War hero returning to a sweetheart he does not recognise. Peter Graves and Carol Raye took the leads in a show which had 283 curtain calls.

Penultimately — but nobody could have guessed it — came **Blue for a Boy**, with lyrics again by Harold Purcell. It opened at His Majesty's Theatre only a month after **Dear Miss Phoebe** got under way with the large rotund figure of cigar-smoking Fred Emney dressed in a blue romper suit and making life a misery for his stepfather and new bride. The arch-clown Richard Hearne added to the fun of a show which ran for

△ In addition to all his other work, Harry Parr Davies also wrote songs for George Formby, the banjulele-playing Lancashire goof who was not at all the gormless person he liked to make out.

more than 650 performances.

In 1953 came Harry's swansong. **The Glorious Days** starred Anna Neagle dreaming she was the reincarnation of several famous women in history, including Nell Gwynn and Queen Victoria. It managed eight months at the Palace but some critics regarded it as a failure.

Although not a stage production, the 1949 film "Maytime in Mayfair" was a musical related to London's West End. Michael Wilding, Anna Neagle, Peter Graves and a young Thora Hird did the honours in a plot which saw the manageress of a dress shop thwarting all her rivals and ultimately winning the day.

According to Harry's sister, Billie he had little social life and lived alone in Knightsbridge. His shyness and phobia of doctors proved fatal, however, for in October 1955, instead of seeking medical help, he took to his bed and died following a perforated ulcer.

It was an unnecessary death and one which robbed the musical theatre of a man in his prime. Only 41 years old, he had many more active years of service ahead of him and, probably because he never acted or sang in his own shows became, quite unfairly, a largely forgotten figure.

Harold Purcell

Christopher Hassall

ERIC MASCHWITZ

According to someone who ought to know, Eric Maschwitz "Had no blazing intellect; thought too quickly; words came too easily; he had no technical understanding of music and his reactions although quick, were often superficial."

A damning indictment of one of the country's most successful men of the theatre? Yes! True? Probably not because the writer was himself, in his 1957 autobiography *No Chip on my Shoulder*! Other people will judge him less harshly because he packed a great deal into his lifetime and gave great enjoyment to millions.

Born at Edgbaston in Birmingham on 10th June 1901, he was educated at Repton and Cambridge. After first going on stage he joined the BBC in 1926 and eventually became Head of Light Entertainment, also enjoying a similar position with the early ITV network.

In between times he led a harum scarum existence involved both with hugely successful musicals and others which flopped miserably. Occasionally broke he was as popular as anyone could wish to be and his circle of friends was a wide one. For someone who allegedly knew little about music he still came up with the lyrics of *"These Foolish Things"* and *"A Nightingale Sang in Berkeley Square"*! Not bad for someone who cared as much for amateur societies as much as his professional associates.

His first job at the BBC was in Outside Broadcasting but his aptitude for writing quickly came to the fore when he and George Posford, with whom he was to produce many musicals, answered an internal request by Val Gielgud for a radio operetta. **Goodnight Vienna** seemed simple fayre to them and they happily accepted £200 for the film copyright. The next thing they knew it was a smash hit movie starring Anna Neagle and Jack Buchanan, the first musical talkie to be made in Britain.

Maschwitz even edited the *Radio Times* before being appointed Variety Director in 1933. From then on there was no holding him back and he was here, there and everywhere, which included the United States. In 1939 he went to Hollywood under contract to MGM and wrote the screenplays of such huge film successes as "Goodbye Mr. Chips" and "Queen of Song". He also managed to persuade the producer of the former to shoot the schoolyard and playing fields scenes at his old school in Derbyshire, when Robert Donat starred in one of the best films ever made.

With the long-running radio series "In Town Tonight", plus the popular "Café Collette" which purported to come from Paris but was actually recorded in a London studio, he was as busy as ever, a fact which contributed to his eventual divorce from the actress Hermione Gingold. In 1936 **Balalaika** proved a great success but **Paprika** flopped. so he simply dressed it up and renamed it **Magyar Melody**, which fared little better.

△ The music to **Starlight Roof** *(1947) was composed by George Melachrino but the stars of the show were (left to right) veteran rotund comedian Fred Emney, the delectable Patricia Kirkwood, and the naturalised Austrian comic at the piano, Vic Oliver, who married Winston Churchill's daughter, Sarah.*

▷ *Eric Maschwitz (left) with Jack Strachey, his collaborator in the famous songs "These Foolish Things" and "A Nightingale Sang in Berkeley Square". Strachey also composed light music, his most famous tune being "In Party Mood" the signature tune of "Housewives' Choice".*

▽ *A rare photograph of a young girl singer who proved a great hit in* **Starlight Roof.** *From a theatrical family she went on to much greater things and the name Julie Andrews soon became famous all round the world.*

△ **In Zip Goes a Million,** *Lancashire window-cleaner Percy Piggott (George Formby) has to spend £1,000,000!*

Throughout the period of hostilities Eric served in the Intelligence Corps as Chief Broadcasting Officer with the 21st Army Group and was demobbed as a Lieutenant Colonel. He still managed to be regularly involved with the theatre, however, and various wartime revues met with mixed success. Sometimes he borrowed other people's music, such as Weber in the film "Invitation to the Waltz", Strauss in **Pink Champagne**, and Chopin in **Waltz Without End**.

His post-war career was a mixture of unexpected failures and triumphs. The 1946 remake of **Nymph Errant** was named **Evangeline** but failed to get off the ground. Then came a surprising double success with **Starlight Roof** and a seemingly old-fashioned operetta called **Carissima** which ran for 466 performances at the Palace Theatre.

Belinda Fair starred Adele Dixon, and was another collaboration with popular theatre composer Jack Strachey but it was **Zip Goes a Million** which really hit the high spots. Conceived specifically for George Formby it opened at the Palace Theatre in October 1951, and achieved 544 performances. In fact Formby only played a small part in its success because he had a heart attack early on and was replaced by fellow Northern comedian Reg 'Confidentially' Dixon.

The final big triumph was **Love From Judy** which managed almost 600 curtain calls at the Saville Theatre in 1952. Two years later theatrical entrepreneur Emile Littler persuaded Maschwitz to turn Arnold Ridley's classic thriller "The Ghost Train" into a musical called **Happy Holiday**, but it failed badly. He knew in advance it was likely to bomb

A selection of ERIC MASCHWITZ Musical Creations	
1932	The Dubarry
1936	Balalaika
1938	Paprika
1939	Magyar Melody
1940	New Faces
1941	Black Vanities
	More New Faces
1942	Waltz Without End
	Evangeline
1943	Flying Colours
1947	Starlight Roof
1948	Carissima
	Masquerade
1949	Belinda Fair
1951	Zip Goes a Million
1952	Love From Judy
1954	Happy Holiday (The Ghost Train)
1955	Romance in Candlelight
1956	Summer Song
1958	Pink Champagne

because it had been such a success as a play and a wartime film starring Richard Murdoch, Arthur Askey and Kathleen Harrison. Littler, however, would not listen to suggestions of how it should be modernised and paid the economic penalty. Maschwitz feared the worst and actually pleaded not have his name associated with the production from the outset.

Romance in Candlelight (1955) could have done better but once again Prince Littler won the argument and lost his money at the Palace. He wanted it be an Edwardian musical while Maschwitz preferred modern Venice. Patricia Burke and Sally Ann Howes did their best but not for long. Maschwitz and Littler parted company but remained friends. A year later **Summer Song**, based on the life and music of Dvorak, reached almost 100 performances, ironically based at the Prince's theatre, with Sally Ann Howes bringing the house down.

In 1958 Eric rejoined the BBC as head of Light Entertainment and had great success with **The Black and White Minstrels** television show and stage musical. Nevertheless,

he recognised he belonged to an older generation and took on more of a father figure role to most of his department. He was well aware of the changing scene and enthusiastically threw himself into writing an entertainment to celebrate the fourth centenary of his old school in which he took part himself, almost 40 years after first treading the boards.

Among the audience were his former headmaster Geoffrey Fisher, later the Archbishop of Canterbury, and fellow pupil the Archbishop of York, Michael Ramsey, who became Fisher's successor at Canterbury in 1961. His autobiography finished at this point with Maschwitz taking a quizzical and critical look at himself in the mirror.

One of his more realistic comments was that in the theatre it is no good complaining if the audience does not attend. If they stay away then you have failed. This may be true economically but many good productions, including some of his own, were simply unlucky. In his own words "A happy man", he died in London on 27th October, 1969.

▷ **Love from Judy** (1952) took nearly 600 curtain calls at the Saville Theatre. Jean Carson is seen here in the star role addressing all the other girls

△ **Romance in Candlelight** (1955) had Roger Dann (left) and Jacques Pils supporting Sally Ann Howes.

▷ **Carissima** (1948) had the famous tenor Lester Ferguson proposing a toast to Elizabeth Theilmann.

THE AMERICAN FIFTIES

As the Forties turned into the Fifties so an invisible barrier went up to separate the new decade from the war. Despite the collapse of many independent British film studios it was a time of hope and optimism for the theatre which believed live shows would always have an audience.

Unfortunately this confidence proved to be unfounded and when the fledgling Independent Television network doubled its capacity during the mid-Fifties it led to the closure of many music halls, cinemas and theatres. Happily, London's West End remained largely untouched and welcomed with open arms a succession of outstanding American musicals. There were also many home-grown successes mentioned elsewhere.

First out of the theatrical traps was Rodgers and Hammerstein's **Carousel** which opened at Drury Lane in June 1950. Among its many memorable numbers were *"June is bustin' out all over"*, *"You'll never walk alone"*, *"If I loved you"*, *"When the children are asleep in bed"* and the rousing *"Carousel Waltz"*.

△ *Mary Martin more than made up for the disappointment of Noel Coward's* **Pacific 1860** *when five years later, in 1951, she starred as Ensign Nellie Forbush in the truly spectacular maritime show* **South Pacific**. *In post-war austerity Britain the bright tropical colours made quite an impact. Among the best-remembered songs are "Bali ha'i", "Younger than springtime", "Honey bun", "Happy talk", "Cockeyed optimist", "Some enchanted evening", "There is nothing like a dame", "Younger than springtime", "I'm in love with a wonderful guy", and "I'm gonna wash that man right out of my hair".*

△ △ ▽ **The King and I** *opened to great acclaim at Drury Lane in October, 1953, and this front cover of* Theatre World *shows the uneasy relationship between the monarch (Herbert Lom) and Anna, the British governess (Valerie Hobson), who tries to educate and reform his feudal kingdom. Although she is largely successful she also becomes romantically entangled with the jealous king. Unfortunately, he dies, but not before he and his heir, the Crown Prince, promise far-reaching changes.*

◁ *Cole Porter wrote both the words and music for* **Kiss Me Kate** *in which he cleverly interwove William Shakespeare's play* The Taming of the Shrew. *It played for 400 performances at the vast Coliseum in 1951. Among the many songs which have stood the test of time are "Wunderbar", "Always true to you in my fashion", "Too darn hot", "Brush up your Shakespeare" and "Why can't you behave?" One of the stars was comedian Sid James who, five years later in 1956, also played the lead in a black comedy film spoof of Shakespeare called "Joe Macbeth".*

△ Cole Porter (1891-1964) was responsible for several successful British shows, including **Nymph Errant, Anything Goes, Can Can, Dubarry was a Lady, Kiss Me Kate,** and **Panama Hattie.**

△ Composer Richard Rodgers (1902-1979), left, worked initially with lyricist Lorenz Hart (1895-1943), then with Oscar Hammerstein (1895-1960), right, with whom he produced the colourful post-war musicals **South Pacific, The King and I, Oklahoma, Flower Drum Song, Carousel** and **The Sound of Music.** Their overwhelming success in London was excellent news for the huge Theatre Royal, Drury Lane, which relied heavily on major musicals to fill its vast auditorium. Ivor Novello had rescued it during the Thirties so when Rodgers and Hammerstein came along with more economic miracles after hostilities ceased it was a massive bonus for everyone.

Next came Cole Porter's **Kiss Me Kate** at the Coliseum in March 1951 whose cast included Adelaide Hall, and also Sidney James and Danny Green singing *"Brush up your Shakespeare"*. Other songs included *"Always true to you in my fashion"* and *"Wunderbar"*.

In November the same year Rodgers and Hammerstein returned to Drury Lane with **South Pacific**, a highly colourful maritime show whose famous songs included *"Bali ha'i"*, *"Some enchanted evening"*, *"There is nothing like a dame"*, *"Honey bun"*, *"Younger than springtime"*, *"I'm gonna wash that man right out of my hair"*, *"I'm in love with a wonderful guy"*, *"Happy talk"*, and *"Cockeyed optimist"*.

Irving Berlin's **Call Me Madam** reached the Coliseum in 1952 but without the foghorn voice of Ethel Merman who had starred on Broadway. The British cast included two unknowns called Arthur Lowe and Shani Wallis, later to find fame elsewhere. The same year also saw an English revival of **Porgy and Bess**, a show originally from the Thirties by George and Ira Gershwin.

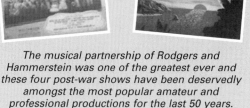

The musical partnership of Rodgers and Hammerstein was one of the greatest ever and these four post-war shows have been deservedly amongst the most popular amateur and professional productions for the last 50 years.

△ *Following the success of* **Oklahoma** *at Drury Lane in 1947, Rodgers and Hammerstein followed it in 1950 with* **Carousel**, *which Time Magazine in New York later described as "The best musical of the 20th Century". It was also Rodgers and Hammerstein's own personal favourite! The hero, Billy Bigelow, is killed in the first half of the show but not before he dreams about his pregnant wife giving birth to "My Boy Bill". Bill eventually turns out to be a girl, however, whom her father returns to visit as a ghost and, in a dramatic testimony to the power of love, instils in both the child and her mother a sense of hope and dignity. Still a great favourite with amateur dramatic societies throughout the land, the show's many memorable numbers include "You'll Never Walk Alone" since adopted by Liverpool Football Club!*

△ **My Fair Lady** *(1958) was based on George Bernard Shaw's "Pygmalion" and deservedly played to packed houses at Drury Lane. Left: Professor Higgins (Rex Harrison) gives an elocution lesson to Covent Garden flower seller Eliza Doolittle (Julie Andrews). Right: Higgins is joined by his friend Colonel Pickering (Robert Coote) while seated is Eliza's aptly-named Cockney father, Doolittle (Stanley Holloway).*

△ **My Fair Lady** *ran for more than 2,200 performances with Professor Higgins (Rex Harrison, third left) keeping a straight face as Eliza Doolittle (Julie Andrews) suddenly forgets her new role as an aristocratic lady at the Ascot Races and lapses into loud broad Cockney vernacular, exhorting a horse to greater action in a most unladylike manner. The rest of the party are scandalised!*

1953 witnessed three big American imports. Lerner and Loewe's **Paint Your Wagon** opened at Her Majesty's Theatre starring father and daughter Bobby and Sally Ann Howes; Frank Loesser's **Guys and Dolls** was staged at the Coliseum; and a third major hit from Rodgers and Hammerstein again went into Drury Lane. With Herbert Lom as the King of Siam and Valerie Hobson as Anna the governess, **The King and I** could not fail. Some of its tunes are still just as famous today, especially *"March of the Siamese children", "Hello young lovers", "I whistle a happy tune"* and *"Shall we dance?"*

Cole Porter's next contribution was **Can Can** (1954), followed up the same year by an original Rodgers and Hart show **Pal Joey**. **Kismet** (1955) was based on the music of Russian composer Igor Borodin, while Adler and Ross's **Pajama Game** starred Edmund Hockridge, Joy Nichols and Max Wall at the Coliseum. Adler and Ross came together

again two years later in 1957, once more at the Coliseum, with **Damn Yankees**. It was 1958, however, which saw the biggest American successes of all.

Leonard Bernstein's **West Side Story** cleared more than 1,000 performances at Her Majesty's but Lerner and Loewe's **My Fair Lady** achieved more than double that at Drury Lane! These two spectacular shows

▷ *Max Wall, Joy Nichols and Edmund Hockridge starred in the British version of* **The Pajama Game** *(1955) which took 578 curtain calls. Long-playing records were by now making all musical shows instantly available to the general public.*

△ *The dramatic final scene in* **West Side Story** *where the leaders of the two rival gangs, the Jets and Sharks, fight to the death. Based on Shakespeare's "Romeo and Juliet" but set in downtown New York, the lyrics were by Stephen Sondheim but the show, which opened in London at Her Majesty's Theatre in December 1958, owed much to the brilliant music of Leonard Bernstein whose impulsive rhythms set a new standard in song.*

could not have been more different. While **West Side Story** was a modern version of Shakespeare's *Romeo and Juliet* set in downtown New York, **My Fair Lady** was set in Edwardian London at Covent Garden Flower Market and the Ascot races, and based on George Bernard Shaw's *Pygmalion*.

In the latter, Julie Andrews and Rex Harrison pitted their wits against each other as Eliza Doolittle and Professor Higgins, while Stanley Holloway gave a memorable performance as Eliza's father. The musical director was Cyril Ornadel who also waved the conductor's baton over many other famous shows during this period.

Most of these American musicals are still enthusiastically performed by amateur operatic societies because of their excellent lyrics and tunes which brightened the severe post-war austerity. Long-playing records had also made their debut at the start of the Fifties so it was not long before the population was buying them in large numbers with the catchy music lodged firmly in the mind.

Teenagers now had Elvis Presley and Bill Haley but mum and dad had **Oklahoma, Annie Get Your Gun, South Pacific, Carousel, Guys and Dolls, Kiss Me Kate, The King and I, My Fair Lady, West Side Story** and many others, including some excellent British shows.

△ **Kismet** *(1955) was a modern Oriental version of Borodin's opera "Prince Igor". It was staged at the Stoll Theatre which was demolished two years later to make way for offices and the new Royalty Theatre.*

THE BRITISH FIFTIES

Despite the overwhelming success and influence of the new post-war Hollywood-style spectaculars from America, a number of unexpected British musicals also hit the high spots during the Fifties.

At the start of the decade George Posford (1906-1976) and Eric Maschwitz (1901-1969) put together **Zip Goes a Million** as a foil for the talents of George Formby who was seeking a change in career. Unfortunately, George suffered a heart attack early on and had to be replaced by his fellow Northern comedian and friend Reg ("Confidentially") Dixon, not to be confused with Reginald Dixon, the organist at the Tower Ballroom, Blackpool. The show was still a success, however, and ran for 544 performances at the Palace.

Laurier Lister was the brains behind a number of contemporary revues including **Tuppence Coloured**, **Penny Plain** and **Airs on a Shoestring**. The latter utilised the many talents of composer Richard Addinsell who also wrote for **Ring Round the Moon** (1950) by Christopher Fry. Two newcomers were Michael Flanders (1922-1975) and Donald Swann (1923-1994), together at both Westminster School and Christ Church, Oxford, but never previously close friends.

They made a splendid combination. Swann, seated at the piano, smaller and outwardly more serious, was perfectly complemented by the burly more extrovert Flanders, who brilliantly compèred proceedings from his wheelchair. He contracted polio during his time as a commando during the war but shamefully was not allowed to complete his unfinished degree at Oxford. He apparently bore little bitterness, though, and the University's loss was the theatre's gain.

Flanders and Swann added a new genre to revue and found their niche in **Oranges and Lemons** (1948), **Pay the Piper** (1954) and two years later, **Fresh Airs** and **At the Drop of a Hat**. This latter production was initially staged privately at the tiny New Lindsey Theatre in Notting Hill but later transferred successfully to the Fortune Theatre in the West End. By popular demand it was followed in 1963 at the Haymarket by **At the Drop of Another Hat**.

There can be few people who have never heard of the *"Hippopotamus"*, *"Gnu"*, *"London Omnibus"* or other Flanders and Swann creations which will last long into the future. Flanders was a giant in reputation but Swann was also a solo composer and song-

△ *Michael Flanders (left) and Donald Swann became famous after their clever animal songs were heard in* **At the Drop of a Hat** *(1957). Although at school and university together they did not become friends until after the war, by which time Flanders was suffering from polio. Amazingly, Oxford refused to allow him to finish his degree because of his disability.*

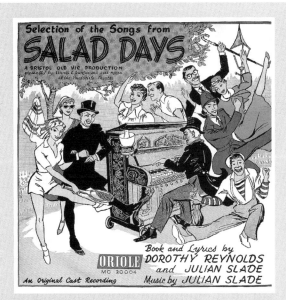

◁ *For some time during the early-Fifties this record of* **Salad Days** *was one of only a handful of LPs to be found in music shops up and down the country. The show's huge success was due in no small measure to its catchy foot-tapping tunes and timeless plot which have easily withstood the test of time. What began as a student romp in Bristol turned into one of the greatest ever British musicals.*

▷ *No one expected* **The Boy Friend** *to run for 2,084 performances but its period costume charm won the hearts of London theatregoers in a most remarkable manner, possibly because many of them could still vividly remember the Twenties in which it was set. It proved to be a hard act to follow for the already established Sandy Wilson and he was never again to scale the heights in the same manner.*

▽ *Like most West End musical successes* **The Boy Friend** *had small beginnings at the Players' Theatre underneath the Charing Cross arches. It later transferred to the Embassy in Hampstead before its record-breaking run at Wyndham's. It also enjoyed extended runs on Broadway before being turned into an MGM film in 1972, starring Barbara Windsor, Twiggy and Christopher Gable.*

△ *French maid Hortense (Violetta Farjeon) sings "It's Nicer in Nice.*

△ *Polly (Anne Rogers, who took over on the first night) is wooed by Tony (Anthony Hayes).*

△ *Everyone who can remember television and theatre from the 1950s will remember both the Tiller Girls and the Television Toppers. Here are the former in a typical high-kicking dance routine from a revue called* **Such is Life** *which ran for 548 performances at the Adelphi. It was a Jack Hylton presentation together with George and Alfred Black. Hylton reinvented himself after the war when he realised that large dance bands had had their day. Turning his back on the touring show band he became a hugely successful theatrical entrepreneur.*

writer whom history may prove to have had a much wider influence than currently thought.

1954 saw the West End birth of two shows which had extraordinary success, neither of which was anticipated in advance. Firstly, Dorothy Reynolds (1913-1978) and Julian Slade (born 1930) worked together at the Bristol Old Vic on a jolly end of term musical called **Salad Days**, a delightful student romp with a magic piano which caused everyone to start dancing. Its appeal to young folk in Bristol resulted in the audience refusing to go home on the final night when the piano was trundled out into the street where everyone joined in!

Impresario Jack Hylton sniffed a success story in the making and immediately brought it to London's Vaudeville Theatre where it deservedly ran for nearly six years, its 2,200 performances far outweighing the expectations of Dorothy Reynolds who thought it might last three weeks! It was a breath of fresh

air and the songs are still as attractive today, especially *"We said we wouldn't look back"*; *"I sit in the sun"*; *"Oh! Look at me"*; *"It's easy to sing"* and *"We're looking for a piano"*.

Amazingly, at the nearby Wyndham's Theatre, 1954 also saw the start of another long-running British musical which, if anything, was even more bizarre in its preparation. Sandy Wilson's **The Boy Friend** was modelled on the Roaring Twenties, in particular the 1925 musical **No No Nanette**. Based on a young ladies' finishing school in Nice, it was a perfect caricature with period costumes playing as vital a role as the affected accents.

During the Fifties if someone did not like a musical then they barracked it. This show received almost no criticism at all but it nearly failed before it started. During the dress rehearsal the night before opening, the leading lady had a breakdown and had to be taken away by ambulance. After the initial shock, a 17-year-old chorus girl called Annie

△ *Sally Anne Howes in* **Summer Song** *(1956), an updated show based on Dvorak's music by Eric Maschwitz (1901-1969). A big name in BBC Light Entertainment and involved in London musicals since 1932, his other Fifties offerings included* **Zip Goes a Million, Love From Judy, Happy Holiday, Romance in Candlelight** *and* **Pink Champagne.**

Rogers stepped forward and said "I can do it!" ... and she did!

Originating at the Players' Theatre under the arches of Charing Cross station, then via the Embassy in Hampstead to Wyndham's in the West End, **The Boy Friend** wowed audiences right up until 1959 by which time it had chalked up more than 2,000 curtain calls. Its best songs are *"I could be happy with you"*; *"The boy friend"*; *"Perfect young ladies"* and *"It's nicer in Nice"*.

In addition to several fine revues, Sandy Wilson's other musical offerings included **Buccaneer, Valmouth** and **Divorce Me Darling** although none came near repeating the success of **The Boy Friend**. It was the same with Reynolds and Slade with **Duenna, Follow That Girl** and **Wildest Dreams**, although **Free as Air** (1957) notched up 417 performances at the Savoy and **Hooray for Daisy** (1960) was revived to great acclaim later in the century.

Another partnership which emerged during the Fifties was David Heneker (1906-2001) and former singer Monty Norman (born 1928), who came together in 1958

with both **Expresso Bongo** and **Irma La Douce**. The former made a creditable 316 performances at the Saville while the latter risqué show ran for more than three years and 1,500 curtain calls at the Lyric. They also did well together with **Make Me An Offer** and **The Art of Living**.

Another person who first appeared during the Fifties was Lionel Bart with **Wally Pone** (1958), based on Ben Jonson's "Volpone". A year later he hit the jackpot with **Fings Ain't What They Used To Be** which ran for 897 performances at the Theatre Royal, Stratford. He also collaborated at the same time with Laurie Johnson on **Lock Up Your Daughters** which was staged at Bernard Miles's Mermaid Theatre.

There were plenty of other British musicals during the Fifties although some lasted only a few weeks. Among the more successful were **Love from Judy** (1952) and no fewer than six Crazy Gang revues at the Victoria Palace. This bunch of ageing but amazing extroverts far outstripped the combined efforts of everyone else, American or British. Their unique mix of buffoonery and nostalgic

△ *Until the advent of Andrew Lloyd-Webber musicals, nobody could match the prolific run of the many* **Crazy Gang** *revues. Spread over 30 years they totalled around 10,000 performances, usually twice nightly which latterly put enormous strain on the ageing stars. This scene from* **Ring Out the Bells** *(1952) shows from left to right: Charlie Naughton, Teddy Knox, Jimmy Nervo, Bud Flanagan, and Jimmy Gold. Much of the post-war music came from Ross Parker but, although retired owing to ill heath, Flanagan's old partner Chesney Allen still played a key background role.*

music proved irresistible and the crowds flocked in.

Bud Flanagan (now with his former partner Chesney Allen as their manager), Jimmy Nervo & Teddy Knox, Charlie Naughton & Jimmy Gold, plus "Monsewer" Eddie Gray played nightly to packed houses in **Together Again** (1947), **Knights of Madness** (1950), **Ring Out the Bells** (1952), **Jokers Wild** (1954), **These Foolish Kings** (1956), **Clown Jewels** (1959) and finally **Young In Heart** (1960). Between them these shows, directed mainly by Ross Parker, added up to more than 7,000 performances, an incredible and unparalleled achievement.

Another "one off" favourite of this period was the incomparable Joyce Grenfell who starred in four different shows in collaboration with her musical partner, Richard Addinsell. Meanwhile, old stalwarts Kenneth Leslie-Smith, Alan Melville and Charles Zwar were still beavering away with various shows, the best of which was **Bet Your Life** (1952) which made 382 appearances at the Hippodrome.

British musicals were in good heart during the Fifties and they were soon to be cheered again when **Oliver!** upstaged everything.

CRAZY GANG
Revues

Crazy Month	1932
Life Begins at Oxford Circus	1935
March Hares	1935
Round About Regent Street	1935
All Alight at Oxford Circus	1936
O-Kay for Sound	1936
London Rhapsody	1937
Many Happy Returns	1937
Swing Is In the Air	1937
These Foolish Things	1938
The Little Dog Laughed	1939
Top of the World	1940
Black Vanities	1941
Hi De Hi	1943
Together Again	1947
Knights of Madness	1950
Ring Out the Bells	1952
Jokers Wild	1954
These Foolish Kings	1956
Clown Jewels	1959
Young in Heart	1960

With the exception of **Many Happy Returns** at the Adelphi and **Hi De Hi** staged at both the Palace and Stoll, all the early shows were at the Palladium then from 1941, exclusively at the Victoria Palace.

THE CRAZY GANG

This remarkable troupe became a national institution and were as daft offstage as they were on it. Their practical jokes were sometimes outrageous and Bud Flanagan once soaked the Western Brothers by puncturing the pipes in their dressing room. The compliment was returned with interest but the monocled duo would never reveal which member of the Gang helped them turn the tables.

△ **Clown Jewels** (1959). Back row from left: "Monsewer" Eddie Gray, Chesney Allen (manager, inset), Jimmy Gold, Teddy Knox and Charlie Naughton; centre Bud Flanagan and visitor Sophie Tucker; front left: Jack Hylton (impresario) and Jimmy Nervo.

△ **Royal Command Performance** (1955).

△ **Young in Heart** (1960).

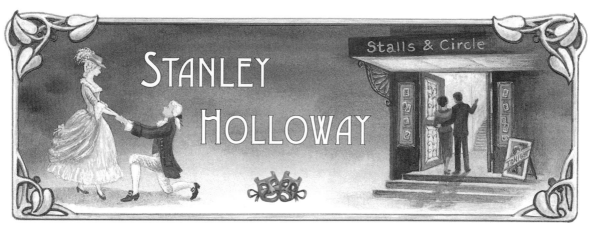

STANLEY HOLLOWAY

S tanley Augustus Holloway was born on 1st October, 1890, at Manor Park in East London, the only son of George and Florrie Holloway. When he joined the school choir the quality of his voice was immediately recognised, and he was offered half-a-crown to sing at a local concert. He was a great success, and with his shiny, cherubic face smiling from above a smart Eton collar, his reputation quickly spread. Billed as "The Boy Soprano", he was soon in demand to provide entertainment at other concert parties.

The inevitable happened of course and his voice broke, by which time Stanley was working at Billingsgate Fish Market. During the evenings he was drawn to the Stratford Empire where he saw some of the all-time greats, including "Little Tich" and the marvellous Marie Lloyd. Enthralled and intoxicated by all he witnessed he visited other London music halls where, he later wrote, "one could see as many as 15 top acts, have a packet of fags, a meat pie and a tram ride home — all for a bob!"

Now a young man with a rich baritone voice, Stanley resumed his singing career and in 1907 left his job at the market and joined a concert-party troupe, **The White Coons**, at Clacton-on-Sea in Essex. Concert-parties, in which the actors dressed up in white pierrot outfits to perform a colourful mixture of songs, sketches and recitations, were a familiar form of entertainment before the First World War. They demanded hard work and great versatility from the actors,

writers and musicians because new material was often needed at a moment's notice and everyone had to play all sorts of roles. For Stanley, it was invaluable experience.

It was during the 1913 summer season that he was spotted by Leslie Henson, then an up-and-coming musical-comedy star who had already made his mark in the West End. Leslie immediately recognised Stanley's potential and invited him to join **Nicely Thanks!**, his new production which was about to tour the music halls. Although he was only earning a few pounds a week, Stanley was thrilled and Henson regarded him as his protégé, the beginning of a lifelong friendship between the two talented men.

When the show's run came to an end, Stanley went to Italy for singing lessons, but after six months in Milan decided that he felt more at home in the down-to-earth world of the music hall. He returned to Clacton, met a young lady called Alice Foran (known as "Queenie") and, in November 1913, they were married. It had been quite a year! Stanley was earning £3 a week, and as he awoke in their rented house on the day after their wedding he was suddenly struck by the thought: "Every penny bun's now going to cost me twopence!"

During the early days of the First World War, Stanley was in South America with another concert-party, **The Grotesques**. However, as he read news reports from the Western Front he was gripped by a terrible feeling of guilt and returned to England to

◁ *Leslie Henson (1891-1957), the star of numerous revues, musical comedies and plays. He became the friend and mentor of Stanley Holloway and gave him great help throughout his show-business career.*

join the Connaught Rangers, eventually seeing action in France. After the war, he made his debut in West End musical comedy at the Winter Garden. **Kissing Time** ran for 430 performances, and **A Night Out**, with Leslie Henson, chalked up more than 300.

It was during a chat in Henson's dressing-room in May 1921 that the idea of staging a pierrot show in a London theatre was first discussed and led to the creation of the legendary **Co-Optimists** which, between 1921 and 1926, took the West End by storm (see Chapter on the Roaring Twenties). It became a national institution, with its good humour, simple songs and happy atmosphere providing audiences with blessed relief after the horrors of the Great War.

By the time **The Co-Optimists** closed for the first time in 1926, Stanley was a star. He returned to musical comedy with **Hit the Deck** at the Hippodrome and **Song of the Sea** at His Majesty's, and was then signed as a solo turn for a couple of weeks at the London Palladium. The show was billed as featuring variety acts, and Stanley was worried that all he planned to do was sing. In the back of his mind was a story he had heard about a soldier at the time of Waterloo who refused to pick up his musket. One night, unable to sleep, he took a pencil and an envelope and started to write. Within 15 minutes he had scribbled down the idea for "*Sam, Pick Oop Tha' Musket*", and created the character who was to add a whole new dimension to his show-business career.

The audience loved the new monologue, and Stanley Holloway came to regard Sam Small as being like a son. In his autobiography *Wiv a Little Bit o' Luck* (1967), Stanley wrote a pleasing character sketch of his stubborn soldier: "A North Country lad, sometimes perky, sometimes dour, but always independent; a tough son of a gun who knows his point of view and his rights and isn't afraid to speak up for them. But also a naive, gentle and lovable character."

When **The Co-Optimists** reformed in 1929, Stanley introduced "Sam" into the show. The monologue was tremendously popular, and when it was put on record thousands of copies were sold. Sam Small became a national figure, and during the Second World War was used by several newspapers in the propaganda battle.

Realising that he had struck gold, Stanley Holloway wrote another monologue, "*Sam Goes to the Palace*", in which Queen Mary pours out the tea and enquires: "How many loomps of sugar, Sam?" When, after one charity matinée, Queen Mary was presented to the cast, she turned to Stanley and said "I'm rather ashamed to admit it, but I never pour the tea!"

Although, over the years, it underwent numerous repairs, Stanley kept the same hair-and-wire moustache that he wore when playing Sam. It became his good-luck charm, and he went to great lengths to ensure he didn't lose it. On one occasion, discovering he had left the theatre without it, he rushed back and, to his relief, discovered the moustache amongst a pile of rubbish at the side of the stage!

When a further revival of **The Co-Optimists** took place, the cast included the talented writer and entertainer Marriott Edgar, half-brother of the popular novelist Edgar Wallace. Inspired by the story of Sam Small, he wrote a monologue about a northern family's visit to the zoo. Stanley wasn't too sure about "*Albert and the Lion*" because, unlike Sam, it didn't have a recurring catch-phrase, but when he was asked to do a turn at a Northern Rugby League dance he decided it was the ideal moment to try it out. The guests at the dinner were still eating

as he began his recital but the clattering of knives and forks soon gave way to silence, followed by laughter and hearty applause. Albert Ramsbottom and "his stick with its 'orse's 'ead 'andle" had arrived! Over the next 10 years, Marriott Edgar wrote many more similar monologues.

Stanley Holloway had begun his film career in a 1921 silent comedy entitled "The Rotter", and during the 1930s appeared in a number of other small productions. Most notable was his role in "Sing As We Go" (1934) when he met Gracie Fields. The two became great friends, and it was "Our Gracie" who persuaded Stanley to go into Variety. This led to a couple of memorable shows at the London Palladium: **Life Begins at Oxford Circus** (1935) with Flanagan and Allen, Jack Hylton and Florence Desmond; and **London Rhapsody** (1937). In both shows he was kept on his toes by those notorious practical jokers, The Crazy Gang.

Sadly, in 1937 Stanley's wife Queenie died. It had been a happy marriage, and one which produced four wonderful children — Joan, Patricia, John and Mary. Stanley threw himself into his work, but as a naturally friendly, talkative, jovial sort of man, he was not the sort of person who could bear to be alone for long. Fortunately he struck up a

close friendship with a young actress whom he had first met in 1935. Violet Lane shared his sense of humour and, as the daughter of a civil engineer in Yorkshire, was refreshingly down to earth. Despite their age difference — "Laney" was more than 20 years younger than Stanley — they got on tremendously well and were married in January, 1939.

They settled at Penn in Buckinghamshire, with Laney giving up her own career to look after her busy husband and creating a comfortable home. She drove him to the theatre when necessary, took care of any secretarial work and skilfully managed his business affairs. Stanley described her as his "prop and cornerstone". They had a son called Julian.

During the 1940s Stanley Holloway made his name in a number of classic British films alongside some of the leading stars of the day. The list is a long one but includes "This Happy Breed" (1944), "The Way Ahead" (1944), "The Way to the Stars" (1945), "Brief Encounter" (1945), "Caesar and Cleopatra" (1945) and "Hamlet" (1948). One of his favourites was "Champagne

▷ Stanley Holloway's famous comic creation in a 1937 film which is largely forgotten today: "Sam Small Leaves Town".

◁ *The Winter Garden, one of many theatres designed by Frank Matcham, was situated to the north of Drury Lane. It was demolished in 1965 and part of the site now houses the New London Theatre (▽) where Andrew Lloyd-Webber's record-breaking "Cats" was staged.*

ALBERTO AZOZ

Charlie" (1944), a story about the music hall in which he starred as the "Great Vance" opposite Tommy Trinder who played George Leybourne. After the war his talents as a character actor enabled him to obtain memorable roles in the famous Ealing comedies "Passport to Pimlico" (1949), "The Lavender Hill Mob" (1951) and "The Titfield Thunderbolt" (1953).

Pantomime, more West End revues, Shakespeare on stage . . . Stanley Holloway's energy and talent knew no bounds. All the many strands of his previous career came memorably together in 1956 when, alongside Rex Harrison and Julie Andrews, he starred on Broadway as Alfred Doolittle in the première of **My Fair Lady**. The show was a sell-out and ran for two years, a triumphant pinnacle to a career that had already seen so many successes. The enthusiasm and gusto he brought to the role were repeated during the London production at Drury Lane (1958,

2000+ performances) and in the film version (1964) with Audrey Hepburn, for which, at the age of 74, he received an Oscar nomination. Stanley Holloway's interpretations of the glorious Lerner and Loewe songs "*Wiv a Little Bit o' Luck*" and "*Get Me to the Church on Time*" have never been bettered.

In 1960, Stanley Holloway was awarded the OBE and remained as busy as ever. He frequently appeared on American television and became a close friend of many international stars, including Danny Kaye, Groucho Marx and Maurice Chevalier. His last major public appearance was at the 1980 **Royal Variety Performance** in a tribute to the Queen Mother on her eightieth birthday.

Stanley Holloway was amongst our country's finest and most versatile entertainers and when he died on 30th January, 1982, one of the last links with the breezy world of the old music hall was finally severed.

STEPHEN GARNETT

JOYCE GRENFELL

The phrase "George — don't do that" will forever be associated with a lady who made us all laugh. The English nursery school teacher reprimanding George was just one of many characters Joyce Grenfell brought to life, her acute powers of observation and mimicry enabling her to add a whole host of other amusing characters to her repertoire.

She was born in London, on 10th February, 1910, to two Americans, Nora and Paul Phipps. Her mother was the youngest sister of Lady Nancy Astor, Britain's first woman MP, while her father was an architect from New York.

She left school at 17 but survived only one term at RADA because she found acting in plays rather dull and had fallen in love with Reggie Grenfell, whom she married in December, 1929. They became regulars at the Savoy Hotel in London, dancing to the music of Carroll Gibbons who once accompanied her on a recording of *"You'd be so Easy to Love"*. It was, however, much later when her recordings became well-known.

It was after she joined *The Observer* newspaper as a radio critic that Joyce developed a talent for mimicry, first taking off a lady speaker she had heard at a WI meeting then imitating the speaker at a friend's dinner party. The impresario Herbert Farjeon was so impressed he asked her to perform in his forthcoming show **The Little Revue** at the Little Theatre, a converted bank near the Strand, where Joyce found herself working alongside Hermione Baddeley. She was the only amateur member of the cast and therefore had to learn quickly. Her W.I. inspired monologue *"Useful and Acceptable Gifts"* featured in the first half of the show and was so good that Herbert asked her to write another which could be included in the second half.

The curtain went up on 19th April, 1939 and the critics were very favourable, singling Joyce out for special praise. Her monologues were, wrote one critic, "the best items in the programme", while another said she received enough applause to "stop the show". A further review hailed her as "The hit of **The Little Revue**".

▷ *The Little Theatre, a converted bank in Adelphi, where Joyce Grenfell began her West End career. It was bombed in 1917 and then blitzed in 1941.*

Even though the war intervened she continued in **The Little Revue** until 1940, combining it with her contribution to the war effort — working in troop canteens, the National Gallery canteen and as a Welfare Officer at the Canadian Red Cross hospital at Cliveden. Joyce was in her element but the Little Theatre was unfortunately blitzed in April 1941 and demolished eight years later.

Next came another Herbert Farjeon revue entitled **Diversion** which took 106 curtain calls at Wyndham's but her outside work prevented her from appearing in Farjeon's 1942 show **Light and Shade** at the Ambassadors. It turned out to be a flop, however, and the impresario appealed for Joyce to step in and save it. She managed to free herself from other commitments and wrote some clever new material but even she was unable to prevent the production's premature closure after only 54 performances.

In 1942, Joyce met Richard Addinsell, composer of the *"Warsaw Concerto"*, and they began a successful musical collaboration which lasted 30 years. Among other songs, they produced *"Nothing New to Tell" You* and *"I'm Going to See You Today"*. In the same year, Joyce took part in an **ENSA** tour of Northern Ireland, followed by an arduous tour of the Middle East and India. In 1946, in recognition of her wartime work, including entertaining the troops, she was awarded the OBE.

Following hostilities she wrote new material for various revues including

▷ Left to right: Cyril Ritchard, Madge Elliott, Joyce Grenfell and Graham Payn performing "The Burchells of Battersea Rise" in Noel Coward's 1945 revue **Sigh No More**.

Noel Coward's **Sigh No More** (1945) and worked with Stephen Potter on BBC radio for which she created many characters, including the nursery school teacher who was later to feature in several monologues.

Joyce's first attempt at writing her own revue came with **Tuppence Coloured** in 1947 collaborating with her cousin Nicholas Phipps. Also in the show, were Elisabeth Welch, Max Adrian and Daphne Oxenford. Four years later came **Penny Plain**, a Laurier Lister revue at St. Martin's.

More theatre appearances followed including **Joyce Grenfell Requests the Pleasure** (1954) which she took to New York the following year. Already a famous film star from comic roles such Miss Gossage in *The Happiest Days of Your Life* and lovesick Ruby Gates in the *St. Trinian's* sagas, she performed solo all over Britain, America, Canada and Australia. Her wide knowledge of music was also aired on the BBC television programme *Face the Music*.

Sadly, in 1973 she was forced to retire from the stage through illness but with characteristic enthusiasm she then completed two volumes of autobiography. In 1979 she was diagnosed with cancer and died on 30th November, aged 69. No fewer than two thousand people attended her thanksgiving service which was held at Westminster Abbey.

ANGELINE WILCOX

THE BLACK & WHITE MINSTREL SHOW

The Black and White Minstrel Show was unique. During the Sixties it won the coveted Golden Rose award at Montreux, and the proud Director of BBC Television at the time (Kenneth Adam) declared: "There are no star names in it . . . the various elements become fused into something bigger. The production has also shown that popular songs need not be vulgar, ruin public taste, or symbolise degeneracy."

How sad, therefore, that the censor's scissors have since consigned it to the cutting room floor on the grounds that it is racially offensive. Now, instead of good, wholesome family entertainment on television we have to suffer programmes which glorify gratuitous violence and portray bad language and obscene humour, all in the name of "progress" — and political correctness!

Although it was primarily a television show, it went out live from the Shepherds Bush Empire and also toured the Provinces before hitting the West End at the Victoria Palace, hence its inclusion in this book.

Its origins began back in 1926 when a new BBC producer was interrupted in his office by a young lad knocking on his door to ask: "Any rats or mice in here?". On being told "No", the youth just grinned and squirted disinfectant over him anyway! The location was the original Savoy Hill studio prior to the BBC's transfer to Broadcasting House; the young producer was Eric Maschwitz, later to become a leading song composer and TV producer. The "rat-catcher" was George Inns, officially a "page boy" but unofficially a jack-of-all-trades who also showed visitors around. In addition to making the tea he produced the famous sound effects of horses' hooves by banging hollow coconut shells on a wooden table, and simulated burning buildings by frying bacon in a pan!

During the early-Thirties, George Inns teamed up with producer Harry S. Pepper to launch the *Kentucky Minstrels*, a non-stop wireless programme of familiar Negro melodies, sung mainly by the BBC Male Chorus under the leadership of Lesley Woodgate. Interspersed with solos and comedy acts, coloured stars like the comedy duo Scott and Whaley were regular contributors.

Radio did not require anyone to "black-up", however, which only came about later when the show transferred successfully onto the stage. Not long into the series Harry Pepper married the programme's musical arranger, Doris Arnold, and together they formed a popular celebrity partnership up until the war, when the whole of broadcasting was thrown into confusion.

In 1948, the *Kentucky Minstrels* came to the small screen via the tiny studios at Alexandra Palace, but producer George Inns

◁ *George Mitchell conducting the Minstrels.*

△ *In 1960 the show toured the provinces and two years later opened at London's Victoria Palace, playing to packed houses. With an unbroken run of more than 4,000 performances it easily made it into the Musicals' "Top Ten".*

was already dreaming of a much larger stage complete with moving cameras. After years of planning, his vision of **The Black and White Minstrel Show** came to fruition in 1957 at, of all places, the television studio constructed at the Earls Court Radio Show.

The obvious choice for the male minstrels was an already well-established outstanding radio group called the George Mitchell Singers, while the experienced and versatile dancing group, the Television Toppers, made their ideal female partners. Initially everyone blacked-up but now it was decided to leave the Toppers with white faces — hence the show's title. Solo artistes included veterans Ike Hatch and G.H. Elliott (who never had any problems describing himself as "The Chocolate Coloured Coon"), plus TV comedian Kenneth Connor and his straight-man foil, Jerry Desmonde. It was enthusiastically received by everyone, both in the flesh and via recorded broadcasts. The following year, George Inns persuaded Eric Maschwitz, now Head of Light Entertainment, that a regular television series would be just the ticket, and so it proved.

The prime-time Saturday evening slot became required family viewing for most of the country's population. No interruptions were allowed as everyone settled down to watch a great musical spectacular. **The Black and White Minstrel Show** had arrived with a vengeance and, ironically, later won the vote for the most popular programme on colour television!

The early shows were broadcast from the BBC Television Theatre, formerly the Shepherd's Bush Empire, and among the guests were Peter Cavanagh ("The Voice of Them All"), Dennis Lotis, Benny Lee, Glen

△ Four well-known stars of the stage show — Leslie Crowther, Valerie Brooks, Stan Stennett and George Chisholm.

Mason and Rosemary Squires. In 1959 Kenneth Connor departed to make *Carry On* films and was replaced by Stan Stennett. Another new arrival was trombonist George Chisholm with his lively comic music group, the Jazzers, creating an outrageously funny personal formula which will forever be associated with the programme.

Among the leading singers were Tony Mercer, John Boulter and Dai Francis —

known as The Three Musketeers — while other members of the cast included the resourceful Leslie Crowther, Valerie Brooks and Penny Nicholls. The essential background music came from Eric Robinson's first-class orchestra. Behind the scenes were extra-quick costume changes, as many as five in a 45-minute show, all overseen by a closely-knit technical crew.

It certainly deserved its sub-title as "The Fastest Show on Television" with Scottish-born George Mitchell, a shy and reserved choirmaster and orchestrator, deserving much of the credit. By 1950 his George Mitchell Glee Club was so popular it took part in a **Royal Variety Performance** at the London Palladium. Although rarely seen on the screen himself, George's sheer professionalism underpinned every production and inspired orchestras and singers to give of their best for more than 30 years.

Following extensive rehearsals the programme went out live. Rarely did anything go wrong, but if it did then George Chisholm quickly came up with something clever to disguise it.

The black-faced Minstrels and the white-faced Toppers always seemed to enjoy themselves and their natural enthusiasm and high spirits infected everyone. Live shows, common then but now a rarity, intimately involved everyone in the studio from producer, performer and cameraman through to the youngest member of the audience. Expectations and adrenalin counts were high, as witnessed by numerous entertainers

◁ *"The Three Musketeers" — top Tony Mercer, centre Dai Francis and below John Boulter.*

down the years, all of whom openly preferred live theatre to studio recordings — because it gave them more of a "buzz".

When the show eventually came to an end it was a reflection of changing tastes more than ageing personnel. Nothing goes on for ever but while **The Black and White Minstrel Show** lasted it was the perfect example of quick-fire family entertainment which amused everyone and upset nobody. That is, until the political lobby came along with nothing better to do than tell us that we ought to be offended and how to complain about it. The writing was on the wall for every innocent show with a touch of character and class and, after an uninterrupted sequence of 21 years, the black greasepaint was removed for the last time in 1978.

Will we ever see another programme like it? Highly unlikely, because it would need to be renamed something like "The Grey and Off-White Minstrels" or the "Multi-Coloured Inter-Ethnic Anti-Racist Non-Sexist String-Players". It doesn't sound quite right!

HUBERT GREGG

Two days after the Second World War broke out, Hubert Gregg enlisted in the Army. Not because of any rush of patriotic fervour but because Neville Chamberlain had announced the closure of all theatres and places of entertainment, thereby killing the livelihoods of many thousands of people. An actor with nowhere to act gets hungry so he rushed down to the Recruiting Office and put his name down — for food! No sooner had he taken the "King's shilling", however, the government had second thoughts but by then it was too late. Hubert had enlisted.

The management of one London theatre tried to get him out to play opposite Alice Delysia in a comedy called *The French For Love* but Hubert was already heading north on a train to join the Lincolnshire Regiment The food was terrible and he said: "I'm going to get lit-up when those lights go up, I can tell you!" It was the germination of a nationally famous song which eventually went as follows:

> *I'm going to get lit-up when the lights go up in London,*
> *I'm going to get lit-up as I've never been before!*
> *You will find me on the tiles,*
> *You will find me wreath'd in smiles,*
> *I'm going to get so lit-up I'll be visible for miles!*
>
> *The city will sit up when the lights go up in London;*
> *We'll all be lit-up as the Fleet was, only more, much more …*
> *And before the party's played out,*
> *They will fetch the Fire Brigade out*
> *To the littest-uppest scene you ever saw!*

Various other verses followed and when someone said "You ought to do something with it" he sent the song to every publisher in London. They all turned it down, however, with comments like "This song has no commercial possibilities". Undeterred and with a superb grasp of the German language Hubert now found himself in London broadcasting twice daily to the enemy. His accent was so good that Goebbels thought he was a German traitor!

Having given up trying to get his song published, in 1941 he tried to sell it to a revue at the Comedy Theatre called **Rise Above It**. Everyone liked it except Hermione Gingold who whined: "We can't sing about getting lit-up when the war's over. We don't know who's going to win!" Hubert tactically withdrew. Two years he was playing and singing the song for fun to the patrons of a London club when Eric Maschwitz walked in.

Apart from being married to Hermione Gingold he was also Director of Light Entertainment at the BBC and suggested contacting George Black who was mounting a show at the Prince of Wales called **Strike A New Note**, starring the comic Sid Field. Visiting Americans flocked in including General Eisenhower, Bing Crosby and Bob Hope. There were fourteen performances a week — twice nightly with two matinées.

It was the idea of brilliant director, Robert Nesbitt, that Zoe Gail should present the song, dressed immaculately in white tie and tails. *"I'm Going To Get Lit-Up"* had not only found its niche but had fallen into the right time slot. Hermione Gingold had done Hubert a big favour. Had the song been sung too early — in 1941 when the Battle of the Atlantic was at its tragic height and few people thought of partying — it would have disappeared as an unacceptable piece of propaganda. Now, in 1943, Rommel was in full retreat and Churchill said "The sun has caught the helmets of our men and we are marching forward to victory".

As the war progressed it was being heard all over London, including the barrel organs! It even made its way into *Hansard* when Lady Astor, who had never had a drink in her life and didn't see why any-body else should, asked the Prime Minister what he thought of the song and was this the dis-graceful way we were going to behave?

Mr. Churchill replied: "I am confident that when the time comes we shall

△ Theatres light up the night in London's West End — but all the lights went out when war was declared on September 3rd, 1939. This picture of Shaftesbury Avenue shows three famous theatres. The Lyric (not to be confused with the Lyric, Hammersmith) opened in 1888; the Apollo (not to be confused with the Apollo Victoria) opened in 1901; and the Globe (originally the Hicks but renamed the Gielgud in 1995) in 1906.
ADINA TOVY

celebrate a victorious peace in a manner worthy of the British nation". Which is what we did! When, after the war, Hubert was invited to meet Churchill, the great man confirmed he had ordered the melody to be broadcast as a signal to members of the Resistance on the Continent that our in-vasion was under way.

On June 13th, 1944 — a year after the success of *"Lit-Up"* — Hubert was on leave in London and tossing around in bed trying to get some sleep when he heard an aircraft approaching. It had a strange intermittent buzz, a noise he hadn't heard before. After a moment he saw what he thought was a plane with its tail on fire crossing the night sky. It passed out of sight, then the engine cut out and a few seconds later there was an

almighty explosion. He actually remem-bered feeling sorry for the pilot — but there wasn't one. It was the first of Hitler's ten German flying bombs launched that night but only four made it across the Channel and just one landed in London; this one — our first "doodle-bug".

London was Hubert's city. He was born within the sound of Bow Bells, which made him a true Cockney. That doodlebug, the first of many, caused him to sit down a few nights later and write a song called *"Maybe It's Because I'm A Londoner"*. Once again, every publisher he sent it to turned it down, so he stuck it in a drawer and forgot about it for a further two years.

One night in 1946, however, Jack Hylton telephoned to ask if he had a song that might suit Bud Flanagan. Jack, now a theatrical entrepreneur, was about to mount a musical at the Victoria Palace called **Together Again**, which would bring the Crazy Gang back to London.

Hubert's first answer was "No", but then he remembered the unwanted song and took out the yellowing manuscript. He was asked to take it right away to His Majesty's Theatre where he sat down at the piano and played it. The show opened in 1947 to rave reviews and Hubert expected the song would now be accepted for publication but again everyone turned it down.

The show ran for a further four years and people were soon whistling the melody in the streets. There was such a public clamour for the sheet music that eventually but very begrudgingly, it was printed by a small subsidiary of a big firm which didn't want its own imprint on the cover.

Amazingly, given its later popularity, the song was not well plugged and because the publisher was strapped for cash, Hubert suggested he might sell copies in the foyer at the Victoria Palace. It didn't happen because Jack Hylton wanted ninepence out of each copy sold — but its full price was only a shilling!

Maybe It's Because I'M A LONDONER

Words & Music by **HUBERT GREGG**

London isn't everybody's cup of tea,
Often you'll hear visitors complain.
Noisy, smoky city, but it seems to me
There's a magic in the fog and rain ...

Maybe it's because I'm a Londoner
That I love London so,
Maybe it's because I'm a Londoner,
That I think of her, wherever I go.
I get a funny feeling inside of me
Just walking up and down —
Maybe it's because I'm a Londoner
That I love London Town.

Apart from the song's original singer, Bud Flanagan's version of *"Maybe It's Because I'm a Londoner"* became associated with many others. Jack Warner made it the theme of his famous *Dixon of Dock Green* television series, whistling it as the introduction to each of the early episodes. It also became popular in Australia, where Arthur Askey sang the opening line as *"Maybe It's Because I'm from Liverpool"!*

Americans, strangely enough, also enjoy singing it. Danny Kaye closed more than one **Royal Variety Performance** by leading the company in it and wrote a new verse for Kirk Douglas and Burt Lancaster to sing at a charity evening at the London Palladium. The oddest rendering, however, was a television performance from the Albert Hall when it was sung with great solemnity by the Omsk-Siberia Choir — in Russian!

In 1981 the new Lord Mayor of London, Sir Ronald Gardner-Thorpe, even took the song as the theme for his "Lord Mayor's Show" — and was kind enough to award Hubert the Freedom of the City!

Hubert Gregg had an amazing memory recall and was probably the last of the great musical men of the London theatre who could quote wartime and even pre-war stories as though they happened only yesterday. He was once on duty at BBC Broadcasting House during the early hours when Winston Churchill phoned to ask if he could have an extra five minutes over his allocated slot to the nation: "... just like

◁ Carroll Gibbons sang Hubert Gregg's songs from the piano at the Savoy Hotel, and was also MD of various shows.

▷ Sid Field's career was short but sharp, starting with Hubert Gregg in **Strike a New Note** at the Prince of Wales in 1943.

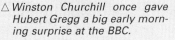

△ Winston Churchill once gave Hubert Gregg a big early morning surprise at the BBC.

Eisenhower did last week!" A somewhat bemused young Hubert assured the Prime Minister that he thought this would be quite acceptable to the Beeb!

Hubert's first wife was Zoe Gail but he later played opposite his second, Pat Kirkwood, in **Chrysanthemum**. Opening in 1956 at the tiny New Lindsey Theatre it later transferred for a run at the Prince of Wales. Although he was an acknowledged expert on musicals Hubert actually directed Agatha Christie's *The Mousetrap* for many years, and also took part in several plays. Latterly he was famous for his radio programme *Thanks for the Memory* in which he would affectionately talk about sitting in his square chair playing CDs which he loved to describe as "shaving mirrors". Each addition always contained one of his own songs which he

played "from me to you".

The grand old man of the London stage died at the age of 89 in March 2004. He never stopped working and attributed his longevity to ginseng and his third wife's cooking. Carmel Lytton survived him with a son and daughter. Sadly, his unpublished autobiography lies gathering dust!

▷ Jack Warner listens to Hubert Gregg singing "Maybe It's Because I'm a Londoner" which became the opening theme of Jack's much-loved "Dixon of Dock Green" BBC television series.

THE SWINGING SIXTIES

For many older people the "Swinging Sixties" represented the beginning of the end for musical tradition. They certainly ushered in huge changes and towards the end of the decade there appeared a number of less salubrious offerings which many found distasteful and would never pay to watch. Others thought differently and felt they offered a new found freedom. The twain would never meet.

Without doubt, however, there was one musical which shone out like a beacon and has remained supreme ever since. **Oliver!** was quite brilliant and turned Lionel Bart into a household name. Despite the difficulties of a large juvenile cast — or possibly because of — it has continued to thrill audiences up and down the country and nearly half a century later shows no sign of abating in popularity.

Bart began his stage career in 1958 with **Wally Pone** at the small Unity theatre. A musical interpretation of Ben Jonson's "Volpone", it ran for a season but a year later he had a big hit with **Fings Aint What They Used To Be** which ran for nearly 900 performances at Stratford East and the Garrick. **Lock Up Your Daughters** (1959) was a joint production with Bernard Miles and Laurie Johnson at the Mermaid theatre, closely followed by **And Another Thing**, a collaboration with Alan Melville and others at the Fortune.

People sang along to Bart's catchy lyrics and tunes and **Oliver!** (1960) broke all box office records with a run of 2618 at the New Theatre. Ron Moody was brilliant as Fagin, Georgia Brown perfect as Nancy, Danny Sewell was nasty Bill Sykes, Paul Whitsun-Jones played Mr. Bumble the beadle, a young Barry Humphries was Mr. Sowerberry the undertaker and Keith Hamshere was one of several boys to play the lead role.

The outstanding songs from **Oliver!** are almost too numerous to list but include *"Food, Glorious Food"*; *"Oliver!"*; *"Boy For Sale"*; *"That's Your Funeral"*; *"Where is Love?"*; *"Consider Yourself"*; *"You've Got to Pick a Pocket or Two"*; *"It's a Fine Life"*; *"Be Back Soon"*; *"Oom-Pah-Pah"*; *"As Long as He Needs Me"*; *"I'd Do Anything"*; *"Who Will Buy?"*; *"As Long as He Needs Me"*; and *"Reviewing the Situation"*. A long list it may be but at the time the whole country was humming the melodies and people still do whenever they watch a new production.

Having had early success on the pop music front, notably writing for Tommy Steele, Bart now embarked on another successful musical and **Blitz!** (1962), based on wartime family experiences, took more than 500 curtain calls at the Adelphi. It was equalled two years later by **Maggie May** at the same venue. Believing he possessed the magic formula Bart now enthusiastically went ahead with an expensive new production based on the adventures of Robin Hood.

Sadly, instead of hitting the bullseye, **Twang!** missed the target at the Shaftesbury in 1965 but instead of pulling the plug Bart poured good money after bad and bankrupted himself. Revivals of **Oliver!** continued but the composer had by now sold the rights. He tried again and contributed to the ironically named **Costa Packet** and **The Londoners** (both 1972) but neither lasted very long at the Theatre Royal, Stratford. A final offering was **Lionel**, a compilation of Bart songs and musicals at the New London in 1977.

The Sound of Music (1961), was a Rodgers and Hammerstein show which many thought the equal of their earlier successes of **Oklahoma**, **South Pacific** and **Carousel**. It ran for 2385 performances at

THEATRE ROYAL, DRURY LANE

Arguably London's premier theatre, Drury Lane has been home to many famous shows and associated with a large number of well-known show business people. Earlier chapters have alluded to its chequered history and this page pays tribute to its role as home to various modern musicals.

◁ *In 1933 Drury Lane hosted **The Three Musketeers**. With lyrics by P.G. Wodehouse and music by Rudolf Friml, it took 240 curtain calls. In 1967 came **The Four Musketeers**, lyrics by Herbert Kretzmer, and music by Laurie Johnson. It lasted for 462 performances and was produced by Bernard Delfont. The stars were Harry Secombe, Elizabeth Larner and Kenneth Connor.*

▷ *Michael Crawford was an amazing entertainer who did all his own stunts. In addition to **Billy** (1974), which ran for 904 performances, he starred in several other London musicals including **Barnum** (1981), **The Phantom of the Opera** (1986) and **The Woman in White** (2004).*

△ *Three giants of the London musical stage. Prince Littler (left) became owner of the Moss Empires Group which included 12 West End theatres. He was also the longest serving manager of Drury Lane. Lew Grade (centre), the brother of theatrical entrepreneur Bernard Delfont, succeeded Littler at Drury Lane and was the father figure behind ATV. Andrew Lloyd Webber (right) had unprecedented success with his musicals and claims five of the 11 longest running shows in the West End. Branching out into ownership with his Really Useful Group he became a huge player in the international Musical market.*

Three more modern Drury Lane shows.

the Palace which was 2000 more than **Flower Drum Song**, an Oriental offering from the same duo which had immediately preceded it. There were no real stars in the original production but Petula Clark played Maria in the 1981 revival at the Victoria Palace. Among the more famous songs are *"Maria"; "My Favourite Things"; "Do-Re-Mi"; "The Lonely Goatherd"; "Sixteen Going on Seventeen"; "Climb Every Mountain";* and *"Edelweiss"*.

Lerner and Loewe hit the high-spots with **Camelot**, a stirring tale of King Arthur and his Knights of the Round Table which held sway for 518 performances at Drury Lane in 1964. Laurence Harvey memorably sang *"How to Handle a Woman"* and the show was revived at the Apollo Victoria in 1982.

Another big-hitter from 1964 was **Robert and Elizabeth** with lyrics by Ronald Millar and music by Ron Grainer. Based on the play "The Barretts of Wimpole Street", the story of Robert and Elizabeth Barrett-Browning, it starred Keith Michell, John Clements and June Bronhill, and achieved 957 performances at the Lyric. A year later came **Charlie Girl** which was a personal triumph for the ageing Anna Neagle, ably assisted by Joe Brown, Hy Hazell and Derek Nimmo. Behind the scenes as its musical director was the seemingly ubiquitous Kenneth Alwyn. 2200 performances at the Adelphi spoke for itself.

Yet another production to pass the 2000 mark was Jerry Bock and Sheldon Harnick's **Fiddler on the Roof** (1967). Lengthy it may have been but the public loved it, with the French actor, Topol, undoubtedly stealing the show at His Majesty's. Richard Hill and John Hawkins' **Canterbury Tales**, based on Nevill Coghill's translation of Geoffrey Chaucer, was quite different but also passed 2000 performances at the Phoenix. The last of the long-runners was **Hair** (1968) but there were many who felt this was not really a musical at all, just an excuse to take off one's clothing in public at the Shaftesbury.

Stephen Sondheim first burst on to the London musical scene when he wrote the

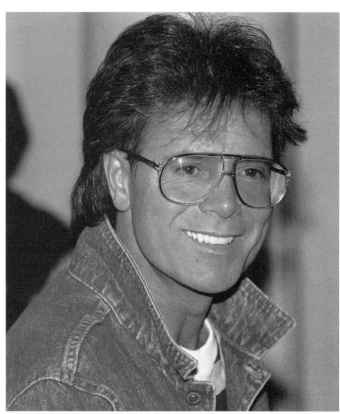

△ *Arguably the most enduring popular music star of all time, certainly in Britain, Cliff Richard continued to be involved with musicals up to, and beyond, pensionable age. His splendid work on stage was complemented off it by unstinting charitable work. From enfant terrible during the Rock 'n' Roll era, he graduated to elder statesman who many younger record producers maliciously, jealously and quite unjustifiably, denigrated. He represented everything good about popular music and it is easy to see why his ever faithful army of fans travelled the length and breadth of the country to watch him perform. Unlike some in show business, his knighthood was richly deserved.*

lyrics to Leonard Bernstein's music for **West Side Story** (1958) but popped up again with both lyrics and the music for the comedy **A Funny Thing Happened on the Way to the Forum** (1963). It was a long title but with a cast including Frankie Howerd, Kenneth Connor, Jon Pertwee and the veterans "Monsewer" Eddie Gray and Robertson Hare ("Oh calamity!") it is hardly surprising that it ran for 762 performances at the Strand. Sondheim followed it up with regular new offerings right up to the end of the century and beyond.

One of the biggest pop stars in the Rock 'n' Roll revolution of the late-Fifties was Tommy Steele. After several hit records he took to the stage in various guises and was the star of David Heneker's **Half a Sixpence** (also 1963). Based on the book *Kipps* by H.G. Wells, it topped 679 performances at

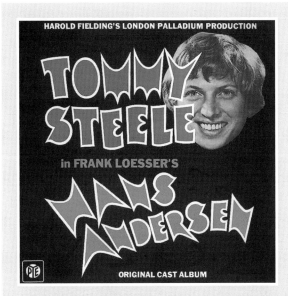

△ Another musical poacher turned gamekeeper was Tommy Steele. From jeans, sideburns, swinging guitars, "Rocking with the Caveman" and "Singing the Blues" in the mid-Fifties — when Lionel Bart was one of his song-writers — he emerged into a highly talented actor and film star who even took on serious roles in Gilbert and Sullivan. **Half a Sixpence** opened at the Cambridge Theatre in 1963 and ran for almost 700 performances. **Hans Andersen** was staged a decade later at the London Palladium — twice the size of the Cambridge — where it played more than 300 times. Like his contemporary Cliff Richard, Tommy Steele continued music-making well past the time most people retire and put their feet up.

the Cambridge with perhaps its best-known song being *"Flash, Bang, Wallop — what a picture"*. It was a triumph for Steele who went on to further stage successes including Frank Loesser's **Hans Andersen** (1974).

Another well-known character who successfully switched careers was Harry Secombe. A genial and humble Christian gent from Swansea, he had everyone in stitches with "The Goon Show" on BBC Radio but could easily change the mood from ridiculous to serious and was the brilliant star of Cyril Ornadel and Leslie Bricusse's **Pickwick** (again 1963). Based on *The Pickwick Papers* by Charles Dickens, Secombe played the title role to perfection and one cannot help but make comparison with his role of Mr. Bumble the Beadle in the film version of **Oliver!** (1968).

Two more big successes of the mid-Sixties were Charles Chilton and Joan Littlewood's **Oh What a Lovely War** staged at Stratford East, and Jerry Herman's American import, **Hello Dolly** produced at Drury Lane. Although very different in character, the former being largely an anti-war effort and the latter a swash-buckling extravaganza, they cleared 501 and 794 performances respectively. Others shows which exceeded 400 curtain calls were Frank Loesser's **Most**

Happy Fella (1960) and **How To Succeed in Business Without Really Trying** (1963); Anthony Newley and Leslie Bricusse's **Stop the World, I Want to Get Off** (1961); Bryan Blackburn's **Come Spy With Me** (1966); **The Four Musketeers** and **Sweet Charity** (1967); Jerry Herman's **Mame** and Burt Bacharach and Hal David's **Promises, Promises** (1969). Other shows worthy of mention include **The Music Man** (*"76 Trombones Led the Big Parade"*); **Jorrocks**; **Cabaret**; **Man of La Mancha**; **Gentlemen Prefer Blondes**; **Anne of Green Gables**; **Sail Away** (Noel Coward); **Instant Marriage**; and **Divorce Me Darling**. Jeremy Taylor's revue **Wait a Minim** was also a big success at the Fortune.

The original aim of this book was to finish at 1970 but it would be churlish not to comment on how the London Musical progressed after that point. It is fair to say that once the Swinging Sixties were over then almost anything went onstage. The purist would say it got worse, the egalitarian would say it got better. What is not in doubt is that many new shows were put on simply to shock and appeal to base instincts. The same could equally be said of films but, happily, a small number of musical giants continued to supply staple family fayre which could be watched by anyone.

The most important was undoubtedly Andrew Lloyd Webber who turned all records on their head, as a glance at Appendix 3 will readily indicate. No fewer than five of the 11 longest-running West End musicals belong to him so his place in history is assured but what was it that made him so successful? He had a good start because his father, William (1914-1982), was a self-effacing romantic academic composer who became Director of the London College of Music and believed that music should be tuneful but concise. His musical pedigree was thus pure thorough-bred but his close friendship with veteran musical composer, Vivian Ellis, also helped. Among his lyricists were Tim Rice and Richard Stilgoe but he was able to harness the best from many others too. Andrew's younger brother, Julian, became a success-ful classical concert cellist who was not afraid to challenge the avant-garde brigade when it came to good music.

Another major influence on late-20th Century musical theatre was Cameron Mackintosh, a major theatrical entrepreneur who did much to promote the cause and it would be interesting to know how history will treat these men who established something of a stranglehold on the musical "Musical" establishment. To their credit they avoided the excesses of the early 21st Century where shame seemed to have been abolished and freedom without responsibility accepted by many as the norm.

Quite where this will all lead no one yet knows but anyone reading this book decades on might wonder how an ordered society where the vast majority of musicals were suitable for children, managed to change into something quite different. Will all the major London theatres survive in their pres-ent form? Probably not but it is interesting to note that by the year 2004, musicals out-numbered plays in the West End for the very first time. The spoken word had finally become subservient to the music.

This remarkable turnabout is partially explained by an explosion of Fringe theatres (see Appendix 4) but also by the dearth of plays suitable for family consumption. Where once they outnumbered musicals by at least four to one, often more, the tables had been turned. One play to buck the trend, however, was Agatha Christie's *The Mousetrap*, which, together with the enor-mous popularity of Lloyd Webber musicals and enduring star entertainers like Cliff Richard, Tommy Steele, Michael Crawford, Elaine Page etc., showed decisively that peo-ple still preferred conservative fayre. The ini-tial success and subsequent revivals of many family musicals also suggest that music crit-ics often, and regularly, get it wrong!

Long live the traditional musical!

FOUR WEST END THEATRE PROGRAMMES

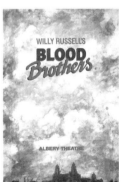

◁ *George Benson and Davy Kaye in* **Belle**, *sub-titled* **The Ballad of Dr. Crippen**, *as depicted in a clever 1961 contem-porary* Punch *cartoon.*

▷ *This logo was very famous during the Sixties and was imme-diately identifiable as* **Oliver!** *the show which broke all records.*

At a time when it is fashionable to listen to music which requires ear plugs — even for those outside the car! — all is not yet lost. Whether a show succeeded or failed often depended on being in the right place at the right time. Many good productions actually flopped through no real fault of their own, so how refreshing that Adrian Wright has released several CDs of long forgotten tuneful musicals when melody was unashamedly the key. His label is cleverly and appropriately titled "Must-Close-Saturday-Records" and is to be warmly applauded when we are told that all that matters today is profitability. "No, No, a thousand times No!"

Evergreen Melodies

This England magazine has produced a series of nostalgic CDs and cassettes about the history of the West End musical. They range in time from early-Edwardian to the 1950s and are available from *This England*, 73 Rodney Road, Cheltenham, GL50 1HT. Ring 01242-537900 for enquiries and a free music catalogue, or order direct on 01242-515156. The 15 recordings are as follows:

SONGS FROM THE SHOWS *Famous songs from London musicals*

▼Tape Ref		CD Ref▼		▼Tape Ref		CD Ref▼
SS1	Edwardian Shows	CS1				
SS2	G & S Overtures	CS2		SS9	Harry Parr Davies	CS9
SS3	G & S Songs	CS3		TL1	The Roaring Forties	CL1
SS4	1st World War Shows	CS4		TL2	Billy Mayerl	CL2
SS5	The Twenties	CS5		TL3	The American Fifties	CL3
SS6	The Thirties	CS6		TL4	Noel Coward	CL4
SS7	Vivian Ellis	CS7		TL5	Show-Stoppers	CL5
SS8	2nd World War Shows	CS8		TL6	The British Fifties	CL6

LONDON THEATRELAND

L ondon's theatreland is a constantly changing scene. Originally most theatres and music halls were nearer the East End but by late-Victorian times they had shifted more towards the centre of town. Many of the buildings were extremely ramshackle and only a handful never suffered serious fire damage — much to their owners' disappointment because insurance payouts sometimes exceeded box office expectations! **The Opera Comique**, home to the first Gilbert and Sullivan operettas, could only be reached by underground passages so it was fortunate there was never a conflagration.

The early post-war map opposite reflects the wartime Blitz — the **Gate**, **Kingsway**, **Little** and the original **Shaftesbury** all being destroyed in 1941, while the **Queen's** was not reopened until 1959. In addition, the famous **Gaiety**, at the junction of Aldwych and the Strand, closed its doors in 1939. Many more changes have since taken place.

The **Hippodrome** became **The Talk of the Town** in 1958 but finally shut in 1982, while the **Windmill** — the only theatre never to close its doors during the war — became a cinema in 1964, followed by the **Saville** in 1970. The **Winter Garden** was demolished in 1960 but from its ashes arose the **New London** theatre, while demolition of the **Stoll**

△ The interior of the **Old Vic** conjures up visions of great artistes and entertainments over the last 200 years.

110

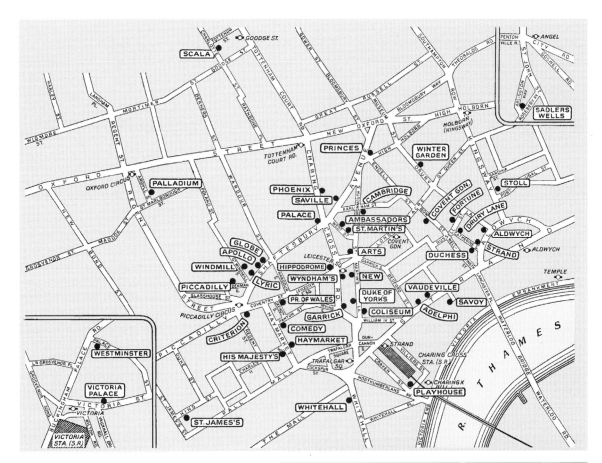

in 1957 resulted in a new office block and theatre called the **Royalty**. The **Globe** is now the **Gielgud**.

On the death of King George VI in 1952, **His Majesty's** once more reverted to **Her Majesty's** while in 1962 the **Prince's** was renamed and became the second **Shaftesbury**. **St. James'** was closed in 1957 and the **Scala**, out on a limb and never really successful, was demolished in 1972. A year later the **New** was renamed the **Albery**.

Many theatres have been associated with famous people and art forms. The **Whitehall** will always be remembered for the brilliant Brian Rix farces between 1950 and 1967 and the glitzy **Palladium** for the post-war ground-breaking Sunday night extravaganzas screened by Independent Television. Pre-war it was also the home of the "Crazy Gang" who later transferred to the **Victoria Palace** where they were succeeded by BBC Television's **Black and White Minstrel Show**. The BBC also had exclusive use of the **Playhouse** theatre between 1951 and 1987.

△ *Twice burnt down, the* **Royal Opera House, Covent Garden**, *has had a new lease of life, including tea dances in the Floral Hall (left).*

111

△ Built on a grand scale, the **London Coliseum** was designed by Frank Matcham. A mythical Roman scene perfectly fits the backdrop.

Most unusually, the **Ambassadors** and **St. Martin's** were actually built as a matching pair at the beginning of the Great War and latterly shared out Agatha Christie's long-running success, *The Mousetrap*. But it was the **Savoy** — built especially by Richard D'Oyly Carte for his Gilbert and Sullivan productions — which caused the biggest sensation, when in 1881 it became the first theatre to use electric light. In 1988 the new D'Oyly Carte Opera Company moved into the **Cambridge** theatre.

For regal connections, however, two theatres stand apart. In 1662 the title **Theatre Royal** was granted to both **Drury Lane** and **Covent Garden**, although the **Haymarket** also managed a royal connection a century later. Both the former theatres, like **Sadler's Wells** and more recently the **Coliseum**, have been closely associated with top ballet and opera companies.

In addition to many smaller theatres, out of picture on the map are the **Old Vic** near Waterloo Station and the **Royal Court** in Sloane Square. The **Royal National Theatre** was established on the South Bank during the Seventies, while in 1982 the **Barbican** opened in the City.

Hopefully, London's Theatreland, which now includes many small club theatres, will continue to flourish, but never totally at the expense of decency and good taste.

△ Originally intended only for the aristocracy or the well-heeled, these splendid boxes at the **Shaftesbury** are similar to many of those constructed in the top Victorian and Edwardian theatres.

△ Sir John Betjeman believed the **Palace** theatre to be "London's noblest surviving building". Situated near Cambridge Circus it is certainly an imposing sight.

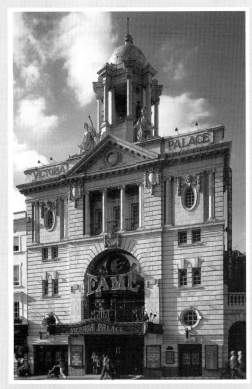

△ The Crazy Gang began their madcap antics at the **Palladium** but post-war transferred to the **Victoria Palace**. It was here they notched up in excess of 7,000 performances in seven smash-hit revues between 1947 and 1960, a truly outstanding achievement.

△ Although the facade of the **London Pavilion** is still an impressive sight near Piccadilly Circus there has been no theatre here since 1934 when it was converted into a cinema.

△ When King George VI died in 1952 **His Majesty's** Theatre reverted to its original Victorian title of **Her Majesty's**.

△ **St Martin's**, and its twin the **Ambassadors**, became famous for Agatha Christie's long-running play "The Mousetrap".

All photographs in this chapter were taken by Alberto Arzoz for the book London Theatres by Mike Kilburn, published by New Holland in 2002.

Although this table does not claim to be comprehensive it does include most of the major shows and also a number of more recent productions (e.g. important pantomimes), from which commercial recordings were made.
It is difficult to distinguish between musical revues and full-length musicals and both have therefore been included. Revues are mostly unnamed but a few associated with famous impresarios merit special mention. Some plays with significant incidental music have been included but revues with little or no music have been omitted.
Many shows had several revivals which are impossible to list in detail, e.g. *Me and My Girl* had at least three separate London repeats before it once again hit the heights in 1985, while Gilbert and Sullivan operettas have been repeated numerous times in London. Among the shows omitted are several short 19th Century musicals which ran together on the same bill and a small number of later shows with deliberately provocative or offensive titles. All these shows had London runs but occasionally reached only the fringes. Librettists and composers are indicated where known, although other people were often involved as well. In the case of revues there were often far too many people to consider. The definite article has been omitted in most cases. Special thanks go to Alexander Gleason who filled in many of the gaps. Anyone who can supply missing data is encouraged to write to the author.

KEY – aka=also known as; rev=revival; extended=extended run; prodn=production; edn=edition; et al=and others

TITLE	YEAR	RUN
1066 and All That (Arkell/Alfred Reynolds)	1935	387
110 In the Shade (Schmidt/Tom Jones)	1967	101
1776 (Sherman Edwards)	1970	168
1954 Palladium Show — revue	1954	54
2 Intimate Revue (Rigby/Fred Elizalde)	1930	17
3p Off Opera (Rice/Thompson/Colvill/Clarke)	1974	season
4000 Brass Halfpennies (Bernard Miles/Frow/Graham)	1965	
42nd Street (Dubin/Warren)	1984	4.5 years
5064 Gerrard (Ayer/Berlin/Comer/Marshall/Murphy/Styler)	1915	194
70 Girls, 70 (Kander/Ebb)	1991	13 weeks
A La Carte (Melville/Zwar) revue	1948	243
A to Z (Trix/Novello) revue	1921	428
Abbacadabra (Black/Ulvaeus/Andersson)	1983	84
Ace of Clubs (Noel Coward)	1950	211
Acorn Antiques (Victoria Wood)	2005	
Ad Lib (Peter Myers/Norman Dannatt)	1948	4 weeks
Adam's Opera (Addinsell/Clemence Dane)	1928	20
Adamless Eden, An (Clarke/Slaughter)	1882	2 months
Adele (Herve/Briquet/Philipp)	1914	20
Adonis (Rice)	1884	110
Adventures of a Bear Called Paddington (Bradley/Johnson/Chappell)	1979	
Adventures of Mr. Toad (Grahame, Chater-Robinson)	1986	Christmas
Afgar (Thompson/David/Cuvillier)	1919	300
After All (Desprez/Cellier)	1878	3 months
After Dark (Duffield/Leslie-Smith) revue	1933	167
After Dinner (Malneck/Signorelli/Kahn) Gwen Farrar revue	1932	15
After the Ball (Noel Coward)	1954	188
After the Girl (Percy Greenbank/Paul Rubens)	1914	105
After the Show (Grahame/Myers/Addison/Dannatt)	1950	14
After the Show (2) (Grahame/Myers/Addison/Dannatt)	1951	
Ages Ago (W.S. Gilbert/Clay)	1868	
Ain't Misbehavin' (Horowitz/Maltby/Fats Waller)	1979	
Airs & Graces (Monckton/Finck/Ross)	1917	115
Airs on a Shoestring (Lister/Addinsell/Flanders/Swann)	1953	772
Aladdin & His Wonderful Lamp (Croft/The Shadows)	1964	
Aladdin (Cole Porter/Coke/Goodwin)	1959	143
Aladdin (Sandy Wilson)	1979	
Aladdin II (Thompson/Herve)	1870	100
Alf's Button (Darlington) revue	1924	111
Alf's Button (Robbins/Abady)	1933	short run
Alice in Wonderland (Savill Clarke/Slaughter)	1886	57
Alice in Wonderland (Savill Clarke/Slaughter) rev.	1927	25
Alice in Wonderland (Carroll/Marleys)	1930	23
Alice in Wonderland (Field/Price)	1932	62
Alice in Wonderland & Through the Looking Glass (Addinsell/Dane)	1943	86
Alice Through the Looking Glass (Carroll/Tilbury)	1903	60
All Abroad (Risque/Rosse)	1895	87
All Alight at Oxford Circus – George Black revue	1936	
All Change Here (Pelissier)	1911	
All Clear — Harold French revue	1939	162
All For Joy (Gilbert Gunn)	1932	23
All in Love (Bruce Geller/Jacques Urbont)	1964	22
All My Eye-Van-Hoe (Hayman/Crook/Talbot/Solomon etc)	1894	9
All Scotch (Herman Darewski)	1915	74
All Square (Melville/Zwar) revue	1963	
All the Winners (Hicks)	1913	144
All You Need Is Love (Lennon/McCartney) revue	2001	
Almond Eye (Soutar/Veasey/Wydiam/Rosse)	1923	24
Always (May/Sprague)	1997	6 weeks
Amasis (Penn/Farady)	1906	200
Ambassador (Hackady/Gohman)	1971	
American Beauty (Morton/Kerker)	1900	69
Amorelle (Boyd-Jones/Serpette)	1904	28
Ancient Britons (A'Beckett/Reed)	1875	3 months
And Another Thing (Melville/Zwar/Dicks/Rudge/Bart/Cryer)	1960	
And On We Go (Rogers/Carter)	1937	21
And So to Bed (Vivian Ellis)	1951	323
Andy Capp (Peacock, Price)	1982	99
Angel Face (Victor Herbert)	1922	13
Ann Veronica (Croft/Cyril Ornadel)	1969	44
Anna Russell (Russell)	1962	
Anne of Green Gables (Montgomery/Harron/Campbell	1969	300
Annie (Charnin/Strouse) not the same Annie as 1967	1978	1485
Annie (Reed/Thornhill) not the same Annie as 1978	1967	398
Annie Get Your Gun (Irving Berlin/D. Fields)	1947	1304
Antarctica	1876	season
Antarctica (Peter Greenwell/Snell)	1957	season
Antelope (Ross/Felix/Lonsadle/Sidney Jones)	1908	22
Any Minute Now (MacLennan/Anderson)	1983	3 weeks
Any Old Thing (Burnaby/Herman Darewski)	1917	
Anyone for England? (Paul McDowell) revue	1965	
Anything Goes (Bolton/Wodehouse/Cole Porter)	1935	261
Anything to Declare?	1971	
Apache (Titheradge/Benatzsky)	1927	164
Applause (Strouse) from the film All About Eve	1972	382
Apple Sauce (Carr/Strachey) revue	1940	462
Arc de Triomphe (Novello/Hassall)	1943	222
Arcadians (Lionel Monckton/Talbot/Wimperis)	1909	809
Are You Lonesome Tonight? (Bleasdale et al)	1985	47 weeks
Are You There? (Edgar Wallace/Leoncavallo)	1913	23
Arlette (Ross/Grey/Novello/Vieu/le Feuvre)	1917	260
Art of Living (Heneker/Monty Norman)	1960	12 months
Artist's Model, An (Sidney Jones/Leslie Stuart)	1895	392
As Dorothy Parker Once Said (Parker/Sandy Wilson)	1969	
As You Were (Herman Darewski) revue	1918	434
Aspects of Love (Lloyd Webber/Hart/Black)	1989	1325
Assassins (Sondheim/Weidman)	1992	9 weeks
At the Drop of a Hat (Flanders/Swann)	1956	759
At the Drop of Another Hat (Flanders/Swann) rev 1965	1963	12 months
At the Lyric (Leslie-Smith/Melville)	1953	
At the Palace (Cryer/Vosburgh/Blackburn) revue	1970	
At the Sign of the Angel (Stevens/Brawn)	1975	short run
At the Silver Swan (James/Samuels/Mackey)	1936	51
Autumn Manoeuvres (Kalman)	1912	75
Babes (Humphrey Carpenter)	1993	5
Babes in the Wood (Croft/The Shadows)	1965	
Babil & Bijou (Boucicault/Planche/Herve/Clay/Riviere)	1872	160
Babil & Bijou (Boucicault/Planche)	1882	167
Baby Bunting (Grey/Ayer)	1919	213
Back Again (Turner/Smith/Weston/Lee)	1919	129
Back to Blighty (Hoare/Braham)	1916	
Balalaika (Posford/Grun/Maschwitz) rev. of Gay Hussar	1936	570
Balkan Princess (Wimperis/Paul Rubens)	1910	176
Ball at the Savoy (Abraham/Hammerstein)	1933	148
Ballyhoo (Walker/Nesbitt)	1932	139
Bamboula (Sirmay/H. Rosenthal/Bolton/Furber/Caesar)	1925	77
Barbe-Bleue (Offenbach)	1883	
Bar-Mitzvah Boy (Jack Rosenthal/Styne/Black)	1978	77
Barnardo (Maxin)	1980	43
Barnum (Stewart/Coleman)	1981	655
Baroness (Cotsford Dick)	1892	13
Bashville (G.B. Shaw/King/Benny Green)	1983	season
Bat Boy (Farley/Fleming/O'Keefe)	2004	

Title	Year	Runs
Battling Butler (Furber/Braham)	1922	238
Beatlemania (Lennon/McCartney)	1979	
Beau Brummel (Harold Simpson)	1933	23
Beautiful Game (Lloyd Webber/Elton)	2000	1 year
Beauty & the Best (Menker/Ashman/Rice)	1997	
Beauty of Bath (Hicks/Taylor/Haines/Norton)	1906	287
Beauty Prize (Kern/Wodehouse/Grossmith)	1923	214
Beauty Spot (Harris/Anderson/James Tate)	1917	152
Beauty Stone (Pinero/Carr/Sullivan)	1898	50
Be-Bop the Ruler (Herzberg)	1990	3 weeks
Beggar Student (Kingston/Millocker)	1884	
Beggar's Opera (Gay)	1728	
Beggar's Opera (John Gay, adapt. Frederic Austin)	1920	1463
Belinda Fair (Strachey/Maschwitz)	1949	131
Belle or Ballad of Dr Crippen (Mankowitz/Norman)	1961	44
Belle Hélène, La (Offenbach) (rev. 1871/1873/1932)	1866	
Belle Hélène, La (Offenbach)	1871	109
Belle of Bond Street (Cook/Monckton/Ross/Aveling)	1914	40
Belle of Brittany (Talbot/Percy Greenbank)	1908	147
Belle of Cairo (Raleigh/Peile)	1896	71
Belle of Mayfair (Hood/Brookfield/Leslie Stuart)	1906	416
Belle of New York (Morton/Kerker)	1898	697
Belle Starr aka The Piecefull Palace	1969	short run
Bells Are Ringing (Styne/Comden/Green)	1957	292
Bells of St Martin's (Douglas Byng)	1952	107
Beloved Vagabond (Locke/Ross/Glass)	1927	107
Bernadette (Hughes)	1990	3 weeks
Best Bib and Tucker (Val Guest/Parr Davies) revue	1942	490
Bet Your Life (Melville/Zwar)	1952	362
Betjemania (Gould/Benedictus)	1976	
Better 'Ole (Herman Darewski)	1917	811
Better Days (Harris/Finck)	1925	135
Better Late — revue by Leslie Julian Jones	1946	211
Betty (Paul Rubens/Ross/Percy Greenbank)	1915	391
Betty in Mayfair (Fraser-Simson)	1925	182
Between Ourselves (Melville/Hackforth/Maschwitz)	1946	
Between the Lines (Ayckbourn/Todd)	1992	20
Beyond Compere (Frankau/Crick/Leonard/C. Burnaby/Gardiner)	1940	
Beyond the Fringe (Cook/Moore/Bennett/Jonathan Miller)	1961	2200
Beyond the Rainbow (Forrest/Trovajoli/Bricusse)	1978	6 months
Biarritz aka John Jenkins in Biarritz (J.K. Jerome/Carr/Ross)	1896	71
Big Ben (Vivian Ellis/A.P. Herbert)	1946	172
Big Boy (Furber/Emney/Carroll Gibbons)	1945	174
Big Business (Waller/Tunbridge)	1937	124
Big Show of 1949 — Palladium revue	1949	114
Big Top ((G. Wright/Brodzsky/April/Parr Davies) revue	1942	139
Billee Taylor (Stephens/Solomon)	1880	83
Billy (Black/Barry)	1974	904
Billy Barnes Revue (Barnes/Rodgers)	1960	
Billy Bishop Goes to War (John Gray)	1981	6 weeks
Billy Elliot (Hall/Daldry/Darling/John)	2005	
Bing Boys Are Here (Ayer/Braham/Novello)	1916	424
Bing Boys on Broadway (Ayer)	1918	562
Bing Girls Are There (Ayer/Gideon)	1917	110
Biograph Girl (Brown/Heneker)	1980	57
Bitch (Dahl/Brown/Senior)	1976	season
Bird Seller (Pepper/Melford/Zeller)	1947	
Bits & Pieces (Petley/Robey et al) revue	1927	167
Bitter Sweet (Noel Coward)	1929	697
Black & White Minstrel Show (George Inns/Gordon)	1962	4344
Black and Blue (Leslie-Smith/Jacobson etc)	1939	305
Black Crook (J. & Harry Paulton)	1872	204
Black Crook (J. & H. Paulton/Clay/Jacobi) rev from 1872	1881	107
Black Mikado (Gilbert & Sullivan)	1975	472
Black Nativity (Langston Hughes)	1962	60
Black Rover (Searelle)	1890	40
Black Vanities (Carr/C Porter/Strachey Jacobson) revue	1941	435
Black Velvet (Park/Butler/Parr Davies) revue	1939	620
Blackbirds (1926, 1934, 1935, 1936) revues	1926	279
Blackbirds of 1934 — revue	1934	193
Blackbirds of 1935 — revue	1935	123
Blackbirds of 1936 (Bloom/Mercer) revue	1936	124
Black New World (McKayle/Freitag/Roberts)	1967	4 weeks
Black-Eyed Susan (Burnand/Lee)	1866	+400
Black-Eyed Susan (Burnand/Lee)	1884	48
Bless the Bride (Vivian Ellis/A.P. Herbert)	1947	886
Blitz! (Lionel Bart)	1962	568
Blockheads (Laurel & Hardy)	1984	short run
Blondel (Rice/Oliver)	1983	292
Blood Brothers (Willy Russell) revived 1988	1983	224
Blood Brothers (Willy Russell) (revived from 1983)	1988	+7300
Blossom Time (Schubert/Clutsam/Tauber) aka Lilac Time	1942	short run
Blue Angel (Gems)	1991	5 weeks
Blue Eyed Susan (F. Osmond Carr)	1892	132
Blue Eyes (Bolton/John/Jerome Kern)	1928	276
Blue for a Boy (Purcell/Parr Davies)	1950	664
Blue Kitten (Harbach/Newman/Duncan/Friml)	1925	140
Blue Magic — revue	1959	436
Blue Mazurka (Graham/Lehar/Friml)	1927	140
Blue Moon (Ellis/Percy Greenbank/Talbot/Rubens)	1905	182
Blue Roses (Desmond Carter/Vivian Ellis)	1931	54
Blue Skies (Ellis) J.W. Jackson revue	1927	192
Blue Train (Stolz/St Helier)	1927	125
Bluebell (revival of Bluebell in Fairyland 1901)	1905	102
Bluebell in Fairyland (Slaughter/Hopwood/Hicks)	1901	294
Blues in the Night (Epps) (after Bessie Smith)	1987	5 weeks
Bob's Your Uncle (Frank Eyton/Noel Gay/Melford)	1948	363
Bobby Get Your Gun (Waller/Tunbridge/Bolton)	1938	92
Boccaccio (Suppé)	1882	129
Bohemian Girl (Balfe)	1843	long run
Bohemian Gyurl (Lutz et al)	1877	117
Boltons Revue (Stranks/Strachey)	1948	
Bombay Dreams (Lloyd Webber/Kapur/Rahman/Black)	2002	extended
Bonita (Peacock/Fraser-Simson)	1911	42
Boodle (Furber/Braham/Herman Darewski)	1925	94
Boogie Nights (Conway)	1998	5 months
Boogie, Woogie, Bubble 'n' Squeak	1982	3 weeks
Boom! Boom! — Basil Brush puppet musical	1977	
Bordello (Moore/Spiro/Frisch)	1974	2 months
Bow Bells (Titheradge/Jeans/Henry Sullivan) revue	1932	232
Bow-Wows (Strachey et al) revue	1927	124
Box 'O Tricks (Forbes/Graham/Haslam/Stamper/Chappelle)	1918	625
Boy (Monckton/Talbot/Ross/Percy Greenbank)	1917	801
Boy Friend (Sandy Wilson)	1953	2084
Boy Friend (Sandy Wilson)	1967	365
Boyband (Peter Quilter)	1999	3 months
Boys from Syracuse (Rodgers/Hart)	1963	3 months
Bran Pie — André Charlot revue	1919	414
Braziliana (Bonfa/Toledo)	1953	32
Bric-a-Brac (Monckton/Finck) revue	1915	385
Bric-a-Brac Will (Fitzgerald/Moss/H. Greenbank/Sapte/Pizzi)	1895	62
Brigadoon (Lerner/Loewe)	1949	685
Brighton Rock (Black/Barry)	2004	
Brighter London (Harris/Finck) revue	1923	593
Bronze Horse (Howard Paul)	1881	187
Bubbling Brown Sugar — revue by various	1977	
Bubbly (Braham) revue	1917	429
Buccaneer (Sandy Wilson)	1953	short run
Buddy — musical biography of Buddy Holly	1989	+5000
Budgie (Black/Shuman)	1988	89
Bugle Call (Sidney Jones/Parker/Bright)	1905	105
Bugsy Malone (Paul Williams/Alan Parker/Dolenz)	1983	300
Burlesque (from play by Hopkins & Watters)	1948	short run
Burning Boat (Phipps/Geoffrey Wright)	1955	12
Business As Usual (Mark/Herman Darewski) revue	1914	295
Butterflies (Read/Robertson)	1908	217
Buzz Buzz (Herman Darewski) revue	1918	612
By Appointment (Stanley/Vernon/Kennedy Russell)	1934	28
By George (George Grossmith) revue	1911	
By Jeeves (Webber/Ayckbourn) revision	1995	3 months
By Jingo — If We Do (Finck) revue	1914	110
By the Way (John/Ellis) revue	1925	341
Bye Bye Birdie (Stewart/Adams/Strouse)	1961	8 months
C'est Chic — revue	1913	
Cabaret (Kander/Ebb)	1968	316
Cabaret Girl (Jerome Kern/P.G. Wodehouse)	1922	361
Cachez Ca! — revue	1913	32
Cage Me a Peacock (Lynd/Leslie/Langley)	1948	337
Cairo (Percy Fletcher/Asche) rev. Mecca from Broadway	1921	267
Calamity Jane (Freeman/Fain/Webster)(rev. Broadway)	1996	
Call It Love (Sandy Wilson)	1960	short run
Call Me Madam (Irving Berlin)	1952	486
Calypso (Hedley Briggs/Ronnie Hill)	1948	
Cambridge Circus (Macdonald/Oddie)	1963	
Camelot (Lerner/Loewe)	1964	518
Can Can (Offenbach/Catto/Grun/Tysh)	1946	
Can Can (Cole Porter)	1954	394
Candide (Bernstein)	1959	60
Canterbury Tales (Coghill/Starkie/Hawkins/Hill)	1968	2080
Captain Beaky (Lloyd/Parker)	1981	
Captain Billy (Cellier/Greenbank)	1891	
Captain Kidd (Hicks/Ross/Leslie Stuart)	1910	34
Captain Therese (Burnand/Bisson/Planquette)	1890	104
Card (Bennett/Hatch/Trent)	1973	130
Careless Rapture (Ivor Novello/Hassall)	1936	295
Carina (Blanchard/Bridgman/Julia Wolff)	1888	116
Carissima (Hans May/Maschwitz)	1948	488
Carmen Jones (Bizet/Hammerstein)	1991	season
Carmen-up-to-Data (Pettitt/Sims/Lutz)	1890	243
Carminetta (Lassailly/Finck/Darewski)	1917	260
Carnaby Street (Hall)	1997	2 weeks
Carnival (Bob Merrill)	1963	28
Carousel (Rodgers/Hammerstein)	1950	566
Carry On London (various)	1973	630
Casanova (Johann Strauss/Benatzky)	1932	429
Cash on Delivery (Hicks)	1917	49
Casino Girl (Harry B. Smith/Englander)	1900	196
Casper the Musical (Marsh/Pickett)	1999	3 months
Casting Vote (Helmore/Slaughter)	1885	1 month
Castle Grim (Allen)	1865	27
Castles in Spain (Mary Brake/Harold Purcell)	1906	50

Castles in the Air (Peck/Wenrich) not the 1911 version	1927	28
Castles in the Air (Ross/Lincke) not the 1927 version	1911	65
Cat and the Fiddle (Kern/Harbach)	1932	219
Catch My Soul (Pohlman/Dean)	1970	+400
Catch of the Season (Hicks/Haines/Taylor)	1904	621
Catherine (Arkell/Tchaikovsky)	1923	217
Cats (Lloyd Webber/T.S. Eliot/Nunn/Stilgoe)	1981	9000
Cattarina (Reece/Clay)	1875	75
Cava, La (Broccoli/O'Keefe)	2000	6 months
Cavalcade (Coward)	1931	405
Centralia (Ishmael/Snape)	1997	3 weeks
Certainly, Sir (Waller/Tunbridge)	1936	20
Chaganog (Ron Moody/Vivian Ellis et al) revue	1964	
Charity Begins At Home (Stephenson/Cellier)	1872	10 seasons
Charlie Girl (Taylor/David Heneker)	1965	2,202
Charlot Show of 1926 (Noel Gay/Addinsell)	1926	87
Charlot's Masquerade (R. Leigh/Hackforth/Strachey/Coates)	1930	84
Charlot's Revue(s) (Coward) (1924/25/26/28/30/35/37)	1924	518
Cheep — Harry Grattan revue	1917	488
Cheerio (C.H. Bovill/Kennedy Russell) revue	1917	181
Chelsea Follies (Charles/Carter/de Bear/Arkell) revue	1930	213
Cherry (M. Gideon)	1920	76
Cherry Girl (Caryll/Hopwood)	1903	215
Cheryomushki (Shostakovich/Pountney)	1994	
Chess (Rice/Anderson/Ulvaeus)	1986	1209
Chicago (Kander/Ebb)	1979	+600
Chicago (Kander/Ebb)	1997	long run
Chieftain (Burnand/Sullivan)	1894	97
Children of Eden (Schwartz/Caird)	1991	3 months
Chilperic (Reece/Marshall/Mansell/Herve)	1870	80
Chinese Honeymoon, A (Talbot/Dance)	1901	1,075
Ching Chow Hi (Offenbach)	1868	
Chitty Chitty Bang Bang (Richard & Robert Sherman)	2002	extended
Chocolate Soldier (Stange/Oscar Straus)	1910	500
Chorus Girls (Keefe/Davis)	1981	4 weeks
Chorus Line (Hamlisch/Kleban)	1976	903
Chox (Cambridge Footlights) revue	1974	
Chrysanthemum (Phillips/Chancellor/Stewart)	1959	148
Chu Chin Chow (Asche/Frederic Norton/Percy Fletcher)	1916	2238
Cigale, La (Burnand/Audran/Crayll)	1890	423
Cigarette (St. Ledger/Hayden Parry)	1892	112
Cinderella (Lacy)	1830	
Cinderella (Dix/Collins/Glover/Weston/Lee)	1919	145
Cinderella (Rodgers/Hammerstein) new version	1958	season
Cinderella (Croft/The Shadows) — new version	1966	
Cinderella the Younger (Thompson Jones/Jonas)	1871	24
Cinder-Ellen Up Too Late (Leslie/Vincent/Lutz/Monckton)	1891	314
Cindy (Brandon)	1968	short run
Cindy-Ella, or I Gotta a Shoe (Caryl Brahms/Ned Sherrin)	1962	
Cinema Star (Graham/Gilbert)	1914	109
Cingalee (Monckton/Percy Greenbank/Ross/Rubens)	1904	365
Circus Girl (H. Greenbank/Monckton/Caryll/Ross/Stuart)	1896	497
City of Angels (Coleman/Gelbert)	1993	30 weeks
Clancarty (West/Wolseley Charles)	1933	23
Clap Hands (various) Canadian revue	1962	
Clari aka Maid of Milan (Payne/Bishop)	1823	6 months
Claude Duval (Stephens/Solomon)	1881	54
Claude Duval (Bowyer/Roberts/Crook/Monckton)	1894	142
Cleopatra (Turner/Graham/Oscar Straus)	1925	110
Cliff — the Cliff Richard Story (Read/Payne)	2003	
Cloakroom Ticket No 3 (J. Wilson/Thompson/Fortuin)	1953	
Cloches de Corneville, Les (Farnie/Reece/Planquette)	1878	705
Clo-Clo (Furber/Graham/Lehar)	1925	95
Closer to Heaven (Harvey/Tennant/Lowe)	2001	6 months
Cloudcuckooland (Ronald Bullock)	1956	season
Clown Jewels — Crazy Gang revue	1959	803
Clowns in Clover (Titheradge/J. Hulbert/Noel Gay/Ellis)	1927	508
Cochran's 1930 Revue (D. Byng)	1930	245
Cochran's 1931 Revue (Coward)	1931	27
Cochran's Revue of 1926 (D. Byng)	1926	148
Cockles & Champagne (Stevens/Heneker)	1954	118
Cockyolly Bird (Dearmer/Shaw)	1914	40
Cocoanuts (Kaufmann/Berlin)	1928	15
Cole (Cole Porter)	1974	
Colette (Dankworth)	1980	47
Come In (L. White/Graham/Clay Smith/F. Godfrey)	1924	28
Come Out Of Your Shell (Leslie Jones/Ensor)	1940	93
Come Out to Play (E. Pola/Watson/Parr Davies/Frankel)	1940	77
Come Over Here (Williams/Sturgess/Hirsch/Johnson)	1913	271
Come Spy With Me (Bryan Blackburn)	1966	468
Comedy in Music (Victor Borge)	1964	
Comedy of Errors (Harris/McNab/Julian Slade)	1956	season
Comic Relief — fund-raising event for charity abroad	1986	
Command Performance (Grey/Waller/Tunbridge)	1933	31
Company (Sondheim)	1972	344
Constance (Robertson/Clay)	1865	18
Contrabandista (Burnand/Sullivan)	1867	72
Conversation Piece (Noel Coward)	1934	177
Coo-ee (Gideon/Wylie/Sampson)	1929	70
Co-optimists (Gideon etc) revue	1921	500
Co-optimists (Gideon etc) revue	1922	232

Co-optimists (Gideon etc) revue	1923	210
Co-optimists (Gideon etc) revue	1924	207
Co-optimists (Gideon etc) revue	1925	203
Co-optimists (Gideon etc) revue	1926	216
Co-optimists (Gideon etc) revue	1929	133
Co-optimists (Gideon etc) revue	1930	99
Co-optimists (Gideon etc) revue	1935	13
Copacabana (Manilow/Sussman/Jack Feldman)	1994	
Corunna (Dewhurst/Hart/Steeye Span)	1971	12
Cosi Fan Tutte (Mozart)	1811	
Costa Packet (Frank Norman/Klein/Bart)	1972	65
Cotton Club (Barron)	1992	6 months
Count of Luxembourg (Franz Lehar/Ross/Hood)	1911	340
Countess Maritza (Douglas/Kalman)	1983	
Country Girl, A (Monckton/Rubens/Ross/P. Greenbank)	1902	729
Cousin From Nowhere (Künneke/Ross/Furber/Tharp)	1923	105
Cowardy Custard (Coward)	1972	
Cowboy Casanova (Tommie Conner)	1950	8
Cox & Box (Burnand/Sullivan)	1867	300
Cradle Will Rock (Blitzstein)	1985	3 weeks
Cranford (Littlewood/Wells/Carl Davis)	1975	26
Cranks (Cranko/Addison)	1955	217
Crazy Days (Carter/Eyton/Billy Mayerl)	1937	78
Crazy for You (Gershwin)	1993	3 years
Crazy Month (George Black revue) Crazy Gang	1932	
Creatures of Impulse (W.S. Gilbert/Randegger)	1871	91
Crest of the Wave (Hassall/Ivor Novello)	1937	203
Crimson Scarf (Farnie/Legouix/Offenbach)	1873	
Crooked Mile (Wildeblood/Greenwell)	1959	164
Crystal Heart (William Archibald/Baldwin Bergerson)	1957	6
Cupid & the Cutlets (Percy Greenbank/Barrow)	1929	
Cups & Saucers (Grossmith sr.)	1878	6 months
Curate's Egg (Ellis/Finck) revue	1922	83
Curse of the Werewolf (Hill/Armit)	1977	24
Cyberjam (Mason/Vanderkolff/Pinney)	2003	3 months
Cymbia (H. Paulton/Williams)	1883	48
Dad's Army (Perry/Croft)	1975	
Dairymaids (Wimperis/Rubens/Tours)	1906	239
Daisy Pulls It Off (Brazil/Deegan)	1983	3 years
Daisy Pulls It Off (Brazil/Deegan) rev. by A. Lloyd Webber	2002	
Damask Rose (G.H. Clutsam)	1930	52
Dames at Sea (Haimsohn/Miller/Wise)	1969	short run
Dames at Sea (Haimsohn/Miller/Wise)	1996	
Damn Yankees (Adler/Ross)	1957	861
Dancin' (Bob Fosse)	1983	88
Dancing City (a Charlot Viennese musical)	1935	65
Dancing Girl (Henry Jones)	1891	310
Dancing Heiress (Grand/Fletcher)	1960	2 weeks
Dancing Mistress (Ross/Percy Greenbank/Monckton)	1912	242
Dancing Viennese (Oscar Straus)	1912	6 weeks
Dancing Years (Hassall/Novello)	1939	187
Dancing Years (Hassall/Novello)	1942	969
Dandy Dan the Lifeguardsman (Slaughter/Hood)	1897	166
Dandy Dick Whittington (Caryll)	1895	124
Dandy Fifth (Sims/Corri)	1898	8 weeks
Daphne (Bayton Power/Turner/Farrell)	1930	
Dark Doings — all-black revue	1933	33
Darling I Love You (Hedley/Acres/Rigby/Mayerl)	1930	147
Dashing Little Duke (Hicks/Ross/Tours)	1909	101
Day in Hollywood, A, Night in the Ukraine, A (Vosburgh/Lazarus)	1979	168
Days of Hope (Goodall/Allen)	1991	6 weeks
De La Folie Pure — revue	1930	94
Dean (Howlett/Campbell)	1977	35
Dear Anyone (Black/Stephens)	1983	65
Dear Little Billie (Carter/Hedley/Strachey)	1925	86
Dear Little Denmark (Rubens)	1909	109
Dear Love (Waller/Tunbridge/Haydn Wood)	1929	132
Dear Miss Phoebe (Harry Parr Davies/Hassall)	1950	283
Decameron '73 (Coe/Griffiths/Sawyer)	1973	69
Decameron Nights (Finck)	1922	370
Decline & Fall (unpublished Cole Porter material) revue	1966	
Dé-dé (Jeans/Christiné)	1922	50
Deja Revue (Olov Wyper/Alan Melville)	1974	
Demon Barber (Cotton/Burke)	1959	39
Demon's Bride (Leterrier/Vanloo/Byron)	1874	48
Derby Day (Alfred Reynolds/A.P. Herbert)	1932	132
Desert Song (Romberg/Harbach/Hammerstein) rev 1967	1927	432
Destry Rides Again (Harold Rome)	1982	40
Dick (Murray/Jakobowski)	1884	29
Dick Deterred (David Edgar/Field)	1974	season
Diversion (Walter Leigh) Farjeon revue	1940	54
Diversion No. 2 (Walter Leigh) revue	1941	106
Divorce Me Darling! (Sandy Wilson)	1964	178
Do I Hear a Waltz? (Sondheim/Rodgers)	1992	12
Do Re Mi (Comden/Green/Styne)	1961	
Do Somethin' Addy Man (Russell/Browne)	1962	25
Dollar Princess (Ross/Fall/Hood)	1909	428
Dolly Varden (Stange/Edwards)	1903	39
Don Juan (Tanner/Lutz/Ross)	1893	221
Don Quixote (H. Paulton/Maltby)	1876	41

Title	Year	Run
Don't Shoot, We're English (Law/Mulcahy/Bentine)	1960	short run
Donna Diana (Marston)	1864	
Donna Luiza (Hood/Slaughter)	1892	4 months
Dora's Doze (Hirtsch)	1914	3 weeks
Dorian (Reeves)	1997	1 week
Doris (Stephenson/Cellier)	1889	202
Dorothy (Stephenson/Cellier)	1886	931
Dover Street to Dixie (H. Darewski) revue	1923	108
Dr. Dolittle (Leslie Bricusse)	1998	12 months
Dr. D. (Colnaghi/Dick)	1885	25
Dracula (Hill/Armit)	1974	77
Dragon of Wantley (Carey/Lampe)	1737	
Drake's Dream (Lynne & Richard Riley)	1977	82
Dubarry (Millocker/Rowland Leigh/Maschwitz)	1932	397
Dubarry Was a Lady (Cole Porter)	1942	178
Dublin Pike Follies — revue	1957	
Duchess of Dantzig (Hamilton/Caryll)	1903	236
Duenna (Sheridan/Alfred Reynolds)	1924	141
Duenna (Sheridan/Julian Slade/Dorothy Reynolds) rev.	1954	134
Earl and the Girl (Caryll/Percy Greenbank/Hicks)	1903	371
Eastward-Ho! (Rodney/Younge)	1894	6
Eastward Ho! (Torrens/Asche/Ansell)	1919	124
Eastward Ho! (Jonson/Schuman/Bicat)	1981	45
Eclipse (Herman Darewski/Gideon/Ross)	1919	117
Edith Piaf, Je Vous Aime — Libby Morris revue	1977	
Eightpence a Mile (Wright/Redstone)	1913	143
El Capitan (Klein/Sousa)	1899	154
Eldorado (Robinson/Clapham/Frank/Asche)	1930	93
Elephant in Arcady, An (Eleanor & Herbert Farjeon)	1938	141
Elidor (Parker/Williams)	1976	season
Elmer Gantry (Brown/Lewis)	1986	4 weeks
Elsie Janis at Home (Janis)	1924	74
Elvis — Jack Good & Ray Cooney revue	1977	
Elvis, the Musical (Jack Good)	1996	
Emerald Isle (Sullivan/German/Hood)	1901	205
Encore (Peter Myers/Norman Dannatt/Sonnie Hale) revue	1948	
Encore Les Dames — revue	1936	
Enfant Prodigue, L' (Carré/Wormser)	1891	13
Enrico (Garinei/Giovannini/Rascel)	1963	2 months
Erb (Peacock/Pett Ridge)	1970	38
Erminie (Bellamy/Paulton/Jakobowski)	1885	154
Escape from Pterodactyl Island (Morris/Jeffrey)	1999	4 weeks
Estrella (Parke/Searelle)	1883	36
Eternal Waltz (Leo Fall)	1911	good run
Eurovision (Luscombe)	1993	2 weeks
Evangeline (Posford/Jacobson/Maschwitz)	1946	32
Eve On Parade — revue	1939	225
Evening with Alan Jay Lerner (Loewe/Bernstein/Lane/Strouse)	1987	
Evening with Beatrice Lillie — revue by various	1954	195
Evening with Hinge & Bracket (St Claire/Logan)	1974	
Ever Green (Rodgers/Hart)	1930	254
Every Good Boy Deserves Favour (Stoppard/Previn)	1978	
Everybody's Doing It (Clarke/Berlin) Bovill/Grossmith revue	1912	354
Evita (A. Lloyd Webber/Rice)	1978	3176
Excelsior (Harwood)	1885	
Exile from Home, An (Fletcher/Hess)	1906	13
Expresso Bongo (Heneker/Monty Norman/More)	1958	316
Eyes & No Eyes (W.S. Gilbert/Reed)	1875	2 months
Faddimir (Ross/Carr)	1889	4
Falka (Farnie/Chassaigne)	1883	157
Fallen Fairies (W.S. Gilbert/German)	1909	51
Fame (Levy/de Silva/Margoshes)	2002	
Fame (Levy/Margoshes)	1995	3 months
Fancy Free (Barbara Gordon/Basil Thomas) revue	1951	370
Fanfare (Carter/Henry Sullivan)	1932	28
Fanny (Harold Rome)	1956	333
Fantasia (Cliff/Illingworth/Gideon)	1921	
Fantasticks (Schmidt/Tom Jones)	1961	44
Far Pavilions (Kaye/Clark/Henderson)	2005	
Farjeon Reviewed (Trewin/Toguri/Walter Leigh)	1975	
Fascinating Aida (Keane/Anderson/Cutts)	1987	6 weeks
Fatinitza (Henry Leigh/Suppé)	1878	
Faust (Reid/Bogdanov)	1979	26
Faust on Toast (Redstone/Gideon/Shephard/Ross/Henderson)	1921	34
Faust-up-to-Date (Sims/Pettitt)	1888	180
Fay O'Fire (Herman/Edward Jones)	1885	16
Fearless Frank (Andrew Davies/Brown)	1979	52
Felix (Oxenford)	1865	
Fenella (Lambelet)	1906	
Ferry Cross the Mersey (Norris/Picot)	1996	1 month
Festen (Norris/Eldridge/Gough/Arditti)	2004	
Fiddler on the Roof (Harnick/Jerry Bock)	1967	2030
Fields of Ambrosia (Higgins/Silvestri)	1996	23
Fifinella (Jackson/Dean)	1919	47
Fig Leaves — Lucien Samett revue	1940	
Fille de Madame Angot (Byron/Lecocq)	1873	
Fine and Dandy (Sherwin/Blore/Byng/Shephard/Nesbitt)	1942	346
Fine Feathers (Parr Davies) revue	1945	578
Fings Aint What They Used To Be (Lionel Bart)	1959	897
Finian's Rainbow (Harburg/Burton Lane)	1947	53
Fiorello! (Harnick/Bock)	1962	56
Fire Angel (Bentley/Haines)	1977	42
First Kiss (Lawrence/Luna)	1924	43
Five Guys Named Moe (Clarke Peters)	1990	4 weeks
Five O'Clock Girl (Bolton/Thompson)	1929	122
Fix (Dempsey/Rowe)	1997	4 weeks
Fleet's Lit Up (Ellis/Bolton)	1938	199
Floodlight (Vivian Ellis) revue	1937	51
Flora (Heard/Gideon/Herman Darewski)	1918	72
Florodora (Leslie Stuart/Rubens/Boyd-Jones)	1899	455
Flower Drum Song (Rodgers/Hammerstein/Joseph Fields)	1960	+300
Flowers for Algernon (David Rogers/Strouse)	1979	29
Flying Colours (de Courville/Pink/Peters) revue	1916	203
Flying Colours (Jeans/Maschwitz) revue	1943	103
Flying Trapeze (Benatzky/Wynne/Carter/Eyton/Furber)	1935	73
Fol-de-Rols (Greatrex Newman/Wolseley Charles) revue	1951	98
Folies Bergère (Hayman/Sheldon/Colerick) revue	1925	121
Folies Bergère Revue (Derval/Gyarmathy/Hurran)	1949	881
Folies Bergère Revue 1951 (Derval/Gyarmathy/Hurran)	1951	579
Follies (Goldman/Sondheim)	1987	18 months
Follies (Pelissier) — at Terry's	1907	108
Follies (Pelissier) — at the Alhambra	1900	
Follies (Pelissier) — at the Apollo	1911	
Follies (Pelissier) — at the Apollo	1908	571
Follies (Pelissier) — at the Apollo	1910	521
Follies (Pelissier) — at the Apollo	1912	
Follies (Pelissier) — at the Palace	1901	
Follies (Pelissier) — at the Queen's Hall	1904	
Follies (Pelissier) — at the Royalty	1907	30
Follies (Sondheim) Royal Festival Hall	2002	
Follies of 1938 (Pelissier)	1938	
Follow a Star (Furber/Ellis)	1930	118
Follow That Girl (Slade/Reynolds)	1960	211
Follow the Crowd (Wimperis/Carrick/Berlin)	1916	144
Follow the Girls (Bolton/Davis/Shapiro/Pascal/Charig)	1945	572
Follow the Star (Daly/Jim Parker)	1975	
Follow the Sun (Dietz/Carter/Schwartz) revue	1936	204
Follow Through (Schwab/de Sylva/Brown/Henderson)	1929	148
Folly To Be Wise (Ellis/Titheradge) J. Hulbert revue	1931	257
Folly To Be Wiser (Ellis/Titheradge) 2nd edn. of above	1931	87
For Adults Only (Pritchett/Cass/Grahame) P. Myers revue	1958	292
For Amusement Only (Pritchett/Cass) Peter Myers revue	1956	698
For Crying Out Loud — revue	1945	351
For Goodness Sake (Gershwin et al)	1923	224
For the Love of Mike (Maltby/Grey/Waller/Tunbridge/Miller)	1931	239
Forbidden Broadway (Alessandrai)	1989	3 months
Forever Plaid (Stuart Ross)	1993	
Forty Thieves (George Colman jr.)	1806	
Forty Years On (Alan Bennett)	1968	
Fosse (Fosse/Maltby/Reinking/Walker) revue	2000	12 months
Fountain of Youth (Robertson/Alfred Reynolds)	1931	46
Four Degrees Over (Wood/Gould)	1966	2 months
Four Musketeers (Kretzmer/Laurie Johnson)	1967	462
Four to the Bar (Blackburn/Ellis/Hill/Dring/Rand/Hughes)	1961	
Four, Five, Six (Hackforth/Spoliansky)	1948	315
Frankenstein (Butler/Newton/Lutz/Martin/Bowyer)	1887	110
Frasquita (Arkell/Lehar)	1925	36
Frederica (Pepper/Ross/Lehar)	1930	110
Free As Air (Slade/Reynolds)	1957	417
French Maid (Slaughter/Hood)	1897	480
Fresh Airs (Flanders/Swann)	1956	163
Fritzi (Stanley/Tucker)	1935	64
Frogs (Sondheim)	1990	2 weeks
From a Jack to a King (Carlton)	1992	14 weeks
Full Swing (Posford/Macrae/Menzies/J. Hulbert/Parr Davies)	1942	468
Fun and Games (Sherwin/Furber) revue	1941	289
Fun and the Fair — Charles Henry revue	1953	9 weeks
Fun of the Fayre (Barratt/Kern/Caldwell/Damerell et al)	1921	239
Fun On the Bristol (Rowe)	1882	
Funny Face (Gershwin brothers)	1928	263
Funny Girl (Styne/Merrill)	1966	109
Funny Side Up — Stanley Lupino revue	1940	217
Funny Thing Happened on the Way to the Forum, A (Sondheim)	1963	762
G.B. (Thornhill/Henderson/Williams/Johnson)	1973	
Gaieties (Gibbons/Furber) revue	1945	179
Gaiety Girl (Sidney Jones/Harry Greenbank)	1893	413
Gavin & the Monster (Williams/Johnson)	1981	78
Gambler (Lewis/Goody/Smith)	1986	10 weeks
Gang Show (Reader) revival of Thirties scout shows	1946	170
Gang Show 1950 (Reader)	1950	
Gangway (Parr Davies/Noel Gay) George Black revue	1941	535
Ganymede & Galatea (Gilbert/Suppé)	1872	
Garrison Theatre (BBC show)	1940	225
Gate Revue (Geoffrey Wright/Bob McDermott/Morgan)	1939	449
Gay Deceivers (Arkell/Simon/Broones)	1935	123
Gay Divorce (Cole Porter)	1933	180
Gay Gordons (G. Jones/H. Darewski/Bovill/ Wimperis/Wodehouse)	1907	229
Gay Lothario (Tours)	1913	4 months
Gay Masquerade (Hajos)	1935	3

Title	Year	Runs
Gay Parisienne — *aka* Girl from Paris (Vousden/Caryll/Dance)	1896	306
Gay Pretenders (Grossmith jr.)	1900	49
Gay Princess (A.P. Herbert/Katscher)	1931	12
Gay Rosalinda (Johann Strauss/Heppner) Die Fledermaus	1945	413
Gay's the Word (Novello/Melville)	1951	504
Geisha (Sidney Jones/Harry Greenbank/Monckton/Philp)	1896	760
Genevieve de Brabant (Farnie/Offenbach)	1871	
Gentleman in Black (W.S. Gilbert/Clay)	1870	26
Gentleman Joe — The Hansom Cabby (Hood/Slaughter)	1895	391
Gentleman's Pastime (Marion Hart)	1958	18
Gentlemen Prefer Anything (Hill/Macaulay/Armit)	1974	34
Gentlemen Prefer Blondes (Styne/Rabin/J'ph Fields/Loos)	1962	223
Georgian Springtime (Beatrice Snell)	1939	
Get a Load of This (Sherwin/Val Guest) revue	1941	698
Gigi (Lerner/Loewe)	1985	242
Gingerbread Man (David Wood)	1977	season
Girl Behind the Counter (Talbot/Johnson/Barratt/P. Greenbank)	1906	141
Girl Called Jo, A (Myers/Grahame/Climie)	1955	141
Girl for the Boy (Hurgon/Arthurs/Rolt/Carr)	1919	86
Girl Friend (Rodgers/Hart/Ellis/Herbert Fields)	1927	421
Girl from Cook's (Hubbell/Gilbert/Burnside/Newman)	1927	38
Girl from Kay's (Cook/Caryll/Ross/Aveling)	1902	432
Girl from Over the Border (Moore/Carse/Locknane/Lawrence)	1908	
Girl from Up There (Morton/Kerker)	1901	102
Girl from Utah (Sidney Jones/Rubens/Ross/P. Greenbank)	1913	195
Girl He Left Behind Him (Sims/Schroter)	1881	2 months
Girl in the Bath (Bath/Gibson/Fulton/Dix)	1918	short run
Girl in the Taxi (Jean Gilbert/Fenn/Wimperis)	1912	385
Girl in the Train (Fall/Ross)	1910	340
Girl of the Year (Jeavons)	1953	
Girl on the Film (Sirmay/Ross/Kollo/Bredschneider)	1913	232
Girl on the Stage (revised version of Little Cherub below)	1906	29
Girl Who Didn't (Eysler/Wimperis)	1913	68
Girlfriends (Howard Goodall)	1987	5 weeks
Girls of Gottenberg (Caryll/Monckton/Ross/Hood)	1907	303
Give a Dog a Bone (Howard/Thornhill/Fraser) rev 1971	1964	
Give Me a Ring (Broones/John)	1933	239
Glamorous Night (Novello/Hassall) rev 1975	1935	243
Glass Slipper (Herbert Farjeon/Clifton Parker)	1944	
Globe Revue (Coward)	1952	
Glorious Days (Parr Davies/Purcell/Nesbitt)	1953	255
Glory (Cross)	1990	3 weeks
Glory Be! (Lineham/Kinlen/Murray)	1961	
Go-Bang (Grossmith jr./Carr/Ross)	1894	159
Godspell (Schwartz) rev 1975	1971	1128
Going Greek (Sammy Lerner/Goodhart/Hoffman/Bolton)	1937	306
Going Places (Ellis/Bolton/Thompson)	1936	44
Going to Town (Melville/Swann/Leslie-Smith/Zwar)	1954	68
Going Up (Harbach/Hirsch)	1918	574
Golden Boy (Adams/Strouse)	1968	118
Golden City (Tore/Mitchell)	1950	140
Golden Moth (Novello/P.G. Wodehouse)	1921	281
Golden Ring (Sims/Clay)	1883	105
Golden Touch (Gilbert/More)	1960	12
Golden Toy (Robert Schumann/Titheradge)	1934	185
Golden Web (Corder/Stephenson)	1893	29
Goldfaden Dream, A (Goldfaden/Kon)	1961	season
Gondoliers (Gilbert & Sullivan)	1889	554
Gone With the Wind (Harold Rome)	1972	398
Good Companions (Addinsell/Graham/Eyton/J.B. Priestley)	1931	331
Good Companions (Priestley/Mercer/Previn)	1974	252
Good Golly Miss Molly (Eaton)	1991	16 weeks
Good Luck (Finck)	1923	262
Good News (Schwab/de Sylva/Henderson/Brown)	1928	132
Good Old Days (Asche/Fletcher)	1925	37
Good Old, Bad Old Days (Newley/Bricusse)	1972	309
Good Road — revue for Moral Rearmament	1948	
Grab Me a Gondola (More/James Gilbert)	1956	673
Grand Duchess of Gerolstein (Kenney/Offenbach)	1867	
Grand Duchess (Brookfield/Ross/Offenbach)	1897	99
Grand Duchess (Robinson/Kenney/Offenbach) rev.	1937	60
Grand Duke (Gilbert & Sullivan)	1896	123
Grand Hotel (Wright/Forrest/Yeston) rev. 2004	1992	135
Grand Mogul (Oxenford/Meadows) not the 1884 version	1881	1
Grand Mogul (Farnie/Audran) not the 1881 version	1884	short run
Grease (Casey/Jacobs)	1973	236
Grease (Jacobs/Casey) also revived 2002	1979	124
Great American Backstage Musical (Bill Solly)	1978	
Great Balls of Fire (David Graham)	1994	
Great Caesar(Grossmith jr/Paul & Walter Rubens)	1899	56
Great Endeavour (Hassall/Mark Lubbock)	1948	
Great Taykin (Law/Grossmith sr.)	1885	87
Great Waltz (Johann Strauss/Korngold/Wright/Forrest)	1970	+600
Greek Slave (Sidney Jones/Harry Greenbank/Ross)	1898	349
Green Old Age (Reece/Clay)	1874	5 weeks
Gretna Green (Ford/Storer)	1890	16
Gulliver's Travels (Frow/Kenny/Oldham)	1968	
Gulliver's Travels (Willie Rushton/Mike d'Abo)	1975	season
Guy Mannering (Terry/Bishop)	1816	
Guys & Dolls (Frank Loesser)	1953	555
Gypsy (Styne/Sondheim)	1973	300
Gypsy Girl (Arundale/Thorpe)	1907	30
Gypsy Love (Lehar/Ross/Hood)	1912	299
Gypsy Princess (Kalman/Stanley)	1921	212
Haddon Hall (Grundy/Sullivan)	1892	204
Hair (Ragni/Rado/MacDermott) rev 1974	1968	1999
Half a Sixpence (Heneker)	1963	679
Half-Past Eight (Wright/Rubens/Percy Greenbank)	1916	143
Handful of Keys (von Memerty/Colyn)	2002	10
Hanky Panky (Arthurs/Max Darewski)	1917	
Hans Andersen (Loesser/Tommy Steele/Beverley Cross)	1974	+300
Hans the Boatman (Greene)	1887	season
Hansel & Gretel (Humperdinck)	1894	161
Happidrome (Park/Parr Davies) Robert Nesbitt revue	1942	224
Happy & Glorious — George Black revue	1944	938
Happy Arcadia (W.S. Gilbert/Clay)	1872	6 months
Happy as a King (Melfords/Emney/Ross Parker)	1953	26
Happy as a Sandbag (Ken Lee) — wartime songs	1975	
Happy Day (Rubens/Sidney Jones/Ross)	1916	241
Happy End (Brecht/Weill)	1965	short run
Happy Family (Ross/Clarke)	1916	41
Happy Go Lucky (Cook/Johnstone)	1926	37
Happy Hampstead (Desprez)	1877	4 weeks
Happy Holiday (*aka* The Ghost Train) (Posford/Maschwitz)	1954	31
Happy Hypocrite (Addinsell/Dane)	1936	68
Happy Returns — C.B. Cochran revue	1938	78
Happy Weekend (Michael Eiseman)	1934	54
Hard Times (Tookey/Thomas)	2000	3 months
Harmony Close (Ronald Cass/Charles Ross)	1956	62
Harvest Time (Venis/Sherman)	1957	season
Hassan (Delius/Flecker)	1923	281
Haste to the Wedding (WS Gilbert)	1892	22
Havana (Leslie Stuart/Ross)	1908	221
Haw-Haw (Parr Davies) Max Miller & Ben Lyon revue	1939	361
He Wanted Adventure (Grey/Waller/Tunbridge)	1933	152
Head Over Heels (Fraser-Simson/Ross/Graham)	1923	113
Heads Up (Rodgers/Hart)	1930	20
Hearts & Diamonds (John/Granichtadten/Max Darewski)	1926	46
Heathcliff (Bronte/rice/Farrar/Richard)	1997	3 months
Heaven's Up (Clyde)	1990	5 weeks
Hedwig & the Angry Inch (Trask)	2000	
Helen! (Offenbach/Korngold/Herbert) *aka* La Belle Helene	1932	194
Hello Dolly (Jerry Herman)	1965	794
Henson's Gaieties (Henson/Ellis)	1945	180
Herbstmanover, Ein (Kalman)	1912	75
Her Excellency (Purcell/Harry Parr Davies)	1949	252
Her Royal Highness (Slaughter/Hood)	1898	56
Here and There (Chappelle) de Courville & Pink revue	1917	107
Here Come the Boys (Kester/Purcell/Sherwin)	1946	330
Here We Are Again (Arkell/de Bear/Newman/W Charles)	1932	22
Here Comes the Bride (Carter/Dietz/Schwartz)	1930	175
Here, There & Everywhere — revue	1918	
Here, There & Everywhere — Robert Nesbitt revue	1947	466
Here's How (Pola/Nesbitt/Walker)	1934	69
He's Coming (Burnand/Reed)	1874	2 months
Heyday (Appleman)	1986	4 weeks
Hiawatha (Longfellow/Bogdanov/Teare)	1981	
Hide and Seek (Vivian Ellis/Bolton/Thompson/Furber)	1937	204
Hi-De-Hi — Jack Hylton revue	1943	340
Hi-De-Hi (Perry/Croft)	1983	84
Hidenseek (Arthur Eliot/Kiefert/Scot-Gatty/Lutz)	1901	50
Hi-Diddle-Diddle (Walker/Nesbitt/D. Byng)	1934	198
High Button Shoes (Styne/Sammy Cahn)	1948	291
High Diplomacy (Reed/Fraser)	1969	172
High Jinks (Harbach/Friml/Rubens/Talbot/Tate/Kern etc)	1916	383
High Society (Eyre/Cole Porter)	1987	47 weeks
High Spirits (Myers/Climie/Grahame/Cass/Pritchett)	1953	
High Spirits (Martin/Gray) book Blithe Spirit by N. Coward	1964	93
High Time — Robert Nesbitt revue	1946	570
Hired Man (Melvin Bragg/Goodall)	1984	164
His Excellency (Carr/W.S. Gilbert)	1894	161
His Girl (Hurgon/Thomas/Burton)	1922	81
His Little Widows (Young/Duncan/Shepherd/Schroeder)	1919	172
His Majesty *aka* Court of Vignolia (Burnand/Lehmann/Mackenzie)	1897	61
His Master's Voice (Anderson)	1983	5 weeks
His Monkey Wife (Sandy Wilson)	1971	28
Hit the Deck (Youmans/Grey/Robin/Herbert Fields)	1927	277
HMS Irresponsible (Cornish/George Byng)	1901	165
HMS Pinafore (Gilbert & Sullivan)	1878	571
Hold Everything (de Sylva/Brown/Henderson)	1929	173
Hold My Hand (Carter/Noel Gay)	1931	212
Hollywood Dreams (Binns)	1982	3 weeks
Home and Beauty (Henry Sullivan/Brodszky/A.P. Herbert)	1937	128
Home and Beauty — revived from 1937	1950	180
Honeymoon Express (Hirtsch) revue	1914	
Honi Soit! (Bovill/Russell) revue	1915	256
Honk! (Stiles/Drewe)	1999	9 months
Honourable Phil (Huntley/Clayton/Samuel)	1908	71
Hooray for Daisy (Slade/Reynolds)	1959	51
Hostage (Behan)	1958	

Title	Year	Runs
Hot Shoe Shuffle (Atkins)	1994	
Hot Stuff (Norris/Kerryson)	1993	25 weeks
Houp-la! (Ayer/Talbot/Percy Greenbank/Wright)	1916	108
House of Cards (Peter Greenwell/Wildeblood)	1963	27
House That Jack Built (Novello/Ellis/Schwartz/Parsons)	1929	270
How D'You Do? (O. Hamilton/Byng/Macrae) Charlot revue	1933	244
How Now Brown Cow? (Paula Stone)	1965	
How to Succeed in Business Without Really Trying (Loesser)	1963	520
Hullabaloo (Lloyd Webber/Rice) Harold Fielding revue	1972	
Hullo America! (Grey/Finck)	1918	358
Hullo London (Grossmith/Clarke)	1910	
Hullo People (revision of Hullo London)	1910	
Hullo Ragtime (Hirsch/Abrahams/Berlin/Ayer/Brown/Gilbert)	1912	451
Hullo Tango (Arthurs/Hirsch/Abrahams/Clarke/Leslie)	1913	485
Humpty Dumpty (Bobby Crush)	1984	
Hunting of the Snark (Mike Batt)	1991	7 weeks
I and Albert (Adams/Strouse)	1972	120
I Do! I Do! (Schmidt/Tom Jones)	1968	166
I Love My Wife (Coleman/Stewart)	1977	401
I'm Getting My Act Together & Taking It On the Road (Cryer/Ford)	1981	8 weeks
Ib & Little Christina (Hood/Leoni)	1901	16
Illustrious Stranger (Kenney/Millengen/Nathan)	1827	1 year
Immortal Hour (Rutland Boughton)	1922	216
Importance (O.Wilde/Sean O'Mahoney-alias John Dean)	1984	29
In Dahomey (Dunbar/Rogers/Cook)	1903	251
In the Lap of the Gods — revue	1963	
In the Midnight Hour (Ryan)	1992	3 weeks
In the Sulks (Desprez/Cellier)	1880	12 months
In Town (Osmond Carr/Ross/Leader)	1892	292
In Town (Osmond Carr/Ross/Leader) second edition	1893	
Incidental Music (Ayckbourn/Todd)	1983	7 weeks
Indiana (Farnie/Audran)	1886	70
Innocent as Hell (Andrew Rosenthal)	1960	13
Instant Marriage (Bob Grant/Laurie Holloway)	1964	366
Intimacy at 8.30 — Peter Myers revue	1954	551
Into the Woods (Lapine/Sondheim)	1990	186
Iolanthe (Gilbert & Sullivan)	1882	398
Ipi Tombi (Lakier/Egnos)	1975	
Irene (Tierney/McCarthy) revived 1976	1920	399
Irma la Douce (Heneker/More/Monty Norman/Monnot)	1958	1512
Iron Harvest (Colin Sell)	1983	4 weeks
Is Your Doctor Really Necessary? (Macaulay)	1973	68
Isabel's a Jezebel (Dumaresq/MacDermott)	1970	short run
Island King (Gawthorne/Garstin)	1922	160
Islander (Marshall/Faraday)	1910	114
It's a Girl (Burrows/Whitefield)	1987	4 weeks
It's All Wrong (Janis/Finck)	1920	112
It's Foolish But It's Fun (Furber/Ellis/Reader/Ridley/Anthony)	1943	469
It's in the Bag (Landeau/George Rubens)	1937	81
It's Time to Dance (Dyrenforth/Roy/L.-Smith/Phillips/Rogers/Roy)	1943	259
Ivanhoe (Sullivan)	1891	155
J'Adore . . . Ca! — revue	1913	
Jack in the Box (Sims/Scott)	1887	88
Jack o' Diamonds (Grey/Maltby/Noel Gay)	1935	126
Jack the Ripper (Pember/de Marne)	1974	228
Jacob's Journey (Rice/Lloyd Webber)	1972	
Jacques Brel Is Alive & Well & Living in Paris (J. Brel)	1968	41
Jailhouse Rock (Bettinson/Janes)	2004	
James & the Giant Peach (Dahl/Chappell)	1983	1 week
Jane Annie (Conan Doyle/J.M. Barrie/Ford)	1893	50
Japs (Harry & Edward Paulton)	1885	3 months
Jaunty Jane Shore (Crook/Robertson)	1894	56
Jazz Train (J.C. Johnson) Mervyn Nelson revue	1955	
Jean Seberg (C. Adler/Hamlisch)	1983	short run
Jeanne (Roden)	1986	3 weeks
Jeanne, Jeannette, Jeanneton (Reece/Larcombe)	1881	88
Jeeves (Ayckbourn/A. Lloyd Webber)	1975	38
Jenny (Grattan/Plunkett/Anderson/Stanley/Stuart)	1922	66
Jenny Jones (Purcell/Parr Davies)	1944	153
Jericho (Ali)	1977	season
Jesus Christ Superstar (Andrew Lloyd Webber/Tim Rice)	1972	3358
Jigsaw (Chappelle/Horan) de Courville/E. Wallace revue	1920	311
Jill Darling (Edgar/Carter/Vivian Ellis)	1934	242
Jingle Jangle (Shaper/Morrow)	1982	1 week
Joan of Arc (Osmond/Shine/Carr/Ross)	1891	287
Joe Lives (Alex Glasgow)	1971	
Joey, Joey (Ron Moody) aka Great Grimaldi, also Joey	1966	22
John, Paul, George, Ringo & Bert (Beatles)	1974	
John, Paul, George, Ringo & Bert (Russell)	1983	2 months
Johnny Jones (Grey/Cuvillier)	1920	349
Johnny the Priest (Powell/Antony Hopkins)	1960	14
Joie de Vivre (Rattigan/Dehn/Stolz)	1960	4
Jokers Wild (Ross Parker) Crazy Gang revue	1954	911
Jolly Jack Tar (H. Darewski)	1918	67
Jolly Roger (Clinton-Baddeley/Mackenzie/Walter Leigh)	1933	199
Jolson (Bettinson/Francis Essex)	1995	5 months
Jorrocks (Heneker)	1966	181
Joseph & the Amazing Technicolor Dreamcoat (Lloyd-Webber/Rice)	1972	243
Joseph & the Amazing Technicolor Dreamcoat — rev.	1991	923
Josephine (Chadwick)	1992	8 weeks
Joy-Bells (Pether/Hazell/Gray/Chappelle) de Courville revue	1919	723
Joyce Grenfell Requests the Pleasure of Your Co. (Addinsell)	1954	12months
Joyce Grenfell — A Miscellany	1957	
Joyce Grenfell (Addinsell/Blezard)	1962 & 1965	
Joy-land (Herman Darewski) de Courville & Pink revue	1915	409
Joyride Lady (Anderson/Carrick/Gilbert)	1914	105
Jubilee Girl (Fordyce/David Rogers/Kaplan)	1956	53
Judgement in Stone (Rendell/Bartlett/Bloomfield)	1992	3 weeks
Judy — musical biography (Wale)	1985	6 weeks
Jukebox (Donnelly)	1983	5 months
Jumble Sale (Arkell/Turner/Braham)	1920	176
Jumpers (Stoppard/Wilkinson)	1972	
Jumping Red Lights (Willett/Taylor)	1991	4
Just a Kiss (Yvain/Carter/Ellis etc)	1926	93
Just Fancy (Wimperis/H. Darewski/Mayo/Harrington)	1920	332
Just So (Drewe/Styles)	1990	2 months
Kat & the Kings (Kramer/Petersen)	1998	6 months
Katinka (Harbach/Davies/Friml)	1923	108
Katja the Dancer (Graham/Gilbert)	1925	505
Keep Smiling (Gordon-Lennox/Berman)	1913	223
Keep Your Hair On (Cranko/Addison)	1958	20
Kern Goes to Hollywood (Kern/Kernan/Vosburgh)	1985	2 months
Kid Boots (McCarthy/Tierney/Ellis)	1926	172
Kid from Stratford (Gordon/Thomas/Manning Sherwin)	1948	235
Kill That Fly! (Tharp/Goldberg/Grant/Gideon) Grossmith revue	1912	201
King & I (Rodgers/Hammerstein) rev 1973	1953	946
King & I (Rodgers/Hammerstein) revival	1979	538
King & I (Rodgers/Hammerstein) revival	2000	20 months
King (Blackford/Angelou/Beaton)	1990	4 weeks
King Kodak (Crook/Slaughter/Solomon/Monckton)	1894	63
King Kong (Williams/Matshikizia)	1961	6 months
King of Cadonia (Sidney Jones/Adrian Ross)	1908	330
King's Jesters (Archie de Bear/Stafford Byrne)	1948	
King's Rhapsody (Hassall/Novello)	1949	881
Kingdom Come (Davey/Parker)	1978	41
Kingdom Coming (Baum/Snyder/Climie/Cass)	1973	14
Kingdom for a Cow (Arkell/Vambery)	1935	18
Kings and Clowns (Bricusse)	1978	34
Kismet (Borodin/Wright/Forrest)	1955	648
Kiss Call (Thompson/Caryll/Ross)	1919	176
Kiss in Spring, A (du Garde Peach/Kalman/Griffiths)	1932	83
Kiss Me Kate (Cole Porter)	1951	501
Kiss Me Kate (Cole Porter) revival	2001	extended
Kiss of the Spiderwoman (Kander/Ebb)	1992	390
Kiss the Sky (Cartwright)	1996	
Kissing Time (Bolton/Wodehouse/Caryll/Grey/Redstone)	1919	430
Kitty Grey (Monckton/Talbot/Rubens/Ross/Piggott/Barratt)	1901	220
Klondyke (Languirand/Charpentier)	1965	
Knight Was Bold (Gordon/Thomas/Parr Davies)	1943	10
Knights of Madness (Ross Parker) Crazy Gang revue	1950	1361
Kong (Harold Kingsley/Baynton Power)	1931	20
Kookaburra (Eric Spear)	1959	42
Kwa Zulu (Ntoni)	1975	
L'Africaine (Burnand/Musgrave)	1865	88
La Cage aux Folles (Jerry Herman)	1986	301
La-Di-Da-Di-Da (Gay/Stanley & Lupino Lane/Ash)	1943	318
Lads of the Village — revue	1917	
Lady at the Wheel (Bricusse/Beaumont)	1958	65
Lady Be Good (Bolton/Thompson/Gershwin brothers)	1926	326
Lady Behave (Stanley Lupino/Horan/Eyton)	1941	401
Lady Day (Dahl)	1987	5 weeks
Lady Luck (Strachey/Rodgers/Carter/Hart/Hedley/Newman/Shephard)	1927	324
Lady Madcap (Rubens/Percy Greenbank)	1904	354
Lady Mary (Lonsdale/Sirmay/Turner/Charig)	1928	181
Lady of the Locket (Hamilton/Fullerton)	1885	120
Lady of the Rose (Romberg/Gilbert/Graham/Lonsdale/Stuart)	1922	507
Lady or the Tiger (Paul/Richmond)	1975	52
Lady Slavey (Dance/Crook)	1894	96
Lady Tatters (Carse/Slaughter)	1907	80
Ladyland (Ponsonby/Lambert)	1904	15
Lancelot the Lovely (Henry/Crook)	1889	66
Land of the Dinosaurs (Hill/Armit)	1974	season
Land of Nod (Chevalier/West)	1898	6
Land of Smiles (Herzer/Lohner-Beda/Franz Lehar)	1931	71
Land of the Christmas Stocking (Foord/Mabel Buchanan)	1945	season
Large As Life — revue	1958	382
Lark Rise (Dewhurst) adapted from the Flora Thompson trilogy	1978	
Larry the Lamb in Toytown (Hulme Beaman/D. Wood/Rankin)	1973	season
Last Sweet Days of Isaac (Gretchen Cryer/Nancy Ford)	1971	season
Last Waltz (Oscar Straus/Arkell/Evett)	1922	288
Late Joys — Victorian music hall	1964	
Late Night Extra (Myers/Dannatt/Grahame) revue	1951	
Latin Quarter (1) — Robert Nesbitt revue	1949	455
Latin Quarter (2) — Robert Nesbitt revue	1950	456
Latin Quarter (3) — Robert Nesbitt revue	1951	468
Latin Quarter (4) — Robert Nesbitt revue (Excitement)	1952	419
Laughing Cavalier (Arkell/Byrne)	1937	38

Title	Year	Runs
Laughing Eyes (H. Darewski)	1919	126
Laughing Husband (Wimperis/Kern/Eysler)	1913	78
Lautrec (Aznavour/Shipman)	2000	short run
League of Notions (Murray/Anderson/Barratt/Ager/Trix)	1921	360
Leap Year (Harris/Finck) Lauri Wylie revue	1924	471
Leave Him To Heaven (Lee)	1976	
Leave It To Me (Cole Porter)	1991	
Lennon — musical biography (Eator)	1985	28 weeks
Leonardo (Moeller/Moeller/Dunlop/Minks)	1993	5 weeks
Les Miserables (Hugo/Kretzmer/Schonberg)	1985	+7500
Les Pres Saint-Gervais	1874	132
Let's Face It (Rich/Morgan/McDermot/G. Wright/Zwar/Lubbock)	1939	
Let's Face It (Cole Porter/Herbert Fields)	1942	348
Let's Make an Opera (Crozier/Britten)	1949	50
Let's Mix It (Joan Byford/Harold Brewer) revue	1940	
Let Yourself Go — Robert Nesbitt revue	1963	
Liberty Ranch (Goldsmith/Brahms/Sherrin)	1972	26
Lido Lady (Rodgers/Hart)	1926	259
Lie Down, I Think I Love You (Davies)	1970	13
Life (Fred Rome/Arkell/Chappelle)	1926	167
Life Begins at Oxford Circus — Crazy Gang revue	1935	
Light & Shade (C. Parker/Reynolds/G. Wright) Farjeon revue	1942	54
Light Blues (Ross/Ambient/Jack Hulbert/Finck)	1916	20
Light Fantastic — revue	1954	2 weeks
Lights Up (Grant/Eyton/Noel Gay) Ronald Jeans revue	1940	114
Lilac Domino (Fitzgerald/Cuvillier)	1918	747
Lilac Time (Schubert/Romberg/Clutsam/Ross)	1922	626
Lili Marlene (Conner/Cutter)	1950	
Lily of Leoville (Murray/Caryll)	1886	41
Lily White Boys (Cookson/Logue/Kinsey/Le Sage)	1960	45
Line One (Ludwig)	1986	2 weeks
Lion King (Elton John/Tim Rice et al)	1999	+2000
Lionel & Clarissa (Bickerstaff/Dibdin)	1768	
Lionel & Clarissa (revised Alfred Reynolds)	1925	171
Lionel (Lionel Bart compilation)	1977	
Lisbon Story (Harry Parr Davies/Harold Purcell)	1943	492
Listen to the Wind (Ellis)	1955	48
Listening In — revue	1922	26
Little Cherub (Hall/Caryll/Tours/Ross)	1906	114
Little Christopher Columbus (Sims/Raleigh/Caryll)	1893	421
Little Doctor Faustus (Byron)	1877	151
Little Dog Laughed (Butler/Gay/Carr/Kennedy) revue	1939	461
Little Duke (Saville & Bolton Rowe, alias Stephenson & Scott)	1878	
Little Dutch Girl, A (Graham/Hicks/Kalman)	1920	207
Little Genius (Harris/Sturgess/Taund/Ronald/Glover)	1896	128
Little Giant (John Pudney)	1972	
Little Girl in Red (Simpson/Stanley)	1921	33
Little Hans Andersen (Hood/Slaughter)	1903	27
Little Jack Sheppard (Stephens/Yardley/Lutz)	1885	155
Little Mary Sunshine (Rick Besoyan)	1962	44
Little Match Girl (Stewart/Strachan)	1991	8 weeks
Little Me (Cy Coleman/Caroline Leigh) rev. 1984	1964	334
Little Michus (Messager/ Percy Greenbank)	1905	401
Little Miss Bluebeard — various	1925	13
Little Miss Nobody (Graham/Godfrey/Ronald)	1898	198
Little Nellie Kelly (Cohan)	1923	265
Little Night Music, A (Sondheim)	1975	406
Little Night Music, A (Sondheim) revival	1995	1 year
Little Old King Cole (Johnson)	1961	205
Little Revue (Walter Leigh/Farjeon)	1939	415
Little Revue Starts at Nine (Finck/Waller/Farjeon)	1923	196
Little Shop of Horrors (Ashman/Mencken)	1983	813
Little Tommy Tucker (Carter/Vivian Ellis/Schwartz)	1930	86
Little Whopper (Harbach/Dudley/Friml)	1920	53
Little Women (Gavin Sutherland)	2002	1 week
Little Women (Howland/Dickstein)	2004	
Living for Pleasure (Macrae/Addinsell)	1958	370
Liza of Lambeth (Willie Rushton/Stringle/Cliff Adams)	1976	110
Lock Up Your Daughters (Miles/Johnson/Bart)	1959	330
Lola (Marshall/Orsini)	1880	36
London Calling! (Noel Coward/Braham) Ron. Jeans revue	1923	316
London Laughs — Jack Hylton revue	1952	1113
London Laughs — Robert Nesbitt revue	1966	
London Revue (Mayerl et al)	1925	77
London Rhapsody (Carr/Kennedy/Weston/Lee) Crazy Gang revue	1937	3 months
London, Paris and New York (Wimperis/H. Darewski)	1920	366
Londoners (Lewis/Bart/Carr)	1972	63
Lonesome Stone (Czekalaski/M & M. Damrow/Hoyt/Palosaari)	1973	
Look Out, It's Sir (Lewis/Klein)	1975	season
Look Who's Here (Ayer) not the 1960 version	1916	130
Look Who's Here (Ted Dicks) not the 1916 version	1960	
Looking Around (Weston/Norworth)	1915	43
Looking For Action (Mathieu) Chicago revue	1963	
Looking Glass (Chappelle/E. Wallace) revue	1924	56
Lord Bateman (Stephens/Solomon)	1875	
Lord Chamberlain Regrets (Myers/Cass/Pritchett)	1961	
Lord of the Manor (Burgoyne)	1780	
Lord Tom Noddy (Carr/Dance)	1896	62
Lost, Stolen or Strayed — A Day in Paris (Stuart)	1897	76
Love & Laughter (Oscar Straus)	1913	65
Love Adrift (Poldini)	1926	21
Love and Law (Latimer/Caryll)	1891	9 months
Love Doctor (Wright/Forrest/D. Byng)	1959	16
Love From Judy (Hugh Martin/Maschwitz/Webster)	1952	594
Love in a Village (Bickerstaff/Arne)	1762	
Love in a Village (revised Alfred Reynolds)	1928	124
Love in the Country (Alfreds/Bowles)	1993	
Love Laughs (Noel Gay/Mayerl/Grey/Newman)	1935	96
Love Lies (Mayerl/S. Lupino/Rigby/Carter/Brody/Sarony)	1929	347
Love Mills (Fonson/Wicheler)	1911	24
Love Race (Stanley Lupino/Clarke/Carter/Mayerl)	1930	237
Love Racket (S. Lupino/Gay/Eyton/Gibbs/Gordon/Thomas)	1943	324
Love's Awakening (Kunneke/Ross)	1922	81
Love's Limit (Galer/Mallandaine)	1866	
Love's Prisoner (Hargreaves)	1925	26
Love's Trickery (Caryll)	1889	3 months
Lovebirds (Grossmith/Percy Greenbank/Raymond Roze)	1904	75
Lovely Lady (Jean Gilbert)	1932	3
Lucky Boy (Ian Douglas/Melachrino)	1953	3
Lucky Break (Furber/Thompson/Archer)	1934	198
Lucky Girl (Furber/Weston/Lee/Charig)	1928	150
Lucky Star aka L'Etoile (Brookfield/Ross/Hopwood/Caryll)	1899	143
Lumber Love (Stiles/Berie & Emmett Adams)	1928	108
Lurette (Desprez/Murray/Offenbach)	1883	83
Lute Song (Hanighen/Scott)	1948	24
Lying Dutchman (Hay/Clements)	1876	48
Lyle the Crocodile (Strouse)	1987	
Lyric Revue (Coward/Swann/Bryant/Zwar)	1951	454
Mack & Mabel (Herman) revival	1995	270
Mack and Mabel (Jerry Herman)	1988	
Madame Favart (Farnie/Offenbach)	1879	502
Madame Pompadour (Lonsdale/Graham/Fall)	1923	467
Madame Sherry (Hugo Felix/Ross/Harbach/Hoschna)	1903	102
Maddie (Keeling/McKenna/Dexter)	1997	5 weeks
Maggie (Lattes/Ross/Thompson/Maltby)	1919	108
Maggie (Wild)	1977	42
Maggie May (Lionel Bart)	1964	501
Magic Carpet (Furber/Melford/Guest/Sherwin)	1943	182
Magic Man, The (Barbara & Anthony D'Amato	1977	24
Magic of Young Houdini	1976	40
Magic Opal aka Magic Ring (Law/Albeniz)	1893	81
Magyar Melody (Posford/Maschwitz/Bolton) aka Paprika	1939	105
Maid Marian (Smith/de Koven)	1892	
Maid of Athens (Pearson/Newton/Carr)	1897	27
Maid of the Mountains (F.-Simson/Graham/Friml) rev1972	1917	1352
Maid to Measure — Leigh Stafford revue	1948	
Make It a Date (Horan/Young/Carr)	1946	140
Make Me an Offer (Monty Norman/Heneker)	1959	267
Mame (Jerry Herman)	1969	443
Mamma Mia (Andersson and Bjorn Ulvaeus)	1999	+2000
Mamselle Tra-La-La (Wimperis/Carrick/Gilbert)	1914	105
Mamzelle Nitouche (Herve)	1893	104
Man About Town (Mee/Carpenter)	1897	18
Man From the East (Yamashta)	1973	short run
Man in the Moon (Springfield/Diamond/Taylor)	1963	
Man of La Mancha (Joe Darion/Mitch Leigh)	1968	253
Man of Magic (Morley/Cash/Wilfred Josephs)	1966	135
Man With a Load of Mischief, The	1968	short run
Mandrake (Alfreds/Bowles)	1970	12
Manteaux Noirs, Les (Parke/Paulton/Bucalossi)	1882	190
Many Happy Returns (Farjeon/Scott et al)	1928	127
Many Happy Returns (Johnny Johnston)	1937	short run
March Hares — Crazy Gang revue	1935	
March of the Falsettos (William Finn)	1987	3 weeks
Mardi Gras (Bragg/Howard/Blaikley)	1976	212
Marie (Richard D'Oyly Carte)	1871	5
Marie Lloyd Story (Farson/Moore)	1967	
Mariette (Oscar Straus/Sacha Guitry)	1929	28
Marigold (Zwar/Alan Melville)	1959	77
Marilyn! (Wilson/Garson)	1983	5 months
Maritana (Wallace)	1843	
Maritza (Kalman/Byng/Stanley) see also Countess Maritza	1938	68
Marjolaine (Asche)	1928	67
Marjolaine, La (Edwards/Lecocq)	1877	2 years
Marjorie (Clifton/Dilley/Slaughter)	1890	193
Marlow (Rost/Horowitz)	1986	4 weeks
Mary Poppins (Travers/R. & B. Sherman/Stiles/Drewe)	2004	
Marriage Market (Anderson/Ross/Jacobi)	1913	423
Marry Me a Little (Lucas/Reno/Sondheim)	1982	22
Martin Guerre (Schonberg/Hardy/Clark/Boublil/Kretzmer)	1996	6 months
Martin Luther King (Lloyd)	1969	
Mary (Harbach/Mandel/Hirsch)	1921	93
Mascotte, La (Farnie/Reece/Audran)	1881	199
Masquerade (Argent)	1982	31
Mata Hari (Lovell/Chappell/Smith)	1982	4 weeks
Matador (Leander/Seago/Jukes)	1991	13 weeks
Matchgirls (Bill Owen/Tony Russell)	1966	119
May Fever (John Morley)	1955	Christmas
Maybe That's Your Problem (Chetwynd/Don Black/Scharf)	1971	18
Mayfair and Montmartre (Gershwin/Yvain/de Sylva)	1922	77
Me and My Girl (Furber/Gay/Rose)	1937	1646

Title	Year	Run
Me and My Girl (revival from 1937) (Noel Gay)	1985	3303
Me Nobody Knows (Schapiro/Friedman)	1973	45
Me, Myself & I (Ayckbourn)	1982	2 seasons
Medal and the Maid (Jessop/S. Jones/Taylor/Rubens/Rollit)	1903	98
Medorah (Ennem/Ansell/Ross)	1920	short run
Meet Me by Moonlight (Dearlove/Whitby)	1957	148
Meet Me on the Corner — revue	1955	25 weeks
Meet Me Victoria (Eyton/Gay)	1944	251
Meg & Mog Show (David Wood)	1981	season
Melita (Kennedy/Piccolomini)	1882	6
Melnotte (Anderson/Tours)	1901	
Melody That Got Lost (Kay North/Nancy Logan/Freeman)	1936	28
Mercenary Mary (Conrad/Friedlander/Caesar/Ellis)	1925	446
Merely Molly (Finck/Joseph Meyer/Graham)	1926	85
Merrie England (Edward German/Hood)	1902	120
Merrily We Roll Along (Sondheim)	1983	24
Merrily we Roll Along (Sondheim)	2000	3 months
Merry Duchess (Sims/Clay)	1883	177
Merry Merry (Archer/Thompson//Tunbridge/Waller/Weston)	1929	131
Merry Peasant (Fall/Hamilton)	1909	69
Merry War (Reece/Johann Strauss)	1882	
Merry Widow (Franz Lehar/Ross/Hood)	1907	778
Merry-Go-Round (Hopwood/Lutz et al)	1899	season
Merveilleuses, Les aka Lady Dandies (Hood/Felix/Ross)	1906	196
Messenger Boy (Caryll/Monckton/Ross/Percy Greenbank)	1900	429
Metropolis (Hughes & Brooks)	1989	6 months
Metropolitan Mikado (G. & S./Beaton/Sherrin)	1985	2 weeks
Miami (St Leger/Haydn Parry)	1893	11
Midsummer Madness (Clifford Bax/Armstrong Gibbs)	1924	128
Mignonette (Brand/Parker)	1889	31
Mikado (Gilbert & Sullivan)	1885	672
Mildred's Well (Burnand/Reed)	1873	3 months
Miller's Daughters (P. Greenbank/Rubens)	1916	36
Millionaire Kid (Eyton/Billy Mayerl)	1931	87
Milord Sir Smith (O'Day/Ross/Jakobowski)	1898	82
Mine Fair Sadie (Alf Fogal)	1960	
Mirette (Messager/Ross/Weatherly)	1894	101
Miss Decima (Burnand/Audran)	1891	191
Miss Esmeralda (Leslie/Mills/Lutz)	1887	87
Miss Hook of Holland (Hurgon/Rubens)	1907	462
Miss Saigon (Schonberg/Boublil/Maltby)	1989	3840
Miss Wingrove (Risque/Talbot)	1905	11
Mister Venus (Galton/Speight)	1958	16
Mitford Girls (Greenwell/Caryl Brahms/Ned Sherrin)	1981	12 weeks
Mixed Grill, A (Talbot)	1914	
Moby Dick (Longden/Kaye)	1992	15 weeks
Mock Turtles (Desprez/Faning)	1881	12 months
Modern Don Quixote (Dance/Crook)	1893	21
Money to Burn (Abineri)	2003	
Monsieur Beaucaire (Lonsdale/Ross/Messager)	1919	221
Monte Carlo (Carlton/Henry Greenbank/Talbot)	1896	76
Monte Christo Junior (Butler/Newton/Lutz)	1886	166
Moonlight is Silver (Addinsell/Dane)	1934	85
Moonshine (Strachey) Arkell & de Bear revue	1940	
More Odds and Ends (Grattan/Edward Jones)	1916	376
More New Faces (Posford/Maschwitz)	1941	
Morocco Bound (Branscombe/Osmond Carr/Ross)	1893	295
Most Happy Fella (Frank Loesser)	1960	464
Mother Earth (Shearer/Thronson)	1972	
Mother of Pearl (A.P. Herbert/Oscar Straus)	1933	181
Mountaineers (Eden/Somerville)	1909	61
Mountebanks (W.S. Gilbert/Cellier)	1892	229
Mousmé (Wimperis/Monckton/Talbot/Percy Greenbank)	1911	209
Mousquetaires, Les (Farnie/Varney)	1880	
Mozart (Guitry/Hahn)	1926	28
Mr. and Mrs (alias Brief Encounter) (Noel Coward/Taylor)	1968	44
Mr. Burke, MP (Gerald Frow)	1960	114
Mr. Cinders (Grey/Newman/Myers/Vivian Ellis) rev 1983	1929	528
Mr. Guffin's Elopement (Law/Grossmith sr.)	1882	season
Mr. Manhattan (Thompson/Bovill/Talbot/Tours/Braham)	1916	221
Mr. Men Musical (Hargreaves/Sircom)	1985	
Mr. Popple of Ippleton (Rubens)	1905	173
Mr. Tower of London — Archie Pitt revue for Gracie Fields	1925	2 years
Mr Whittington (Grey/Newman/Furber/Green/Waller/Tunbridge)	1934	298
Mr. Wix of Wickham (Seddon/Everard/Tours)	1902	
Mrs. Tucker's Pageant (Hill/Klein)	1981	49
Mrs. Wilson's Diary (John Wells/Taylor/Ingrams)	1967	
Mummy's Tomb (Ken Hill)	1980	
Murderous Instincts (Cinda Fox)	2004	1 week
Music at Midnight (Offenbach/Bolton/H. Purcell/May)	1950	
Music Box Revue (Berlin) Sam Harris revue	1923	119
Music Box Show — revue	1960	
Music in the Air (Kern/Hammerstein)	1933	275
Music Man (Meredith Willson)	1961	395
Mutiny (Essex/Crane)	1985	60 weeks
Mutt & Jeff (West/Jack Hylton)	1921	
My Aunt's Secret (Burnand/Molloy)	1872	3 months
My Brother's Sister (Palmer)	1890	
My Darling (Seymour Hicks/Haines/Taylor/Baker/Wodehouse)	1907	71
My Fair Lady (Lerner/Loewe)	1958	2281
My Girl (Tanner/Ross/Carr)	1896	183
My Lady Frayle (Wimperis/Pemberton/Talbot/Finck)	1916	130
My Lady Molly (Sidney Jones/Jessop/Percy Greenbank/Taylor)	1903	342
My Lucky Day (John Dellacey/Robin Baker)	1951	
My Mimosa Maid (Hurgon/Rubens)	1908	83
My Nieces (Percy Greenbank/Talbot)	1921	172
My One and Only (Gershwin brothers) based on Funny Face	2002	
My Sister and I (Carter/Eyton/Benatzky/Grossmith)	1931	8
My Son John (John/O. Straus/Ellis/Graham/ Carter/Thompson)	1926	255
My Sweetheart (Meader/Gill)	1883	163
Mynheer Jan (Harry & Edward Paulton/Jakobowski)	1887	35
Mysteries (Caddick/Tams et al)	1982	
Mystery of Edwin Drood (Rupert Holmes)	1987	68
Mystical Miss aka The Charlatan (Klein/Sousa)	1899	2 months
Nadgy (Murray/Chassaigne)	1888	162
Napoleon (Williams/Sabiston)	2000	4 months
Naughty Nancy (Bath/Preston/Lyon/Davidson)	1902	77
Naughty Nero (Ross/Barratt)	1906	
Naughty Princess (Cuvillier/Ross/Turner)	1920	263
Nautch Girl (Dance/Solomon)	1891	200
Nell Gwynne (Farnie/Planquette)	1884	86
Nelly Neil (McLellan/Caryll)	1907	107
Nemesis (HB Farnie/Offenbach)	1873	262
Never Mind the Bullocks (Lee/Dowie)	1979	season
New Aladdin (Monckton/Tours/Caryll/P. Greenbank/ Ross/Grossmith)	1906	203
New Ambassadors Revue (Diana Morgan/Bob McDermott)	1941	
New Ambassadors Revue (Strachey et al)	1942	
New Ambassadors Revue (Posford)	1943	
New Barmaid (Bowyer/Sprague/Crook)	1896	259
New Corsican Brothers (Raleigh/Slaughter)	1889	36
New Cranks (Cranko/David Lee)	1960	
New Faces (Strachey/Maschwitz/Sherwin/Connor)	1940	257
New Moon (Romberg/Hammerstein/Mandel/Schwab)	1929	148
New Whirligig — revue	1920	
Newmarket (Boyd-Jones/Crook/Capel/Plumpton et al)	1896	58
Nice Goings On (Schwartz/Furber/Eyton)	1933	221
Nicholas Nickleby (Oliver) also known as Smike	1980	
Nickleby & Me (Brahms/Sherrin)	1975	44
Nicolette (Frost/Lark/Barrow)	1925	12
Night & the Laughter — Robert Nesbitt & Joan Davis revue	1946	168
Night & the Music — Robert Nesbitt revue	1945	686
Night Birds (Anderson/Johann Strauss)	1911	133
Night in Venice, A (Strauss)	1944	
Night Out (Redstone/Grey/Grossmith/Miller/Gideon/Porter)	1920	311
Nights at the Comedy (Farson) music hall	1964	
Nightingale (Martin-Harvey/Sax/Rohmer/Kennedy Russell)	1947	55
Nightingale (Strouse)	1982	4 weeks
Nightshriek (Ward) based on Macbeth	1986	3 weeks
Nina Rosa (Harbach/Romberg/Caesar)	1931	111
Nine (Yeston/Coppit)	1996	3 months
Nine O'Clock Revue (Hamilton/Simpson/Harvey/Lillie)	1922	385
Nine Sharp (Walter Leigh) Farjeon revue	1938	405
Nineteen-Naughty-One (Ronald Frankau/Monte Crick)	1941	170
Nippy (Billy Mayerl/Wimperis/Melford/Eyton)	1930	137
No Cards (W.S. Gilbert/Reed)	1869	
No Sky So Blue (Grant/Horan)	1938	40
No Strings (Taylor/Richard Rodgers)	1963	short run
No Way to treat a Lady (Cohen)	1998	3 weeks
No, No, Nanette (Youmans/Irving Caesar/Harbach)	1925	665
No, No, Nanette (Youmans/Caesar/Harbach) revival	1973	277
Noddy in Toyland (Blyton/Phil Green) seasonal prodns.	1954	Christmas
Noel & Gertie (Coward/Sheridan Morley)	1983	4 weeks
Noel & Gertie (Coward/Sheridan Morley)	1986	3 weeks
No Song, No Supper (Prince Hoare)	1790	
Not Likely! (Grossmith/Gordon-Lennox)	1914	305
Not To Worry (Stanley Daniels)	1962	
Notre Dame de Paris (Plamondon/Cocciante/Jennings)	2000	5 months
Now and Then (Turner/Graves)	1921	76
Now's the Time (Lennox/Bovill/Max Darewski/Redstone)	1915	147
Nunsense (Dan Goggins)	1987	9 months
Nutmeg & Ginger (Julian Slade)	1991	8 weeks
Nymph Errant (Romney Brent/Cole Porter)	1933	154
Nymphs and Satires (various) Leon Gluckman revue	1965	short run
O Mistress Mine (Cole Porter/Ben Travers)	1936	11
Odd Spot (Titheradge/Santon/Broones)	1924	106
Odds & Ends (Grattan/Jones)	1914	259
Off the Record — revue	1954	702
Officers' Mess (Hurst/Strong)	1905	8
Officers' Mess (Braham/Burnaby)	1918	200
Oh, Be Careful (revival of Mamselle Tra-La-La 1914)	1915	33
Oh, Boy! (Jack Good) — based on TV show	1979	
Oh, Calcutta (various)	1970	+2300
Oh! Coward — Roderick Cooke revue	1975	
Oh Don't Dolly! (Pemberton/Ponsonby/Burnand/Dorlay)	1919	36
Oh, Kay! (Gershwin bros/Bolton/P.G. Wodehouse)rev1974	1927	214
Oh, Joy! (Kern/Bolton/Wodehouse)	1919	167
Oh, Julie (Shephard/Brooke/Sullivan/Herman Darewski)	1920	143
Oh Mr Porter (Cole Porter compilation)	1977	
Oh, My Papa! (Montagu/Burkhard)	1957	45
Oh! Oh! Delphine (McLellan/Caryll)	1913	174

Title	Year	Runs
Oh, What a Lovely War! (Charles Chilton/Joan Littlewood)	1963	501
Oh, What a Night (compilation musical)	1999	10 weeks
Oh! You Letty (Sharon)	1937	71
O-Kay for Sound (Weston/Lee/Gay/Carr/Kennedy)		
Crazy Gang	1936	
Oklahoma! (Rodgers/Hammerstein)	1947	1543
Old Chelsea (Walter Ellis/Tysh/Grun/Richard Tauber)	1943	95
Old Man of Lochnagar (Wood)	1986	1 week
Oliver Grumble (Dance)	1886	30
Oliver! (Lionel Bart)	1960	2618
Oliver! (rev from 1960)	1967	331
Oliver! (rev from 1960)	1977	1152
Oliver! (rev from 1960)	1994	600
Olivette (Farnie/Audran)	1880	466
Omar Khayyam (Liza Lehmann/Grieg)	1923	86
On Condition (Reece/Lutz)	1883	15 months
On Duty (Herman Darewski)	1914	13
On Jhelum River (Fraser/Amy Woodforde-Finden)	1909	6
On the Brighter Side (Gilbert/Myers/Grahame)	1961	
On the Level (Millar/Grainer)	1966	118
On the March (Yardley/Stephenson/F. & C. Clay/Crook)	1896	77
On the Town (Comden/Green/Bernstein) rev 2005	1963	63
On the Twentieth Century (Comden/Green/Coleman)	1980	165
On With the Dance (Coward/Braham/D. Byng)	1925	229
On With the Show — Lawrence Wright revue	1933	57
On With the Show (Hill/Morgan/MacDermott/G. Wright)	1935	
On Your Toes (Rodgers/Hart) revived 1963	1937	104
Once On This Island (Flaherty)	1994	145
Once Upon a Mattress (Mary Rodgers/Marshall Barer)	1960	38
Once Upon a Song (Newell/Mittleman)	1992	3 weeks
Once Upon a Time (Newell/Webb)	1972	26
One Damn Thing After Another (Rodgers/Hart)	1927	237
One Girl (Grey/Adamson/Youmans)	1933	45
One Mo' Time (various)	1981	12 months
One Night Stand (Harding)	1981	47
One Over the Eight (Cook/Law/Mulcahy)	1961	
One to Another — revue	1959	
One, Two, Three (Wigram/Spoliansky)	1947	198
Only Girl (Blossom/Thompson/Victor Herbert)	1915	107
Only in America (Stoller/Leiber)	1980	
Open Your Eyes (Duke/Gibbons/Dyrenforth/Knox/Jackson)	1930	24
Operette (Noel Coward)	1938	133
Oranges & Lemons (Flanders/Swann/Sandy Wilson/Lister)	1948	116
Orchid (Caryll/Monckton/Ross/P. Greenbank/Tanner/Rubens)	1903	559
Orchids and Onions (Jayne Ogden)	1941	
Oriana (Albery/Clay)	1873	18
Orlando Dando (Slaughter/Hood)	1898	
Orpheus in the Underground (Offenbach/Noyes/Tree)	1911	70
Orpheus in the Underworld (Offenbach)	1865	76
Oscar (Clutton/Landi)	1992	2 weeks
Oscar (Mike Read)	2004	1
Our Agency (Brummell/Matchem)	1886	7
Our Day Out (Russell)	1983	4 weeks
Our Diva (Ferrier/Carre/Roger/Rae)	1886	48
Our House (Firth)	2002	
Our Island Home (W.S. Gilbert/Reed)	1870	4 weeks
Our Liz (Aller/Thayer/Clayton/West)	1923	8
Our Man Crichton (Kretzmer/J.M. Barrie/David Lee)	1964	208
Our Miss Gibbs (Monckton/Caryll/Ross/P. Greenbank/Tanner)	1909	636
Our Nell (Parker/Arkell/Fraser-Simson/Novello)	1924	140
Out of the Blue (Tokura/Sand/Gilmore)	1994	
Out of the Bottle (Thompson/Grey/Levant/Vivian Ellis)	1932	106
Out of this World (Cole Porter)	1991	10
Over She Goes (Carter/Eyton/Stanley Lupino/Billy Mayerl)	1936	248
Over the Moon (Ellis)	1953	156
Over the Page (Vivian Ellis) John Murray Anderson revue	1932	82
Oxford Blazers (Watkyn/Ensor/Spurgin/Sayer) revue	1932	12
Pacific 1860 (Noel Coward)	1946	129
Pacific Overtures (Weidman/Wheeler/Sondheim)	1987	10 weeks
Pacific Overtures (Sondheim)	2003	
Padlock (Bickerstaff/Dibdin)	1768	
Paganini (Lehar/A.P. Herbert)	1937	59
Pageant of the People (du Garde Peach/Charles Williams)	1946	
Paint Your Wagon (Lerner/Loewe)	1953	477
Painting the Town — revue	1955	373
Pajama Game (Adler/Jerry Ross)	1955	578
Pal Joey (Rodgers/Hart)	1954	245
Palace of Pearl (Murray/Younge)	1886	48
Palladium Pleasures (Wylie/Newman/Jeans/Lofthouse/Ellis)	1926	312
Palladium Variety — revue	1962	
Pamela (Wimperis/Norton)	1917	172
Panama Hattie (Herbert Fields/de Sylva/Cole Porter)	1943	308
Pantomime Rehearsal (Clay/Edward Jones)	1891	438
Papa's Wife (Hicks/Terriss/Phillips)	1895	season
Paprika (Maschwitz/Posford) aka Magyar Melody 1939	1938	11
Paquita (Reece/Mallandaine)	1871	13
Pardon My French — revue	1953	758
Paris by Night — revue	1955	890
Paris in London (M. & D. Parsons/Reynolds/Penso)	1932	21
Paris to Piccadilly — revue	1952	850
Passing Show (Wimperis/Flers/Finck/Norton)	1914	351
Passing Show of 1915 (Wimperis/Carrick/Finck/Norton)	1915	143
Passion (Sondheim/Lapine)	1996	232
Passion Flower Hotel (Mankowitz/Peacock/John Barry)	1965	148
Patience (Gilbert & Sullivan)	1881	578
Patricia (MacKail/Stanley/Melford/Gwyther/Titheradge)	1924	160
Patsy Cline (Worthy)	1994	
Paul & Virginia (Cobb)	1800	
Paul Jones (Farnie/Planquette)	1889	370
Paulette (Harry S. Pepper/England/Claude Hulbert)	1932	32
Pay the Piper (Flanders/Swann) Laurier Lister revue	1954	20
Pearl Girl (Caryll/Hood/Talbot/Felix)	1913	254
Peep Show (Harris/Valentine/James Tate)	1921	421
Peg (David Heneker)	1984	146
Peggy (Grossmith/Leslie Stuart/Bovill)	1911	270
Peggy Ann (Herbert Fields/Rodgers/Hart)	1927	134
Peggy Machree (Bidwell/Esposito/Lucas)	1904	35
Peggy Sue Got Married (Leichtling/Gaudio)	2001	2 months
Pell-Mell (Grey/Wright/Ayer)	1916	298
Penny Plain (Phipps/Grenfell/Addinsell) Laurier Lister revue	1951	443
Pepita (Paulton/Lecocq)	1888	102
Perchance to Dream (Novello)	1945	1022
Perichole, La (Offenbach)	1875	
Persian Princess, A (Barrow/S. Jones/P. Greenbank/Horne)	1909	68
Personals (Mencken/Schwartz)	1998	4 weeks
Pet of Newmarket (Mooney/Bossche)	1885	6
Peter Pan (J.M. Barrie/Moose Charlap)	1985	73
Peter Pan (J.M. Barrie/Chater-Robinson)	1994	
Petit Faust (Farnie/Herve)	1870	
Petronella (Turner/Gliddon)	1906	8
Phantom of the Opera (Hart/A. Lloyd Webber)	1986	+5000
Phantom Violin (McBurney/Complicite)	1988	4 months
Phil the Fluter (Heneker/French)	1969	125
Philomel (Clifford Bax/Jefferson)	1932	21
Phi-Phi (Thompson/Grey/Christiné)	1922	133
Piccadilly Hayride (Dick Hurran/Park)	1946	778
Pick-a-Dilly — revue	1916	284
Pickwick (Cyril Ornadel/Bricusse)	1963	694
Pieces of Eight (L. Johnson/S. Wilson/Law/Mulcahy/Pinter)	1959	429
Pied Piper (Gordon Vivian/James Stevens)	1962	42
Pilgrim (McCulloch)	1975	short run
Pink Champagne (Maschwitz/Grun) aka Die Fledermaus	1958	
Pink Lady (McLellan/Caryll)	1912	124
Pinkie and the Fairies (Robertson/Norton)	1908	73
Pins & Needles (Pink/de Courville/Chappelle)	1921	242
Pippin (Stephen Schwartz)	1973	2 months
Pirates of Penzance (Gilbert & Sullivan)	1880	363
Plain and Fancy (Horwitt/Hague)	1956	217
Playing the Game (Younge/Flaxman/Eplett/Edward Jones)	1896	5
Please Teacher (Browne/Weston/Lee/Waller/Tunbridge)	1935	300
Please! (Titheradge/MacGunigle/Ellis/Croom-Johnston)	1933	108
Pleasures of Paris — revue	1957	850
Plume de Ma Tante (Robert Dhery)	1955	700
Pocahontas (Grundy/Solomon)	1884	24
Pocahontas (Kermit Goell)	1963	12
Point (Harry Nilsson)	1976	season
Polly (John Gay/Austin) sequel to The Beggars Opera	1922	324
Polly (Mortimer/Solomon)	1884	69
Polynesia (Gawthorne/Garstin)	1924	24
Pom ((Bucalossi)	1876	30
Popkiss (alias Rookery Nook) (Heneker/John Addison)	1972	65
Poppy (Stephen Jones/Samuels/Donnelly)	1924	188
Poppy (Monty Norman/Nicholls)	1982	97
Porgy & Bess (Gershwin brothers) 1935 American opera	1952	142
Postillion! (Adolphe Adam)	1837	
Pot Luck (Braham/Duffield/Trix/Weston/Lee)	1921	284
Pot Luck — revue	1958	7 weeks
Poupée, La (Sturgess/Audran)	1897	576
Premise — revue	1962	172
Present Arms (Thompson/Eyton/Noel Gay)	1940	225
Present from the Corporation, A (Sadler/Wood/Gould)	1967	3
Pretty Girls of Stillberg	1842	
Pretty Peggy (Rose/Austin/Adams)	1920	168
Pride of the Regiment (Clinton-Baddeley/Mackenzie/W. Leigh)	1932	52
Prima Donna, La (Farnie/Murray/Mattei)	1889	60
Primrose (Carter/George Gershwin/Bolton/Grossmith)	1924	255
Prince of Borneo (Joseph Herbert/Edward Jones)	1899	31
Prince of Pilsen (Pixley/Luders)	1904	160
Princess Caprice (Craven/Beswick/Percy Greenbank/Fall)	1912	265
Princess Charming (Sirmay/Waller/Bennett/Wimperis/Wylie)	1926	362
Princess Ida (Gilbert & Sullivan)	1884	246
Princess of Kensington, A (German/Hood)	1903	115
Princess of Trebizonde (Kenney/Offenbach)	1870	
Princess Toto (W.S. Gilbert/Clay)	1876	48
Prisoners at the Bar (Oxenford/Meadows)	1880	
Private Lives (Coward)	1930	101
Privates on Parade (Nichols/King)	1977	208
Promises, Promises (Neil Simon/Bacharach/David)	1969	560
Pull Both Ends (King/Schroeder)	1972	36
Pump Boys & Dinettes (Foley/Hardwick/Morgan/Monk et al)	1984	50 weeks
Punch Bowl (Berlin/Gershwin/Mayerl/de Sylva etc)	1924	565
Punch Revue (Vida Hope)	1955	

Puppets (Titheradge/Novello)	1924	254
Purple Emperor (T., C. & H. Austin)	1909	
Push and Go — Mark/de Courville/Herman Darewski revue	1915	359
Puss in Petticoats (Offenbach)	1867	
Puss-Puss (Duffield/Smith/Weston/Lee)	1921	156
Quaker (Dibdin)	1775	
Quaker Girl (Monckton/Ross/Percy Greenbank/Tanner)	1910	536
Queen High (Schwab/de Sylva/Gensler/Green)	1926	198
Queen of Brilliants (Thomas/Jakobowski)	1894	41
Queenie (Ted Willis/Manning/Laird)	1967	20
Quick March (Leslie/Allison)	1870	2 months
Quiz Kid (Jimmy & Nin Thompson	1959	31
Ragged Child (Nield/Taylor/Whatley)	1988	
Ragtime (Ahrens/McNally/Flaherty)	2003	
Rainbow (E Wallace/de Courville/Scott/Grey/Gershwin)	1923	113
Rainbow Square (Robert Stolz/Bolton/Harold Purcell)	1951	146
Rat Pack, Live from Las Vegas (Sebastian)	2004	
Ratepayers Iolanthe (G. & S./Beeton/Sherrin)	1984	2 months
Rats (Braham/Mahoney) Ronald Jeans revue	1923	258
Razzle-Dazzle (Herman Darewski/Klein) de Courville/Pink	1916	408
Re:Joyce (Addinsell/Joyce Grenfell)	1988	6 months
Rebel (Francechild)	1986	3 weeks
Rebel Maid (Dalton/Montague Phillips)	1921	114
Red Hussar (Stephens/Solomon)	1889	175
Red Mill (Victor Herbert)	1920	64
Red, Bright and Blue — Charlot's non-stop revue	1937	38 days
Rendezvous — revue	1952	28
Rent (Larson)	1998	6 months
Restoration (Bond/Bicat)	1981	62
Return to the Forbidden Planet (Bob Carlton)	1984	1516
Revudeville — regular revues at the Windmill Theatre	1933	4 weeks
Rhoda (Parke/Mora)	1886	13
Rhyme & Reason (Ronald Vowles/David Griffiths)	1950	
Ride! Ride! (Thornhill/Thwaites)	1976	
Riki Tiki (Stiles/Kunneke)	1926	18
Ring Out the Bells (Ross Parker) Crazy Gang revue	1952	987
Ring Round the Moon (Addinsell/Christopher Fry)	1950	682
Ring Up (Blore/Melford/Allen/Ivy St Helier etc)	1921	136
Rink (Ebb/Kander)	1988	38
Rio Rita (McCarthy/Tierney)	1930	59
Rip-Off — revue	1976	1940
Rip Van Winkle (Farnie/Planquette)	1882	328
Rise Above It (L. Jones/Melville/Sherwin/V. Guest/Connor)	1941	380
Rise and Shine (Astaire/Stolz/Youmans/De Sylva/ Mercer)	1936	44
Rivals! (Monsell/Hughes)	1935	86
Riverdance (Flatley)	2002	
Riverside Nights (Austin/Reynolds/Arne)	1926	238
Rob Roy MacGregor (Pocock/Davy)	1818	
Robert & Elizabeth (Millar/Ron Grainer)	1964	957
Robert the Devil (W.S. Gilbert)	1868	
Robey en Casserole (H.B. Hedley/Waller)	1921	108
Robin, Prince of Sherwood (Fenn/Howarth)	1993	
Rock Carmen (Hughes/Hendler)	1972	
Rockets (Henry/Tunbridge) — Herman Darewski revue	1922	490
Rocking the Town — revue	1956	397
Rocky Horror Show (Richard O'Brien)	1973	2960
Romance (John Spurling/Charles Ross)	1971	6
Romance in Candlelight (Coslow/Maschwitz)	1955	53
Romany Love (H. Myers/V. Herbert/W. & G. Forrest)	1947	
Romp (Bickerstaff)	1778	
Rose and the Ring (Slaughter)	1890	4 weeks
Rose and the Ring (Thackeray/Carter/Cox)	1923	42
Rose and the Ring (Thackeray/Marilier/Belloc/Cox/C. Bax)	1928	52
Rose and the Ring (John Dalby)	1964	Christmas
Rose Marie (Harbach/Hammerstein/Friml/Stothart)	1925	851
Rose of Persia (Sullivan/Hood)	1899	213
Rosiere, La (Monkhouse/Jakobowski)	1893	41
Rosina (Brooke/Shield)	1782	
Rosy Rapture (Crook/Herman Darewski/Kern/Mark)	1915	79
Rothomago (Farnie/Solomon/Bucalossi/Serpette/Jacobi)	1879	98
Round About Regent Street — Crazy Gang revue	1935	+400
Round in 50 (Finck/Tate/Monckton)	1922	471
Round Leicester Square (Myers/Cass/McPherson) revue	1963	
Round the Map (McLellan//Finck/Burnaby/Grey/Carrick/Rice)	1917	219
Roundabout (Eyton/Attiwill/Horan)	1949	27
Royal Exchange — (All the Kings Horses) (Herendeen/Horan)	1935	10
Royal Roundhead (Seton/Harris)	1897	30
RSVP (De Bear/O'Neill/Newman/R. Leigh/Addinsell)	1926	297
Ruddigore (Gilbert & Sullivan)	1887	288
Ruddy George, or Robin Redbreast (Taylor/Percy Reeve)	1887	
Runaway Girl, A (Hopwood/H. Greenbank/Caryll/Monckton)	1898	593
Runaway Love (Barry Lupino/Eyton/Billy Mayerl)	1939	195
Running Riot (Furber/Shephard/Bolton/Ellis)	1938	207
Ruy Blas & the Blasé Roué (Leslie/Clark/Lutz)	1889	282
Sail Away (Noel Coward)	1962	252
Saint, She Ain't, A (King/Vosburgh)	1999	5 months
Salad Days (Julian Slade/Dorothy Reynolds) rev 1964	1954	2329
Sally (Kern/Grey/Bolton)	1921	387
Samarkand (Piffard/Ferrari)	1972	season
Sammy Cahn's Songbook (Cahn) Bernard Delfont revue	1974	
Samples (Tate/Herman Darewski/Berlin/Gideon/Schwartz)	1915	242

San Toy (Morton/Sidney Jones/Harry Greenbank/Ross)	1899	768
Saturday Night (Sondheim)	1997	season
Saturday Night Fever (Bee Gees)	1998	long run
Sauce Piquante (Landeau/Douglas Byng)	1950	
Sauce Tartare (Landeau/Fase/Parsons)	1949	433
Saucy Jack & the Space Vixens (Mann)	1998	2 months
Savoy Follies (de Bear/Arkell/Charles)	1932	61
Scapa (Hugh Hastings)	1962	44
Scarlet Feather (Harry Greenbank/Lecocq)	1897	short run
School (Robertson/Phillips)	1957	22
School Girl (Hamilton/Potter/Stuart)	1903	333
Scoop (Joan Davis/Heneker)	1942	70
Scrooge (Bricusse)	1996	3 months
Second Little Revue Starts at Nine (Simson/Arkell/Furber/Baynes/Ellis)	1924	174
Secret Diary of Adrian Mole, Aged 13¾ (Townsend/Howard/Blaikley)	1984	61 weeks
Secret Garden (Morgan/Markwick)	1987	5 months
Secret Garden (Norman/Simon)	2001	4 months
See You Again (Sandy Wilson)	1952	
See You Inside (various) Barry Cryer revue	1963	
See You Later (Sandy Wilson)	1951	
Seeing Stars (Bolton/Thompson/John/Broones)	1935	236
See-Saw (Braham/Novello/Redstone et al)	1916	158
See-See (Sidney Jones/Tours/Ross)	1906	152
Sensational Novel (W.S. Gilbert/Reed)	1871	6 months
Sentry (Caryll)	1890	6 weeks
Sergeant Brue (Wood/Hall/Liza Lehmann)	1904	280
Seven Brides for Seven Brothers (Johnny Mercer/de Paul)	1985	extended
Shake Your Feet (Acres/Astaire/Gershwin/Gibbons/Strachey)	1927	201
Shall We Reverse? — revue	1935	42
Shamus O'Brien (Jessop/Graves/Stanford)	1896	82
Shanghai (Duncan/Wylie/Witmark)	1918	131
Share My Lettuce (Statham/Gowers/Bamber Gascoigne)	1957	301
She Loves Me (Harnick/Bock) revived 1994	1964	189
She Shall Have Music (Eyton/Frankau/Fry/Monte Crick)	1934	72
She Smiled at Me (Allon Bacon) formerly Caste	1956	4
Shell Out — de Courville/Pink/Herman Darewski revue	1915	315
Shephard Show (Parr Davies/D. Byng/Purcell/Blore)	1946	174
Shephard's Pie (Sherwin/Furber) 2nd edn 1941	1939	356
Sherlock Holmes (Bricusse)	1989	3 months
Shockheaded Peter (Hoffman/Huge/Stout/Jacques)	2002	2 months
Shop Girl (Caryll/Monckton/Ross/Dam) rev. 1920	1894	546
Show Boat (Kern/Hammerstein)	1928	350
Show's the Thing (Pitt/Courtney)	1929	292
Showboat (Kern/Hammerstein) revival from Broadway	1971	909
Showman (Shield/Hase)	1976	47
Side by Side by Sondheim (Sondheim/Sherrin/Bernstein/Rodgers/Styne)	1976	781
Siege of Belgrade (Cobb)	1791	
Sigh No More (Coward)	1945	213
Silver Curlew (Eleanor Farjeon/Clifton Parker)	1949	season
Silver Patrol (Thayer/Bruce Sievier)	1940	75
Silver Slipper (Risque/Stuart)	1901	197
Silver Wings (Titheradge/Furber/Waller/Tunbridge/Mayerl)	1930	170
Simply Heavenly (Langston Hughes/David Martin) rev 2004	1958	16
Sing a Rude Song (Brahms/Sherrin)	1970	71
Singin' in the Rain (Brown/Freed)	1983	894
Sitting Pretty (Furber/Sherwin)	1939	15
Six for Gold (Brown/Reed)	1984	30
Six of One (Essex et al) revue	1963	
Six Pairs of Shoes (Lubbock/Spear/Mayerl/H. Roy/Ullman etc.)	1944	23
Skirts (Loesser) US Forces production	1944	
Sky High (de Courville/Simpson/Smith/Chappelle/Ross)	1925	309
Sky High (Melville) revue	1942	149
Sky High (Chappelle/Pether/Squire)	1948	108
Slave (Morton/Bishop)	1816	
Sleak (C.P. Lee)	1977	27
Slice of Saturday Night, A (Heather brothers)	1989	21 months
Slings & Arrows (Sandy Wilson et al)	1948	141
Slow Drag (Kreitzer)	1997	
Smike (Oliver) also known as Nicholas Nickleby	1980	
Smile (Haslam/Randall/Scott/E. Wallace/ Chappelle/H. Darewski)	1917	206
Smilin' Through (John Hanson/Constance Cox)	1972	28
Smith Family (Grey/Logan/Page/Ayer)	1922	131
Smokey Joe's Café (Lieber/Stoller)	1996	2 months
Snap (Titheradge/Jeans/Duffield/Ayer/Hupfeld)	1922	230
Snoopy — The Musical (Schulz/Grossman/Hackady)	1983	14 months
Snowman (Slaughter)	1899	68
So Much to Remember (Whyte/F. Fielding/Myers) revue	1963	short run
So This is Love (Stanley Lupino/Rigby/Brody/Hedley)	1928	321
Society Ltd. (Branscombe/Carrington)	1920	20
Soldier Boy (Young/Edgar Wallace/Romberg/Chappelle)	1918	372
Some (Grattan/Harris/Valentine/Tate)	1916	273
Some Like It Hot (Styne/Merrill)	1992	12 weeks
Someone Like You (Clark/Shipman)	1990	4 weeks
Something for the Boys (Cole Porter)	1944	
Something in the Air (Jack Hulbert/Sherwin/Purcell/Kester)	1943	499
Something Nasty in the Woodshed (Manley/Transem)	1965	20

Somewhere in England (Furber/J. Hulbert/Will Hay/Ayer)	1939	
Song & Dance (Don Black/Lloyd Webber)	1982	781
Song of Norway (Lazarus/Wright/Forrest/Grieg)	1946	526
Song of Singapore (Frandsen/Garin/Hipkens/Lockhart)	2001	10 weeks
Song of the Drum (Thompson/Bolton/V. Ellis/Finck/Carter)	1931	131
Song of the Sea (Wimperis/Wylie/Kunneke)	1928	158
Songbook (Monty Norman/Julian More)	1979	208
Songs for Stray Cats (Franceschild)	1985	3 weeks
Sons o'Guns (Thompson/Donahue/Connolly/ Swanstrom/Davis/Coot)	1930	211
Sophie! The Last of the Red Hot Mommas (Kops)	1990	3 months
Sorcerer (Gilbert & Sullivan)	1877	175
Sound of Music (Rodgers/Hammerstein)	1961	2385
South Pacific (Rodgers/Hammerstein)	1951	792
South Pacific (Rodgers/Hammerstein) revival	1988	12 months
Southern Maid, A (Fraser-Simson/Furber/ Calthrop/Novello/Graham/Ross)	1920	306
Space Family Robinson (Julian & Stephen Butler)	2002	
Space Is So Startling (P. & A. Howard/Allen/Broadhurst)	1962	
Spectre Knight (Albery/Cellier)	1878	6 months
Spend, Spend, Spend (Greene/Brown)	1999	11 months
Splinters — revue	1919	37
Sporting Love (Stanley Lupino/Billy Mayerl)	1934	302
Spread a Little Happiness (Vivian Ellis)	1992	3 weeks
Spread It Abroad (Walker/Strachey/Marvell) Farjeon revue	1936	209
Spring Chicken (Grossmith/Caryll/Monckton/ P. Greenbank/Ross)	1905	401
Spring Maid (Henry & Robert Smith/Reinhardt)	1911	2 months
Stage Door Canteen — BBC wartime review	1943	
Stairway to Heaven (Metchear/Morgan)	1994	
Stand and Deliver (Mankowitz/Norman)	1972	14
Stand Up and Sing (Furber/Jack Buchanan/Charig/Ellis)	1931	325
Star is Torn (Archer/Fisher)	1982	4 weeks
Starlight Express (Stilgoe/Lloyd Webber)	1984	7406
Starlight Roof (Melachrino/Maschwitz/Brooks/Rome)	1947	649
Stars In Your Eyes — revue	1960	season
Starting Here, Starting Now (Shire/Maltby)	1984	4 weeks
Stiffkey Scandals of 1932 (Wright/Wood)	1969	12
Still Dancing (Wimperis/Ellis) Ronald Jeans revue	1925	113
Stomp (Cresswell/McNicholas) no dialogue	2002	extended
Stop Flirting (Daly/Lannin/G. & I. Gershwin/de Sylva) 2 edns	1923	418
Stop Press (Whitley/Berlin/Schwartz/Dietz)	1935	148
Stop the World, I Want to Get Off (Newley/Bricusse)	1961	478
Stop! In the Name of Love (Eyers/Findlay/Harmer)	1987	12 weeks
Stop-Go! (Blatt/Ayer/D. Byng)	1935	110
Streamline (Vivian Ellis/A.P. Herbert) Ronald Jeans revue	1934	178
Street Cries (Binns)	1997	5 weeks
Street Singer (Lonsdale/F.-Simson/St Helier/P. Greenbank)	1924	360
Streets of London (Boucicault/Carpenter/Barnett)	1980	122
Strike a Light (Adcock/Caleb/Taylor)	1966	30
Strike a New Note (Hubert Gregg et al) George Black revue	1943	661
Strike It Again (Hubert Gregg et al) revue	1945	438
Strike Up the Music (Douglas Byng et al)	1941	48
Student Prince (alias Old Heidelberg)(Romberg/Donnelly)	1926	96
Suburban Strains (Ayckbourn/Todd)	1981	31
Such Is Life — Jack Hylton/George & Alfred Black revue	1955	548
Sugar Babies (Fields/McHugh/Allen/Rigby) compilation	1988	4 months
Sugar & Spice (Hackforth/L. Julian Jones/Treford/Mann)	1948	
Sultan of Mocha (Jarrett/Cellier)	1876	47
Summer Holiday (Gyngell/Haddigan) — Cliff Richard film	1997	3 months
Summer Madness (Macor)	1991	
Summer Song (Dvorak/Maschwitz/Grun/Kraft)	1956	90
Sumurun (Freska/Hollander)	1911	
Sun Never Sets (Cole Porter/Leslie-Smith)	1938	35
Sunday in the Park with George (Lapine/Sondheim)	1990	4 months
Sunny (Harbach/Kern/Hammerstein)	1926	363
Sunny River (Romberg/Hammerstein/Harbach)	1943	2 months
Sunset Boulevard (Black/Hampton/Lloyd Webber)	1993	1529
Sunshine Girl (Rubens/Raleigh/P. Greenbank/Wimperis)	1912	336
Sunshine of the World (Cuvillier)	1920	49
Suzette (Hurgon/Arthurs/Max Darewski)	1917	255
Swan Down Gloves (Nigel Hess/Billie Brown)	1981	22
Swan Esther & the King (Oliver/Munns)	1983	26
Swan with Topping (Donald Swann/Frank Topping)	1980	short run
Sweeney Todd (Sondheim)	1980	157
Sweeney Todd (Sondheim)	2002	extended
Sweet and Low (Melville/Gregg/Wright/Strachey/Posford)	1943	264
Sweet Broken Heart (Burrows)	1991	
Sweet Charity (Dorothy Fields/Cy Coleman)	1967	484
Sweet Lorraine (Peters)	1994	
Sweet William (Bill Solly)	1956	season
Sweet Yesterday (Leaver/Dyrenforth/Kester/Leslie-Smith)	1945	196
Sweeter and Lower (Zwar/Wright/Melville)	1944	870
Sweetest and Lowest (Zwar/Melville)	1946	791
Sweetheart Mine (Wylie/Lupino Lane/Gay/Eyton)	1946	323
Swing Along (Thompson/Furber/Broones/ Bolton/John)	1936	311
Swing Along — Robert Nesbitt revue	1963	
Swing Is In the Air — Crazy Gang revue	1937	
Swinging Down the Lane — revue	1959	343
Swinging the Gate (Morgan/McDermot/G. Wright/Zwar)	1940	126
Swing Along — Palladium revue	1963	

Sybil (Graham/Jacobi)	1921	346
Sylvia (Dyrenforth/Carroll Gibbons)	1927	51
Sylvia the Forest Flower (Mallandaine)	1866	
Sylvia's Lovers (Rolt/Gordon-Lennox)	1919	103
T. Zee (O'Brien/Hartley)	1976	38
Tabs (Jeans/Novello/Lillie/Thayer/Donaldson/Lefeuvre)	1918	268
Tails Up (Braham/Burnaby/Wright/Turner)	1918	467
Take It Easy (Timberg)	1937	27
Take It From Us (radio show Take It From Here)	1950	570
Tale of Istanbul (Erol Gunayadin)	1971	
Talk of the Town — revue	1954	656
Talk of the Town (Hicks/Haines/MacCunn/Baker)	1905	100
Taming of the Shrew (Addinsell)	1937	
Tantivy Towers (A.P. Herbert/Dunhill)	1931	170
Tap Dance on a Telephone Line (Franceschild)	1981	6 weeks
Tarantara-Tarantara (Gilbert & Sullivan/Taylor)	1975	
Teeth 'n' Smiles (Tony Hare/Tony & Nick Bicat)	1975	
Tell Her the Truth (Waller/Tunbridge/Weston/Lee)	1932	234
Tell Me More (Thompson/Wells/de Sylva/Gershwin bros)	1925	263
Tell Me on a Sunday (Black/Lloyd Webber)	2003	
Telling the Tale (Blow/Hoare/Braham)	1918	90
Tess of the D'Urbevilles (Fry/Hardy)	1985	3 weeks
Tess of the D'Urbevilles (Hardy/Edwards/Fleming)	1999	2 months
That's a Good Girl (Charig/J. Meyer/Furber/Carter/I. Gershwin)	1928	363
That's a Pretty Thing (Stanley Lupino/Noel Gay/Carter)	1933	103
Theodore & Co (Rubens//Novello/Kern/Harwood/Ross/Grey)	1916	503
These Foolish Kings — Crazy Gang revue	1956	882
These Foolish Things (Magidson/Wrubel/Mills) Crazy Gang	1938	
Thespis (Gilbert & Sullivan)	1871	63
They're Playing Our Song (Neil Simon/Hamlisch/Sager)	1980	
Thirty Thieves (Risque/Edward Jones)	1901	42
This and That (James Tate)	1916	48
This is the Army (Irving Berlin) US Services production	1943	
This Year of Grace (Coward/D Byng)	1928	316
This'll Make You Whistle (Goodhart/Sigler/Hoffman)	1936	190
Thomas and the King (Williams/Harbert)	1975	short run
Thoroughly Modern Millie (Tesori/Scanlan)	2003	
Three Caskets (Snell/Greenwell)	1961	season
Three Cheers (Grattan/Herman Darewski/Ross)	1916	190
Three Cheers Robert Nesbitt revue	1953	14 weeks
Three Graces (Lehar/Travers)	1924	121
Three Kisses (Talbot/Percy Greenbank)	1907	32
Three Little Maids (Rubens/Talbot/Rubens/P. Greenbank)	1902	348
Three Musketeers (McGuire/Friml/Grey/P.G. Wodehouse)	1930	240
Three Musketeers (Frow/Kenny Graham)	1963	
Three Musketeers (Bruce Lacey & the Alberts)	1966	
Three Sisters (Kern/Hammerstein)	1934	72
Three Waltzes (Morgan/McDermott/Oscar Straus)	1945	189
Threepenny Opera (Kurt Weill/Blitzstein) rev 1972	1956	140
Thurber Carnival (Don Elliott) James Thurber revue	1962	
Time (Daniels/Dave Clark)	1986	
Tin Pan Ali (Taylor/Nield)	1979	2 weeks
Tina (Graham/Rubens/Haydn Wood/Percy Greenbank)	1915	277
Tip-Toes (Bolton/Thompson/Gershwin brothers)	1926	182
Tita in Thibet aka Brum (Desprez)	1879	long runs
Toad of Toad Hall (Fraser-Simson/Milne)	1930	36
Together Again — Crazy Gang revue	1947	1566
Tom Brown's Schooldays (Joan & Jack Maitland/Andrews)	1972	76
Tom Jones (R. Courtneidge/Thompson/German/Taylor)	1907	110
Tom Sawyer (Tom Boyd)	1960	18
Tomfoolery (Lehrer/Robin Ray/Mackintosh)	1980	
Tommy (Townshend/The Who)	1979	118
Toni (Furber/Graham/Hirsch)	1924	248
Tonight at 8.30 — Noel Coward revue	1936	157
Tonight's the Night (Thompson/Rubens/Percy Greenbank)	1915	460
Tonight's the Night (Ben Elton/Rod Stewart)	2003	
Top of the World (Park/Leslie-Smith/Parr Davies)	1940	short run
Topsy & Eva (Herman Darewski/David/Burnaby/Styles)	1928	89
Topsy Turvy (David/Burnaby/Styles/Herman Darewski)	1917	88
Topsyturveydom (W.S. Gilbert/A. Cellier)	1874	3 weeks
Toreador (Caryll/Monckton/Rubens/Ross/P. Greenbank)	1901	675
Toto (Anderson/Morgan/Archibald Joyce)	1916	77
Touch & Go (Jean & Walter Kerr/Gorney)	1950	352
Tough at the Top (Vivian Ellis/A.P. Herbert)	1949	154
Town Talks (Vivian Ellis)	1936	77
Toymaker of Nuremberg (Ross/Strong/Glass)	1930	32
Tra-La-La-Tosca (Burnand/Pascal)	1890	45
Transatlantic Rhythm (Henderson/Irving Caesar/Carter)	1936	75
Travelling Music Show (Newley/Bricusse)	1978	short run
Treasure Island (Ornadel/Miles/Shaper/Wilson)	1973	season
Treasure Trove (Offenbach)	1869	
Trelawny (Julian Slade/Aubrey Woods/Powell)	1972	177
Trevallion (Phillips/Malcolm Morley)	1956	4
Trial by Jury (Gilbert & Sullivan)	1875	128
Tricks (Titheradge/Simson/Trix/Copeland)	1925	61
Trip to Chicago (John Sheridan)	1893	50
Trip to Chinatown (Hoyt)	1894	125
Troubadour (Lombardi/Holder)	1978	76
Tulip Time (Worton & Hubert David/Parker/Sievier/Wark)	1935	425
Tuppence Coloured — Laurier Lister revue	1947	274

FAMOUS LONDON SHOWS & MUSICALS
CHRONOLOGICAL AND THEATRES LIST

Please read the complementary notes on the Alphabetical List and also the Theatres Guide.

Special thanks go to Alexander Gleason who researched and provided a great deal of information and also to Philip Scowcroft and Terry Brown. Anyone who can supply missing data is encouraged to write to the author.

KEY – aka/also known as; rev/revival; extended/extended run; prodn/production; edn/edition; et al/also

TITLE	YEAR	THEATRE	RUN
Beggar's Opera	1728	Lincoln's Inn Fields	63
Dragon of Wantley	1737	Covent Garden	
Love in a Village	1762	Covent Garden	37
Lionel & Clarissa	1768	Covent Garden	11
Padlock	1768	Drury Lane	54
Waterman	1774	Haymarket	
Quaker	1775	Drury Lane	
Romp	1778	Covent Garden	
Lord of the Manor	1780	Drury Lane	
Rosina	1782	Covent Garden	
No Song, No Supper	1790	Covent Garden	
Siege of Belgrade	1791	Drury Lane	
Paul & Virginia	1800	Covent Garden	
Who Wants a Guinea?	1805	Covent Garden	
Forty Thieves	1806	Drury Lane	
Cosi Fan Tutte	1811	King's	
Guy Mannering	1816	Covent Garden	
Slave	1816	Covent Garden	
Rob Roy MacGregor	1818	Covent Garden	
Clari aka Maid of Milan	1823	Covent Garden	6 months
Illustrious Stranger	1827	Drury Lane	1 year
Cinderella	1830	Covent Garden	
Village Coquettes	1836	St. James'	
Postillion!	1837	St. James'	
Pretty Girls of Stillberg	1842	Haymarket	
Bohemian Girl	1843	Drury Lane	long run
Maritana	1843	Drury Lane	
Donna Diana	1864	Princess'	
Castle Grim	1865	Royalty	27
Constance	1865	Covent Garden	18
Felix	1865	Royalty	1 month
L'Africaine	1865	Royal Strand	88
Orpheus in the Underworld	1865	Her Majesty's	76
Windsor Castle	1865	Royal Strand	43
Belle Hélène, La	1866	Adelphi	
Black-Eyed Susan	1866	Royalty	+400
Love's Limit	1866	Royalty	6 weeks
Sylvia the Forest Flower	1866	Royalty	1 month
Contrabandista	1867	St. George's Opera House	72
Cox & Box	1867	Adelphi	300
Grand Duchess of Gerolstein	1867	Covent Garden	
Puss in Petticoats	1867	St. George's Opera House	
Ages Ago	1868	Gallery of Illustration	
Ching Chow Hi	1868	St. George's Opera House	
Robert the Devil	1868	Gaiety	
No Cards	1869	Gallery of Illustration	
Treasure Trove	1869	St. George's Hall	
Aladdin II	1870	Gaiety	100
Chilperic	1870	Lyceum	80
Gentleman in Black	1870	Charing Cross	26
Our Island Home	1870	Gallery of Illustration	4 weeks
Petit Faust	1870	Lyceum	
Princess of Trebizonde	1870	Gaiety	
Quick March	1870	New Queen's	2 months
Belle Helene, La	1871	Gaiety	109
Cinderella the Younger	1871	Gaiety	24
Creatures of Impulse	1871	Court	91
Genevieve de Brabant	1871	Islington Philharmonic	+100
Marie	1871	Opera Comique	5
Paquita	1871	New Royalty	13
Sensational Novel	1871	Gallery of Illustration	6 months
Thespis	1871	Gaiety	63
Babil & Bijou	1872	Covent Garden	160
Black Crook	1872	Alhambra	204
Charity Begins At Home	1872	Gallery of Illustration	10 seasons
Ganymede & Galatea	1872	Gaiety	
Happy Arcadia	1872	Gallery of Illustration	6 months
My Aunt's Secret	1872	Gallery of Illustration	3 months
Very Catching	1872	Gallery of Illustration	9 months
Vie Parisienne, La	1872	Holborn	
Crimson Scarf	1873	Haymarket	
Fille de Madame Angot	1873	St. James'	season
Mildred's Well	1873	Gallery of Illustration	3 months
Nemesis	1873	Strand	262
Oriana	1873	Globe	18
Demon's Bride	1874	Alhambra	48
Green Old Age	1874	Vaudeville	5 weeks
He's Coming	1874	St. George's Hall	2 months
Les Pres Saint-Gervais	1874	Criterion	132
Topsyturveydom	1874	Criterion	3 weeks
Vert-Vert	1874	St. James'	
Whittington	1874	Alhambra	112
Ancient Britons	1875	St. George's Hall	3 months
Cattarina	1875	Charing Cross	75
Eyes & No Eyes	1875	St. George's Hall	2 months
Lord Bateman	1875	Alhambra	6 weeks
Perichole, La	1875	St. James'	
Trial by Jury	1875	Royalty	+300
Zoo	1875	St. James'	4 weeks
Antarctica	1876	Strand	season
Don Quixote	1876	Alhambra	41
Lying Dutchman	1876	Strand	48
Pom	1876	Royalty	30
Princess Toto	1876	Strand	48
Sultan of Mocha	1876	St. James'	47
Voyage Dans La Lune, Le	1876	Alhambra	
Bohemian Gyurl	1877	Gaiety	117
Happy Hampstead	1877	Royalty	4 weeks
Little Doctor Faustus	1877	Gaiety	151
Marjolaine, La	1877	Royalty	2 years
Sorcerer	1877	Opera Comique	175
Wildfire	1877	Alhambra	season
After All	1878	Opera Comique	3 months
Cloches de Corneville, Les	1878	Folly	705
Cups & Saucers	1878	Opera Comique	6 months
Fatinitza	1878	Alhambra	
HMS Pinafore	1878	Opera Comique	571
Little Duke	1878	Philharmonic	
Spectre Knight	1878	Opera Comique	6 months
Madame Favart	1879	Strand	502
Rothomago	1879	Alhambra	98
Tita in Thibet aka Brum	1879	Royalty	long runs
Billee Taylor	1880	Imperial	83
In the Sulks	1880	Opera Comique	1 year
Lola	1880	Olympic	36
Mousquetaires, Les	1880	Globe	
Olivette	1880	Strand	466
Pirates of Penzance	1880	Opera Comique	363
Prisoners at the Bar	1880	Royalty	
Black Crook	1881	Alhambra	107
Bronze Horse	1881	Alhambra	187
Claude Duval	1881	Olympic	54
Girl He Left Behind Him	1881	Vaudeville	2 months
Grand Mogul	1881	Royalty	1
Jeanne, Jeannette, Jeanneton	1881	Alhambra	88
Mascotte, La	1881	Comedy	199
Mock Turtles	1881	Savoy	1 year
Patience	1881	Opera Comique/Savoy	578
Adamless Eden, An	1882	Opera Comique	2 months
Babil & Bijou	1882	Alhambra	167
Boccaccio	1882	Comedy	129
Fun On the Bristol	1882	Olympic	
Iolanthe	1882	Savoy	398
Manteaux Noirs, Les	1882	Avenue	190
Melita	1882	Royalty	6
Merry War	1882	Alhambra	
Mr. Guffin's Elopement	1882	Toole's	season

Title	Year	Theatre	Run
Rip Van Winkle	1882	Comedy	328
Vicar of Bray	1882	Globe	69
Wreck of the Pinafore	1882	Opera Comique	4
Barbe-Bleue	1883	Comedy	
Cymbia	1883	Royal Strand	48
Estrella	1883	Gaiety	36
Falka	1883	Comedy	157
Golden Ring	1883	Alhambra	105
Lurette	1883	Avenue	83
Merry Duchess	1883	Royalty	177
My Sweetheart	1883	Grand/Strand	163
On Condition	1883	Opera Comique	15 months
Vie, La	1883	Avenue	123
Virginia & Paul	1883	Gaiety	29
Beggar Student	1884	Alhambra	
Black-Eyed Susan	1884	Alhambra	48
Dick	1884	Globe/Gaiety	29
Grand Mogul	1884	Comedy	short run
Nell Gwynne	1884	Avenue	86
Pocahontas	1884	Empire	24
Polly	1884	Novelty/Empire	69
Princess Ida	1884	Savoy	246
Casting Vote	1885	Prince's	1 month
Dr. D.	1885	Royalty	25
Erminie	1885	Comedy	154
Excelsior	1885	Comedy	
Fay O'Fire	1885	Opera Comique	16
Great Taykin	1885	Toole's	87
Japs	1885	Novelty	3 months
Lady of the Locket	1885	Empire	120
Little Jack Sheppard	1885	Gaiety	155
Mikado	1885	Savoy	672
Pet of Newmarket	1885	Holborn	6
Vicar of Wide-Awake-Field	1885	Gaiety	121
Adonis	1886	Gaiety	110
Alice in Wonderland	1886	Prince of Wales	57
Dorothy	1886	Gaiety	931
Indiana	1886	Avenue	70
Lily of Leoville	1886	Comedy	41
Monte Christo Junior	1886	Gaiety	166
Oliver Grumble	1886	Novelty	30
Our Agency	1886	Avenue	7
Our Diva	1886	Opera Comique	48
Palace of Pearl	1886	Empire	48
Rhoda	1886	Comedy	13
Frankenstein	1887	Gaiety	110
Hans the Boatman	1887	Terry's	season
Jack in the Box	1887	Strand	88
Miss Esmeralda	1887	Gaiety	87
Mynheer Jan	1887	Comedy	35
Ruddigore	1887	Savoy	288
Ruddy George, or Robin Redbreast	1887	Toole's	
Carina	1888	Opera Comique	116
Faust-up-to-Date	1888	Gaiety	180
Nadgy	1888	Avenue	162
Pepita	1888	Toole's	102
Yeomen of the Guard	1888	Savoy	423
Doris	1889	Lyric	202
Faddimir	1889	Vaudeville	4
Gondoliers	1889	Savoy	554
Lancelot the Lovely	1889	Avenue	66
Love's Trickery	1889	Lyric	3 months
Mignonette	1889	Royalty	31
New Corsican Brothers	1889	Royalty	36
Paul Jones	1889	Prince of Wales	370
Prima Donna, La	1889	Avenue	60
Red Hussar	1889	Lyric	175
Ruy Blas & the Blasé Roué	1889	Gaiety	282
Black Rover	1890	Globe	40
Captain Therese	1890	Prince of Wales	104
Carmen-up-to-Data	1890	Gaiety	243
Cigale, La	1890	Lyric	423
Gretna Green	1890	Opera Comique	16
Marjorie	1890	Prince of Wales	193
My Brother's Sister	1890	Gaiety	
Rose and the Ring	1890	Prince of Wales	4 weeks
Sentry	1890	Lyric	6 weeks
Tra-La-La-Tosca	1890	Royalty	45
Captain Billy	1891	Savoy	
Cinder-Ellen Up Too Late	1891	Gaiety	314
Dancing Girl	1891	Haymarket	310
Enfant Prodigue, L'	1891	Prince of Wales	13
Ivanhoe	1891	Royal Opera House	155
Joan of Arc	1891	Opera Comique/Gaiety	287
Love and Law	1891	Lyric	9 months
Miss Decima	1891	Criterion/Prince of Wales	191
Nautch Girl	1891	Savoy	200
Pantomime Rehearsal	1891	Terry's/Shaftesbury/Toole's	438
Baroness	1892	Royalty	13
Blue Eyed Susan	1892	Prince of Wales	132
Cigarette	1892	Lyric	112
Donna Luiza	1892	Prince of Wales	4 months
Haddon Hall	1892	Savoy	204
Haste to the Wedding	1892	Criterion	22
In Town	1892	Prince of Wales	292
Maid Marian	1892	Prince of Wales	3 months
Mountebanks	1892	Lyric	229
Don Juan	1893	Gaiety	221
Gaiety Girl, A	1893	Prince of Wales/Daly's	413
Golden Web	1893	Lyric	29
Jane Annie	1893	Savoy	50
In Town	1893	Gaiety	
Little Christopher Columbus	1893	Lyric	421
Magic Opal aka Magic Ring	1893	Lyric/Prince of Wales	81
Mamzelle Nitouche	1893	Trafalgar Square	104
Miami	1893	Princess's	11
Modern Don Quixote	1893	Strand	21
Morocco Bound	1893	Shaftesbury/Trafalgar Square	295
Rosiere, La	1893	Shaftesbury	41
Trip to Chicago	1893	Vaudeville	50
Under the Clock	1893	Royal Court	78
Utopia Limited	1893	Savoy	245
All My Eye-Van-Hoe	1894	Trafalgar Square	9
Chieftain	1894	Savoy	97
Claude Duval	1894	Prince of Wales	142
Eastward-Ho!	1894	Opera Comique	6
Go-Bang	1894	Trafalgar	159
Hansel & Gretel	1894	His Majesty's	161
His Excellency	1894	Lyric	161
Jaunty Jane Shore	1894	Royal Strand	56
King Kodak	1894	Terry's	63
Lady Slavey	1894	Avenue	96
Mirette	1894	Savoy	101
Queen of Brilliants	1894	Royal Lyceum	41
Shop Girl	1894	Gaiety	546
Trip to Chinatown	1894	Toole's	125
Wapping Old Stairs	1894	Vaudeville	35
All Abroad	1895	Criterion	87
Artist's Model, An	1895	Daly's/Lyric	392
Bric-a-Brac Will	1895	Lyric	62
Dandy Dick Whittington	1895	Avenue	124
Gentleman Joe — The Hansom Cabby	1895	Prince of Wales	391
Papa's Wife	1895	Lyric	season
Belle of Cairo	1896	Court	71
Biarritz aka John Jenkins in Biarritz	1896	Prince of Wales	71
Circus Girl	1896	Gaiety	497
Gay Parisienne aka Girl from Paris	1896	Duke of York's	306
Geisha	1896	Daly's	760
Grand Duke	1896	Savoy	123
Little Genius	1896	Shaftesbury	128
Lord Tom Noddy	1896	Garrick	62
Monte Carlo	1896	Avenue	76
My Girl	1896	Gaiety/Garrick	183
New Barmaid	1896	Avenue	259
Newmarket	1896	Opera Comique	58
On the March	1896	Prince of Wales	77
Playing the Game	1896	Strand	5
Shamus O'Brien	1896	Opera Comique	82
Weather Or No	1896	Savoy	209
White Silk Dress	1896	Prince of Wales	133
Dandy Dan the Lifeguardsman	1897	Lyric	166
French Maid	1897	Terry's/Vaudeville	480
Grand Duchess	1897	Savoy	99
His Majesty aka Court of Vignolia	1897	Savoy	61
Lost, Stolen or Strayed — A Day in Paris	1897	Duke of York's	76
Maid of Athens	1897	Opera Comique	27
Man About Town	1897	Avenue	18
Poupée, La	1897	Prince of Wales	576
Royal Roundhead	1897	St. George's Hall	30
Scarlet Feather	1897	Shaftesbury	short run
Wizard of the Nile	1897	Shaftesbury	short run
Yashmak	1897	Shaftesbury	121
Beauty Stone	1898	Savoy	50
Belle of New York	1898	Shaftesbury	697
Dandy Fifth	1898	Duke of York's	8 weeks
Greek Slave, A	1898	Daly's	349
Her Royal Highness	1898	Vaudeville	56
Land of Nod	1898	Royalty	6
Little Miss Nobody	1898	Lyric	198
Milord Sir Smith	1898	Comedy	82
Orlando Dando	1898	Grand, Fulham	
Runaway Girl, A	1898	Gaiety	593
El Capitan	1899	Lyric	154
Florodora	1899	Lyric	455
Great Caesar	1899	Comedy	56
Lucky Star aka L'Etoile	1899	Savoy	143
Merry-Go-Round	1899	Coronet	season
Mystical Miss aka			

Title	Year	Theatre	Run	Title	Year	Theatre	Run	Title	Year	Theatre	Run
The Charlatan	1899	Comedy	2 months	Lady Tatters	1907	Shaftesbury	80
Prince of Borneo	1899	Strand	31	Merry Widow	1907	Daly's	778
Rose of Persia	1899	Savoy	213	Miss Hook of Holland	1907	Prince of Wales	462
San Toy	1899	Daly's	768	My Darling	1907	Hicks	71
Snowman	1899	Lyceum	68	Nelly Neil	1907	Aldwych	107
American Beauty	1900	Shaftesbury	69	Three Kisses	1907	Apollo	32
Casino Girl	1900	Shaftesbury	196	Tom Jones	1907	Apollo	110
Follies at the Alhambra	1900	Alhambra		Antelope	1908	Waldorf	22
Gay Pretenders	1900	Globe	49	Belle of Brittany	1908	Queen's	147
Messenger Boy	1900	Gaiety	429	Butterflies	1908	Apollo	217
Bluebell in Fairyland	1901	Vaudeville	294	Follies at the Apollo	1908	Apollo	571
Chinese Honeymoon, A	1901	Strand	1,075	Girl From Over the Border	1908	King's Hammersmith	
Emerald Isle	1901	Savoy	205	Havana	1908	Gaiety	221
Follies at the Palace	1901	Palace		Honourable Phil	1908	Hicks	71
Girl From Up There	1901	Duke of York's	102	King of Cadonia	1908	Prince of Wales	330
Hidenseek	1901	Globe	50	My Mimosa Maid	1908	Prince of Wales	83
HMS Irresponsible	1901	Strand	165	Pinkie and the Fairies	1908	Her Majesty's	73
Ib & Little Christina	1901	Savoy	16	Waltz Dream, A	1908	Hicks	146
Kitty Grey	1901	Apollo	220	Arcadians	1909	Shaftesbury	809
Melnotte	1901	Coronet		Dashing Little Duke	1909	Hicks	101
Silver Slipper	1901	Lyric	197	Dear Little Denmark	1909	Prince of Wales	109
Thirty Thieves	1901	Terry's	42	Dollar Princess	1909	Daly's	428
Toreador	1901	Gaiety	675	Fallen Fairies	1909	Savoy	51
Willow Pattern	1901	Savoy	16	Merry Peasant	1909	Strand	69
You and I	1901	Vaudeville	188	Mountaineers	1909	Savoy	61
Country Girl, A	1902	Daly's	729	Our Miss Gibbs	1909	Gaiety	636
Girl from Kay's	1902	Apollo/Comedy	432	On Jhelum River	1909	Aldwych	6
Merrie England	1902	Savoy	120	Persian Princess, A	1909	Queen's	68
Mr Wix of Wickham	1902	Brough, Stratford East		Purple Emperor	1909	King's Hammersmith	
Naughty Nancy	1902	Savoy	77	Balkan Princess	1910	Prince of Wales	176
Three Little Maids	1902	Apollo/Prince of Wales	348	Captain Kidd	1910	Wyndham's	34
Water Babies	1902	Garrick	100	Chocolate Soldier	1910	Lyric	500
Alice Through the				Follies at the Apollo	1910	Apollo	521
Looking Glass	1903	New	60	Girl in the Train	1910	Vaudeville	340
Cherry Girl	1903	Vaudeville	215	Hullo London	1910	Empire	
Dolly Varden	1903	Avenue	39	Hullo People	1910	Empire	
Duchess of Dantzig	1903	Lyric	236	Islander	1910	Apollo	114
Earl and the Girl	1903	Adelphi/Lyric	371	Quaker Girl	1910	Adelphi	536
In Dahomey	1903	Shaftesbury	251	Two Merry Monarchs	1910	Savoy	43
Little Hans Andersen	1903	Adelphi	27	All Change Here	1911	Alhambra	
Madame Sherry	1903	Apollo	102	Bonita	1911	Queen's	42
Medal and the Maid	1903	Lyric	98	By George	1911	Empire	
My Lady Molly	1903	Terry's	342	Castles in the Air	1911	Scala	65
Orchid	1903	Gaiety	559	Count of Luxembourg	1911	Daly's	340
Princess of Kensington, A	1903	Savoy	115	Eternal Waltz	1911	Hippodrome	good run
School Girl	1903	Prince of Wales	333	Follies at the Apollo	1911	Apollo	
Amorelle	1904	Comedy	28	Love Mills	1911	Globe	24
Catch of the Season	1904	Vaudeville	621	Mousmé	1911	Shaftesbury	209
Cingalee	1904	Daly's	365	Night Birds	1911	Lyric	133
Follies at the Queen's Hall	1904	Queen's Hall		Orpheus in the Underground	1911	His Majesty's	70
Ladyland	1904	Avenue	15	Peggy	1911	Gaiety	270
Lady Madcap	1904	Prince of Wales	354	Spring Maid	1911	Whitney	2 months
Lovebirds	1904	Savoy	75	Sumurun	1911	Coliseum	
Peggy Machree	1904	Wyndham's	35	Where the Rainbow Ends	1911	Savoy	69
Prince of Pilsen	1904	Shaftesbury	160	Autumn Manouevres	1912	Adelphi	75
Sergeant Brue	1904	Strand/Prince of Wales	280	Dancing Mistress	1912	Adelphi	242
Veronique	1904	Apollo	495	Dancing Viennese	1912	Coliseum	6 weeks
Bluebell	1905	Aldwych	102	Everybody's Doing It	1912	Empire	354
Blue Moon	1905	Lyric	182	Follies at the Apollo	1912	Apollo	
Bugle Call	1905	Wyndham's	105	Girl in the Taxi	1912	Lyric	385
Little Michus	1905	Daly's	401	Gypsy Love	1912	Daly's	299
Miss Wingrove	1905	Strand	11	Herbstmanover, Ein	1912	Adelphi	75
Mr Popple of Ippleton	1905	Apollo/Shaftesbury	173	Hullo, Ragtime	1912	Hippodrome	451
Officers' Mess	1905	Terry's	8	Kill That Fly!	1912	Alhambra	201
Spring Chicken	1905	Gaiety	401	Pink Lady	1912	Globe	124
Talk of the Town	1905	Lyric	100	Princess Caprice	1912	Shaftesbury	265
White Chrysanthemum	1905	Criterion	179	Sunshine Girl	1912	Gaiety	336
Amasis	1906	New	200	Wedding Morning	1912	Little	15
Beauty of Bath	1906	Aldwych/Hicks	287	All the Winners	1913	Empire	144
Belle of Mayfair	1906	Vaudeville	416	Are You There?	1913	Prince of Wales	23
Castles in Spain	1906	Royalty	50	Cachez Ca!	1913	Middlesex Varieties	32
Dairymaids	1906	Apollo	239	C'est Chic	1913	Middlesex Music Hall	
Exile from Home, An	1906	Savoy	13	Come Over Here	1913	Opera House (Stoll)	271
Fenella	1906	Coliseum		Eightpence a Mile	1913	Alhambra	143
Girl Behind the Counter	1906	Wyndham's	141	Gay Lothario	1913	Empire	4 months
Little Cherub aka				Girl from Utah	1913	Adelphi	195
Girl on the Stage	1906	Prince of Wales	114	Girl on the Film	1913	Gaiety	232
Merveilleuses, Les aka				Girl Who Didn't	1913	Lyric	68
Lady Dandies	1906	Daly's	196	Hullo, Tango	1913	Hippodrome	485
Naughty Nero	1906	Oxford		J'Adore .. Ca!	1913	Middlesex Varieties	
New Aladdin	1906	Gaiety	203	Keep Smiling	1913	Alhambra	223
Petronella	1906	Great Queen Street	8	Laughing Husband	1913	New	78
See-See	1906	Prince of Wales	152	Love & Laughter	1913	Lyric	65
Two Naughty Boys	1906	Gaiety	18	Marriage Market	1913	Daly's	423
Venus	1906	Empire		Oh! Oh! Delphine	1913	Shaftesbury	174
Vicar of Wakefield	1906	Prince of Wales	37	Pearl Girl	1913	Shaftesbury	254
Yellow Fog Island	1906	Terry's	20	What Ho! Daphne	1913	Tivoli	
Follies at the Royalty	1907	Royalty	30	Adele	1914	Gaiety	20
Follies at Terry's	1907	Terry's	108	After the Girl	1914	Gaiety	105
Gay Gordons	1907	Aldwych	229	Belle of Bond Street	1914	Adelphi	40
Girls of Gottenberg	1907	Gaiety	303	Business As Usual	1914	Hippodrome	295
Gypsy Girl	1907	Waldorf	30	By Jingo – If We Do	1914	Empire	110

128

Title	Year	Theatre	Performances
Cinema Star	1914	Shaftesbury	109
Cockyolly Bird	1914	Court/Little	40
Dora's Doze	1914	Palladium	3 weeks
Honeymoon Express	1914	Oxford	
Jigsaw	1914	Hippodrome	
Joyride Lady	1914	New	105
Mamselle Tra-La-La	1914	Lyric	105
Mixed Grill, A	1914	Empire	
Not Likely!	1914	Alhambra	305
Odds & Ends	1914	Ambassadors	259
On Duty	1914	Playhouse	13
Passing Show	1914	Palace	351
5064 Gerrard	1915	Alhambra	194
All Scotch	1915	Apollo	74
Betty	1915	Daly's	391
Bric-a-Brac	1915	Palace	385
Honi Soit!	1915	Pavilion	256
Joy-land	1915	Hippodrome	409
Looking Around	1915	Garrick	43
Now's the Time	1915	Alhambra	147
Oh Be Careful	1915	Garrick	33
Only Girl	1915	Apollo	107
Passing Show of 1915	1915	Palace	143
Push and Go	1915	Hippodrome	359
Rosy Rapture	1915	Duke of York's	79
Samples	1915	Playhouse/Vaudeville	242
Shell Out	1915	Comedy	315
Tina	1915	Adelphi	277
Tonight's the Night	1915	Gaiety	460
Watch Your Step	1915	Empire	275
Whirl of the Town	1915	Palladium	
Back to Blighty	1916	Oxford	
Bing Boys Are Here	1916	Alhambra	424
Chu Chin Chow	1916	His Majesty's	2238
Flying Colours	1916	Hippodrome	203
Follow the Crowd	1916	Empire	144
Half-Past Eight	1916	Comedy	143
Happy Day	1916	Daly's	241
Happy Family	1916	Prince of Wales	41
High Jinks	1916	Adelphi	383
Houp-la!	1916	St. Martin's	108
Light Blues	1916	Prince of Wales	20
Look Who's Here	1916	London Opera House	130
Miller's Daughters	1916	London Opera House	36
More Odds and Ends	1916	Ambassadors	376
Mr Manhattan	1916	Prince of Wales	221
My Lady Frayle	1916	Shaftesbury	130
Pell-Mell	1916	Ambassadors	298
Pick-a-Dilly	1916	Pavilion	284
Razzle-Dazzle	1916	Drury Lane	408
See-Saw	1916	Comedy	158
Some	1916	Vaudeville	273
Theodore & Co	1916	Gaiety	503
This and That	1916	Comedy	48
Three Cheers	1916	Shaftesbury	190
Toto	1916	Duke of York's	77
Vanity Fair	1916	Palace	265
We're All In It	1916	Empire	
Young England	1916	Daly's	278
Airs & Graces	1917	Palace	115
Any Old Thing	1917	Pavilion	
Arlette	1917	Shaftesbury	260
Beauty Spot	1917	Gaiety	152
Better 'Ole	1917	Oxford	811
Bing Girls Are There	1917	Alhambra	110
Boy	1917	Adelphi	801
Bubbly	1917	Comedy	429
Carminetta	1917	Prince of Wales	260
Cash on Delivery	1917	Palace	49
Cheep	1917	Vaudeville	488
Cheerio	1917	Pavilion	181
Hanky Panky	1917	Empire	
Here and There	1917	Empire	107
Lads of the Village	1917	Oxford	
Maid of the Mountains	1917	Daly's	1352
Pamela	1917	Palace	172
Round the Map	1917	Alhambra	219
Smile	1917	Garrick	206
Suzette	1917	Globe	255
Topsy Turvy	1917	Empire	88
Yes, Uncle!	1917	Prince of Wales	626
Zig-Zag	1917	Hippodrome	648
As You Were	1918	Pavilion	434
Bing Boys on Broadway	1918	Alhambra	562
Box 'O Tricks	1918	Hippodrome	625
Buzz Buzz	1918	Vaudeville	612
Flora	1918	Prince of Wales	72
Girl in the Bath	1918	King's Hammersmith	short run
Going Up	1918	Gaiety	574
Here, There & Everywhere	1918	Comedy	
Hullo, America!	1918	Palace	358
Jolly Jack Tar	1918	Prince's	67

Title	Year	Theatre	Performances
Lilac Domino	1918	Empire	747
Officers' Mess	1918	St. Martin's	200
Shanghai	1918	Drury Lane	131
Soldier Boy	1918	Apollo	372
Tabs	1918	Vaudeville	268
Tails Up	1918	Comedy	467
Telling the Tale	1918	Ambassadors	90
U.S.	1918	Ambassadors	312
Valentine	1918	St. James'	87
Very Good, Eddie	1918	Palace	341
Violette	1918	Lyric	57
Afgar	1919	Pavilion	300
Baby Bunting	1919	Shaftesbury	213
Back Again	1919	Ambassadors	129
Bran Pie	1919	Prince of Wales	414
Cinderella	1919	Drury Lane	145
Eastward Ho!	1919	Alhambra	124
Eclipse	1919	Garrick	117
Fifinella	1919	Scala	47
Girl for the Boy	1919	Duke of York's	86
His Little Widows	1919	Wyndham's	172
Joy-Bells	1919	Hippodrome	723
Kiss Call	1919	Gaiety	176
Kissing Time	1919	Winter Garden	430
Laughing Eyes	1919	Shaftesbury	126
Maggie	1919	Oxford	108
Monsieur Beaucaire	1919	Prince's	221
Oh Don't Dolly!	1919	Criterion	36
Oh, Joy!	1919	Kingsway	167
Splinters	1919	Savoy	37
Sylvia's Lovers	1919	Ambassadors/Duke of York	103
Whirligig	1919	Palace	441
Who's Hooper?	1919	Adelphi	349
Beggar's Opera	1920	Lyric Hammersmith	1463
Cherry	1920	Apollo	76
Irene	1920	Empire	399
It's All Wrong	1920	Queen's	112
Jigsaw	1920	Hippodrome	311
Johnny Jones	1920	Alhambra	349
Jumble Sale	1920	Vaudeville	176
Just Fancy	1920	Vaudeville	332
Little Dutch Girl, A	1920	Lyric	207
Little Whopper	1920	Shaftesbury	53
London, Paris and New York	1920	Pavilion	366
Medorah	1920	Alhambra	short run
Naughty Princess	1920	Adelphi	263
New Whirligig	1920	Palace	
Night Out	1920	Winter Garden	311
Oh, Julie	1920	Shaftesbury/Prince's	143
Pretty Peggy	1920	Prince's	168
Red Mill	1920	Empire	64
Society Ltd.	1920	Scala	20
Southern Maid, A	1920	Daly's	306
Sunshine of the World	1920	Empire	49
Wild Geese	1920	Comedy	112
Young Visiters	1920	Court	105
A to Z	1921	Prince of Wales	428
Cairo	1921	His Majesty's	267
Co-optimists	1921	Royalty	500
Fantasia	1921	Queen's	
Faust on Toast	1921	Gaiety	34
Fun of the Fayre	1921	Pavilion	239
Golden Moth	1921	Adelphi	281
Gypsy Princess	1921	Prince of Wales	212
League of Notions	1921	New Oxford	360
Little Girl in Red	1921	Gaiety	33
Mary	1921	Queen's	93
Mutt & Jeff	1921	King's Hammersmith	
My Nieces	1921	Queen's/Aldwych	172
Now and Then	1921	Vaudeville	76
Peep Show	1921	Hippodrome	421
Pins & Needles	1921	Royalty	242
Pot Luck	1921	Vaudeville	284
Puss-Puss	1921	Vaudeville	156
Rebel Maid	1921	Empire	114
Ring Up	1921	Royalty	136
Robey en Casserole	1921	Alhambra	108
Sally	1921	Winter Garden	387
Sybil	1921	Daly's	346
Windmill Man	1921	Victoria Palace	
Angel Face	1922	Strand	13
Battling Butler	1922	New Oxford	238
Cabaret Girl	1922	Winter Garden	361
Co-optimists	1922	Prince of Wales	232
Curate's Egg	1922	Ambassadors	83
Decameron Nights	1922	Drury Lane	370
Dé-dé	1922	Garrick	50
His Girl	1922	Gaiety	81
Immortal Hour	1922	Regent	216
Island King	1922	Adelphi	160
Jenny	1922	Empire	66
Lady of the Rose	1922	Daly's	507

Title	Year	Theatre	Runs
Last Waltz	1922	Gaiety	288
Lilac Time	1922	Lyric	626
Listening In	1922	Apollo	26
Love's Awakening	1922	Empire	81
Mayfair and Montmartre	1922	New Oxford	77
Nine O'Clock Revue	1922	Little	385
Phi-Phi	1922	Pavilion	133
Polly	1922	Kingsway	324
Rockets	1922	Palladium	490
Round in 50	1922	Hippodrome	471
Smith Family	1922	Empire	131
Snap	1922	Vaudeville	230
Whirled Into Happiness	1922	Lyric	246
Almond Eye	1923	New Scala	24
Beauty Prize	1923	Winter Garden	214
Brighter London	1923	Hippodrome	593
Catherine	1923	Gaiety	217
Co-optimists	1923	Prince of Wales	210
Cousin From Nowhere	1923	Queen's	105
Dover Street to Dixie	1923	Pavilion	108
For Goodness Sake	1923	Shaftesbury	224
Good Luck	1923	Drury Lane	262
Hassan	1923	His Majesty's	281
Head Over Heels	1923	Adelphi	113
Katinka	1923	Shaftesbury	108
Little Nellie Kelly	1923	New Oxford	265
Little Revue Starts at Nine	1923	Little	196
London Calling!	1923	Duke of York's	316
Madame Pompadour)	1923	Daly's	467
Music Box	1923	Palace	119
Omar Khayyam	1923	Court	86
Our Liz	1923	Alhambra	8
Rainbow	1923	Empire	113
Rats	1923	Vaudeville	258
Rose and the Ring	1923	Wyndham's	42
Stop Flirting	1923	Shaftesbury/Strand	418
Yes!	1923	Vaudeville	118
You'd Be Surprised	1923	Royal Opera House	270
Alf's Button	1924	Prince's	111
Charlot's Revue	1924	Prince of Wales	518
Come In	1924	Queen's	28
Co-optimists	1924	Palace	207
Duenna	1924	Lyric Hammersmith	141
Elsie Janis at Home	1924	Queen's	74
First Kiss	1924	New Oxford	43
Leap Year	1924	Hippodrome	471
Looking Glass	1924	Vaudeville	56
Midsummer Madness	1924	Lyric Hammersmith	128
Odd Spot	1924	Vaudeville	106
Our Nell	1924	Gaiety	140
Patricia	1924	His Majesty's/Strand	160
Polynesia	1924	Coliseum	24
Poppy	1924	Gaiety	188
Primrose	1924	Winter Garden	255
Punch Bowl	1924	Duke of York's	565
Puppets	1924	Vaudeville	254
Second Little Revue Starts at Nine	1924	Little	174
Street Singer	1924	Lyric	360
Three Graces	1924	Empire	121
Toni	1924	Shaftesbury	248
Whirl of the World	1924	Palladium	627
Yoicks!	1924	Kingsway	271
Bamboula	1925	His Majesty's	77
Better Days	1925	Hippodrome	135
Betty in Mayfair	1925	Adelphi	182
Blue Kitten	1925	Blue Kitten	140
Boodle	1925	Empire	94
By the Way	1925	Apollo	341
Cleopatra	1925	Daly's	110
Clo-Clo	1925	Shaftesbury	95
Co-optimists	1925	His Majesty's	203
Dear Little Billie	1925	Shaftesbury	86
Folies Bergère	1925	Palladium	121
Frasquita	1925	Prince's	36
Good Old Days	1925	Gaiety	37
Katja the Dancer	1925	Gaiety	505
Lionel & Clarissa	1925	Lyric	171
Little Miss Bluebeard	1925	Wyndham's	13
London Revue	1925	Lyceum	77
Love's Prisoner	1925	Adelphi	26
Mercenary Mary	1925	Hippodrome	446
Mr. Tower of London	1925	Alhambra/Winter Garden	2 years
Nicolette	1925	Duke of York's	12
No, No, Nanette	1925	Palace	665
On With the Dance	1925	Pavilion	229
Rose Marie	1925	Drury Lane	851
Sky High	1925	Palladium	309
Still Dancing	1925	Pavilion	113
Tell Me More	1925	Winter Garden	263
Tricks	1925	Apollo	61
Blackbirds of 1926	1926	Pavilion	279
Charlot Show of 1926	1926	Prince of Wales	87
Cochran's Revue of 1926	1926	Pavilion	148
Co-optimists	1926	His Majesty's	216
Happy Go Lucky	1926	Prince of Wales	37
Hearts & Diamonds	1926	Strand	46
Just a Kiss	1926	Shaftesbury	93
Kid Boots	1926	Winter Garden	172
Lady Be Good	1926	Empire	326
Lido Lady	1926	Gaiety	259
Life	1926	Palladium	167
Love Adrift	1926	Gaiety	21
Merely Molly	1926	Adelphi	85
Mozart	1926	Gaiety	28
My Son John	1926	Shaftesbury	255
Palladium Pleasures	1926	Palladium	312
Princess Charming	1926	Palace	362
Queen High	1926	Queen's	198
Riki Tiki	1926	Gaiety	18
Riverside Nights	1926	Lyric H'smith/Ambassadors	238
RSVP	1926	Vaudeville	297
Student Prince aka Old Heidelberg	1926	His Majesty's	96
Sunny	1926	Hippodrome	363
Tip-Toes	1926	Winter Garden	182
Turned Up	1926	New Oxford	89
Vaudeville Vanities	1926	Vaudeville	107
Wildflower	1926	Shaftesbury	114
Yvonne	1926	Daly's	280
Alice in Wonderland & Through the Looking Glass	1927	Savoy	25
Apache	1927	Palladium	164
Beloved Vagabond	1927	New	107
Bits & Pieces	1927	Prince's	167
Blue Mazurka	1927	Daly's	140
Blue Skies	1927	Vaudeville	192
Blue Train	1927	Prince of Wales	125
Bow-Wows	1927	Prince of Wales	124
Castles in the Air	1927	Shaftesbury	28
Clowns in Clover	1927	Adelphi	508
Desert Song	1927	Drury Lane	432
Girl Friend	1927	Palace	421
Girl from Cook's	1927	Gaiety	38
Hit the Deck	1927	Hippodrome	277
Lady Luck	1927	Carlton	324
Oh, Kay!	1927	His Majesty's	214
One Dam Thing After Another	1927	Pavilion	237
Peggy Ann	1927	Daly's	134
Shake Your Feet	1927	Hippodrome	201
Sylvia	1927	Vaudeville	51
Up With the Lark	1927	Adelphi	92
Vagabond King	1927	Winter Garden	480
White Birds	1927	His Majesty's	80
Adam's Opera	1928	Old Vic	20
Blue Eyes	1928	Piccadilly	276
Charlot's Revue	1928	Vaudeville	92
Cocoanuts	1928	Garrick	15
Funny Face	1928	Prince's	263
Good News	1928	Carlton	132
Lady Mary	1928	Daly's	181
Love in a Village	1928	Lyric	124
Lucky Girl	1928	Pavilion	150
Lumber Love	1928	Lyceum	108
Many Happy Returns	1928	Duke of York's	127
Marjolaine	1928	Gaiety	67
Rose and the Ring	1928	Apollo/Playhouse	52
Show Boat	1928	Drury Lane	350
Song of the Sea	1928	His Majesty's	158
So This is Love	1928	Winter Garden	321
That's a Good Girl	1928	Hippodrome	363
This Year of Grace	1928	Pavilion	316
Topsy & Eva	1928	Gaiety	89
Virginia	1928	Palace	223
Vogues & Vanities	1928	Holborn Empire	short run
Will o'the Whispers	1928	Shaftesbury	68
Yellow Mask	1928	Carlton	218
Bitter Sweet	1929	His Majesty's	697
Coo-ee	1929	Vaudeville	70
Co-optimists	1929	Vaudeville	133
Cupid & the Cutlets	1929	Q	
Dear Love	1929	Palace	132
Five O'Clock Girl	1929	Hippodrome	122
Follow Through	1929	Dominion	148
Hold Everything	1929	Palace	173
House That Jack Built	1929	Adelphi	270
Love Lies	1929	Gaiety	347
Mariette	1929	His Majesty's	28
Merry Merry	1929	Carlton/Lyceum	131
Mr. Cinders	1929	Adelphi	528
New Moon	1929	Drury Lane	148
Show's the Thing	1929	Victoria Palace/Lyceum	292
Vie Parisienne, La	1929	Lyric Hammersmith	224
Wake Up and Dream	1929	Pavilion	263

Title	Year	Theatre	Performances	Title	Year	Theatre	Performances
White Camellia	1929	Daly's	62	Music in the Air	1933	His Majesty's	275
Yankee at the Court of King Arthur, A	1929	Daly's	43	Nice Goings On	1933	Strand	221
2 Intimate Revue	1930	Duchess	17	Nymph Errant	1933	Adelphi	154
Alice in Wonderland	1930	Savoy	23	One Girl	1933	Hippodrome	45
Charlot's Masquerade	1930	Cambridge	84	On With the Show	1933	Prince's	57
Chelsea Follies	1930	Victoria Palace	213	Please!	1933	Savoy	108
Cochran's 1930 Revue	1930	Pavilion	245	Revudeville No. 32	1933	Windmill	4 weeks
Co-optimists	1930	Hippodrome	99	That's a Pretty Thing	1933	Daly's	103
Damask Rose	1930	Savoy	52	Blackbirds of 1934	1934	Coliseum	193
Daphne	1930	King's Hammersmith		By Appointment	1934	New	28
Darling I Love You	1930	Gaiety	147	Conversation Piece	1934	His Majesty's	177
De La Folie Pure	1930	Victoria Palace	94	Golden Toy	1934	Coliseum	185
Eldorado	1930	Daly's	93	Happy Weekend	1934	Duke of York's	54
Ever Green	1930	Adelphi	254	Here's How	1934	Saville	69
Follow a Star	1930	Winter Garden	118	Hi-Diddle-Diddle	1934	Comedy	198
Frederica	1930	Palace	110	Jill Darling	1934	Saville	242
Heads Up	1930	Palace	20	Lucky Break	1934	Shaftesbury	198
Here Comes the Bride	1930	Piccadilly	175	Moonlight is Silver	1934	Queen's	85
Little Tommy Tucker	1930	Daly's	86	Mr. Whittington	1934	Hippodrome/Adelphi	298
Love Race	1930	Gaiety	237	She Shall Have Music	1934	Saville	72
Nippy	1930	Prince Edward	137	Sporting Love	1934	Gaiety	302
Open Your Eyes	1930	Piccadilly	24	Streamline	1934	Palace	178
Private Lives	1930	Phoenix	101	Three Sisters	1934	Drury Lane	72
Rio Rita	1930	Prince Edward	59	Why Not Tonight?	1934	Palace	136
Seven Dwarfs	1930	Cambridge	short run	Yes, Madam?	1934	Hippodrome	302
Silver Wings	1930	Dominion	170	Yours Sincerely	1934	Daly's	16
Sons o'Guns	1930	Hippodrome	211	1066 and All That	1935	Strand	387
Three Musketeers	1930	Drury Lane	240	Anything Goes	1935	Palace	261
Toad of Toad Hall	1930	Lyric	36	Blackbirds of 1935	1935	Coliseum	123
Toymaker of Nuremberg	1930	Kingsway	32	Charlot's Char-a-bang	1935	Vaudeville	101
Walk This Way	1930	Winter Garden	149	Co-optimists	1935	Palace	13
Wonder Bar	1930	Savoy	210	Dancing City	1935	Coliseum	65
Blue Roses	1931	Gaiety	54	Flying Trapeze	1935	Alhambra	73
Cavalcade	1931	Drury Lane	405	Fritzi	1935	Adelphi/Shaftesbury	64
Cochran's 1931 Revue	1931	Pavilion	27	Gay Deceivers	1935	Coliseum	123
Folly To Be Wise	1931	Piccadilly	257	Gay Masquerade	1935	Prince's	3
Folly To Be Wiser (2nd edn)	1931	Piccadilly	87	Glamorous Night	1935	Drury Lane	243
For the Love of Mike	1931	Saville	239	Jack o' Diamonds	1935	Gaiety	126
Fountain of Youth	1931	Lyric Hammersmith	46	Kingdom for a Cow	1935	Savoy	18
Gay Princess	1931	Kingsway	12	Life Begins at Oxford Circus	1935	Palladium	
Good Companions	1931	His Majesty's	331	Love Laughs	1935	Hippodrome	96
Hold My Hand	1931	Gaiety	212	March Hares	1935	Palladium	
Kong	1931	Cambridge	20	On With the Show	1935	Gate	
Land of Smiles	1931	Drury Lane	71	Please Teacher	1935	Hippodrome	300
Millionaire Kid	1931	Gaiety	87	Rivals!	1935	Kingsway	86
My Sister and I	1931	Shaftesbury	8	Round About Regent Street	1935	Palladium	+400
Nina Rosa	1931	Lyric	111	Royal Exchange aka All the King's Horses	1935	His Majesty's	10
Song of the Drum	1931	Drury Lane	131	Seeing Stars	1935	Gaiety	236
Stand Up and Sing	1931	Hippodrome	325	Shall We Reverse?	1935	Comedy	42
Tantivy Towers	1931	New	170	Stop-Go!	1935	Vaudeville	110
Viktoria and Her Hussar	1931	Palace	100	Stop Press	1935	Adelphi	148
Waltzes from Vienna	1931	Alhambra	607	Tulip Time	1935	Alhambra	425
White Horse Inn	1931	Coliseum	651	Twenty to One	1935	Coliseum	383
After Dinner	1932	Gaiety	15	All Alight at Oxford Circus	1936	Palladium	
Alice in Wonderland	1932	Little	62	At the Silver Swan	1936	Palace	51
All For Joy	1932	Piccadilly	23	Balalaika	1936	Adelphi/His Majesty's	570
Ballyhoo	1932	Comedy	139	Blackbirds of 1936	1936	Gaiety	124
Bow Bells	1932	Hippodrome	232	Careless Rapture	1936	Drury Lane	295
Casanova	1932	Coliseum	429	Certainly, Sir	1936	Hippodrome	20
Cat and the Fiddle	1932	Palace	219	Encore Les Dames	1936	Prince of Wales	
Crazy Month	1932	Palladium		Follow the Sun	1936	Adelphi	204
Derby Day	1932	Lyric Hammersmith/Comedy	132	Going Places	1936	Savoy	44
Dubarry	1932	Her Majesty's	397	Happy Hypocrite	1936	His Majesty's	68
Fanfare	1932	Prince Edward	28	Melody That Got Lost	1936	Phoenix	28
Helen!	1932	Adelphi	194	O-Kay for Sound	1936	Palladium	
Here We Are Again	1932	Lyceum	22	O Mistress Mine	1936	St. James	11
Kiss in Spring, A	1932	Alhambra	83	Over She Goes	1936	Saville	248
Lovely Lady	1932	Phoenix	3	Rise and Shine	1936	Drury Lane	44
Out of the Bottle	1932	Hippodrome	106	Spread It Abroad	1936	Saville	209
Over the Page	1932	Alhambra	82	Swing Along	1936	Gaiety	311
Oxford Blazers	1932	Little	12	This'll Make You Whistle	1936	Palace/Daly's	190
Paris in London	1932	Comedy	21	Tonight at 8.30	1936	Phoenix	157
Paulette	1932	Savoy	32	Town Talks	1936	Vaudeville	77
Philomel	1932	Ambassadors	21	Transatlantic Rhythm	1936	Adelphi	75
Pride of the Regiment	1932	St. Martin's	52	Two Bouquets	1936	Ambassadors	301
Savoy Follies	1932	Savoy	61	Your Number's Up	1936	Gate	
Tell Her the Truth	1932	Saville	234	And On We Go	1937	Savoy	21
Wild Violets	1932	Drury Lane	291	Big Business	1937	Hippodrome	124
Words & Music	1932	Adelphi	164	Crazy Days	1937	Shaftesbury	78
After Dark	1933	Vaudeville	167	Crest of the Wave	1937	Drury Lane	203
Ball at the Savoy	1933	Drury Lane	148	Floodlight	1937	Saville	51
Beau Brummel	1933	Saville	23	Going Greek	1937	Gaiety	306
Clancarty	1933	Winter Garden	23	Grand Duchess	1937	Savoy	60
Command Performance	1933	Saville	31	Hide and Seek	1937	Hippodrome	204
Dark Doings	1933	Leicester Square	33	Home and Beauty	1937	Adelphi	128
Gay Divorce	1933	Palace	180	It's in the Bag	1937	Saville	81
Give Me a Ring	1933	Hippodrome	239	Laughing Cavalier	1937	Adelphi	38
He Wanted Adventure	1933	Saville	152	London Rhapsody	1937	Palladium	3 months
How D'You Do?	1933	Comedy	244	Many Happy Returns	1937	Adelphi	short run
Jolly Roger	1933	Savoy	199	Me and My Girl	1937	Victoria Palace	1646
Mother of Pearl	1933	Gaiety	181	Oh! You Letty	1937	Palace	71

Title	Year	Theatre	Runs
On Your Toes	1937	Palace	104
Paganini	1937	Lyceum	59
Red, Bright & Blue (Charlot's			
non-stop Revue)	1937	Vaudeville	38 days
Swing Is In the Air	1937	Palladium	
Take It Easy	1937	Palace	27
Bobby Get Your Gun	1938	Adelphi	92
Elephant in Arcady, An	1938	Kingsway	141
Fleet's Lit Up	1938	Hippodrome	199
Follies of 1938	1938	Saville	
Happy Returns	1938	Adelphi	78
Maritza	1938	Palace	68
No Sky So Blue	1938	Savoy	40
Nine Sharp	1938	Little	405
Operette	1938	His Majesty's	133
Paprika	1938	His Majesty's	11
Running Riot	1938	Gaiety	207
Sun Never Sets	1938	Drury Lane	35
These Foolish Things	1938	Palladium	
Under Your Hat	1938	Palace	512
Wild Oats	1938	Prince's	260
All Clear	1939	Queen's	162
Black and Blue	1939	Hippodrome	305
Black Velvet	1939	Hippodrome	620
Dancing Years	1939	Drury Lane/Adelphi	187/969
Eve On Parade	1939	Garrick	225
Gate Revue	1939	Gate/Ambassadors	449
Georgian Springtime	1939	Embassy	
Haw-Haw	1939	Holborn	361
Let's Face It	1939	Chanticleer	
Little Dog Laughed	1939	Palladium	461
Little Revue	1939	Little	415
Magyar Melody	1939	His Majesty's	105
Runaway Love	1939	Streatham Hill/Saville	195
Shephard's Pie	1939	Prince's	356
Sitting Pretty	1939	Prince's	15
Somewhere in England	1939	Lyric	
Who's Taking Liberty?	1939	Whitehall	54
Beyond Compere	1940	Duchess	
Come Out Of Your Shell	1940	Embassy/Criterion	93
Come Out to Play	1940	Wimbledon/Phoenix	77
Diversion	1940	Wyndham's	54
Funny Side Up	1940	His Majesty's	217
Garrison Theatre	1940	Palladium	225
Let's Mix It	1940	Playhouse	
Lights Up	1940	Savoy	114
Moonshine	1940	Vaudeville	
New Faces	1940	Comedy	257
Present Arms	1940	Prince of Wales	225
Silver Patrol	1940	New	75
Swinging the Gate	1940	Ambassadors	126
Top of the World	1940	Palladium	short run
Up and Doing - 2 edns.	1940	Saville	503
Black Vanities	1941	Victoria Palace	435
Diversion No. 2	1941	Wyndham's	106
Fun and Games	1941	Prince's	289
Gangway	1941	Ambassadors	535
Get a Load of This	1941	Hippodrome	698
Lady Behave	1941	His Majesty's	401
(More) New Faces	1941	Apollo	
New Ambassadors Revue	1941	Ambassadors	
Nineteen-Naughty-One	1941	Prince of Wales	170
Orchids and Onions	1941	Comedy	
Rise Above It	1941	Q/Comedy	380
Shephard's Pie - 2nd edn	1941	Prince's	356
Strike Up the Music	1941	Coliseum	48
Best Bib and Tucker	1942	Palladium	490
Big Top	1942	His Majesty's	139
Blossom Time	1942	Lyric	short run
Dubarry Was a Lady	1942	His Majesty's	178
Fine and Dandy	1942	Saville	346
Full Swing	1942	Palace	468
Happidrome	1942	Prince of Wales	224
Let's Face It	1942	Hippodrome	348
Light and Shade	1942	Ambassadors	54
New Ambassadors Revue	1942	Ambassadors	
Scoop	1942	Vaudeville	70
Sky High	1942	Phoenix	149
Twenty to One	1942	Victoria Palace	408
Waltz Without End	1942	Cambridge	181
Wild Rose	1942	Prince's	205
Alice in Wonderland & Through			
the Looking Glass	1943	Scala	86
Arc de Triomphe	1943	Phoenix	222
Flying Colours	1943	Lyric	103
Hi-De-Hi	1943	Palace	340
It's Foolish but It's Fun	1943	Palace	469
It's Time to Dance	1943	Winter Garden/Lyric	259
Knight Was Bold	1943	Piccadilly	10
La-Di-Da-Di-Da	1943	Victoria Palace	318
Lisbon Story	1943	Hippodrome	492
Love Racket	1943	Victoria Palace	324
Magic Carpet	1943	Prince's	182
New Ambassadors Revue	1943	Ambassadors	
Old Chelsea	1943	Prince's	95
Panama Hattie	1943	Piccadilly	308
Something in the Air	1943	Palace	499
Stage Door Canteen	1943	Piccadilly	
Strike a New Note	1943	Prince of Wales	661
Sunny River	1943	Piccadilly	2 months
Sweet and Low	1943	Ambassadors	264
This is the Army	1943	Palladium	
Glass Slipper	1944	St. James'	
Happy & Glorious	1944	Palladium	938
Jenny Jones	1944	Hippodrome	153
Meet Me Victoria	1944	Victoria Palace	251
Night in Venice, A	1944	Cambridge	
Six Pairs of Shoes	1944	Playhouse	23
Skirts	1944	Cambridge	
Something for the Boys	1944	Coliseum	
Strike It Again	1944	Prince of Wales	438
Sweeter and Lower	1944	Ambassadors	870
Big Boy	1945	Saville	174
Fine Feathers	1945	Prince of Wales	578
Follow the Girls	1945	His Majesty's	572
For Crying Out Loud	1945	Stoll	351
Gaieties	1945	Winter Garden	179
Gay Rosalinda	1945	Palace/Prince's	413
Henson's Gaieties	1945	Winter Garden/Saville	180
Land of the Christmas			
Stocking	1945	Duke of York's	season
Night & the Music	1945	Coliseum	686
Perchance to Dream	1945	Hippodrome	1022
Sigh No More	1945	Piccadilly	213
Sweet Yesterday	1945	Adelphi	196
Three Waltzes	1945	Prince's	189
Under the Counter	1945	Phoenix	665
Better Late	1946	Garrick	211
Between Ourselves	1946	Playhouse	
Big Ben	1946	Adelphi	
Can Can	1946	Adelphi	32
Evangeline	1946	Cambridge	172
Gang Show	1946	Stoll	170
Here Come the Boys	1946	Saville	330
High Time	1946	Palladium	570
Make It a Date	1946	Duchess	140
Night & the Laughter	1946	Coliseum	168
Pacific 1860	1946	Drury Lane	129
Pageant of the People	1946	Stoll	
Piccadilly Hayride	1946	Prince of Wales	778
Shephard Show	1946	Prince's	174
Song of Norway	1946	Palace	526
Sweetest and Lowest	1946	Ambassadors	791
Sweetheart Mine	1946	Victoria Palace	323
Wizard of Oz	1946	Winter Garden	
Annie Get Your Gun	1947	Coliseum	1304
Apple Sauce	1947	Palladium	462
Boltons Revue	1947	Boltons	
Bird Seller	1947	Palace	
Bless the Bride	1947	Adelphi	886
Finian's Rainbow	1947	Palace	53
Here, There & Everywhere	1947	Palladium	466
Nightingale	1947	Prince's	55
Oklahoma!	1947	Drury Lane	1543
One, Two, Three	1947	Duke of York's	198
Romany Love	1947	His Majesty's	
Starlight Roof	1947	Hippodrome	649
Together Again	1947	Victoria Palace	1566
Tuppence Coloured	1947	Lyric Hammersmith/Globe	274
A La Carte	1948	Savoy	243
Ad Lib	1948	Chepstow	4 weeks
Bob's Your Uncle	1948	Saville	363
Boltons Revue	1948	Boltons	
Burlesque	1948	Prince's	short run
Cage Me a Peacock	1948	Strand	337
Calypso	1948	Playhouse	
Carissima	1948	Palace	488
Encore	1948	Chepstow	
Four, Five, Six	1948	Duke of York's	315
Good Road	1948	His Majesty's	
Great Endeavour	1948	Drury Lane	
High Button Shoes	1948	Hippodrome	291
Kid from Stratford	1948	Prince's/Winter Garden	235
King's Jesters	1948	King's Hammersmith	5 weeks
Lute Song	1948	Winter Garden	24
Maid to Measure	1948	King's Hammers'th/Cambridge	
Oranges & Lemons	1948	Lyric Hammersmith/Globe	116
Sky High	1948	Palladium	108
Slings & Arrows	1948	Comedy	141
Sugar & Spice	1948	St Martin's	
What Goes On?	1948	Players'	
Belinda Fair	1949	Saville	131
Big Show of 1949	1949	Palladium	114
Brigadoon	1949	His Majesty's	685

Title	Year	Theatre	Runs
Folies Bergère	1949	Hippodrome	881
Her Excellency	1949	Hippodrome/Saville	252
King's Rhapsody	1949	Palace	881
Latin Quarter (1)	1949	Casino	455
Let's Make an Opera	1949	Lyric Hammersmith	50
Roundabout	1949	Saville	27
Sauce Tartare	1949	Cambridge	433
Silver Curlew	1949	Arts	season
Tough at the Top	1949	Adelphi	154
Ace of Clubs	1950	Cambridge	211
After the Show	1950	Watergate	14
Blue for a Boy	1950	His Majesty's	664
Carousel	1950	Drury Lane	566
Cowboy Casanova	1950	Stratford East	8
Dear Miss Phoebe	1950	Phoenix	283
Gang Show 1950	1950	King's Hammersmith	
Golden City	1950	Adelphi	140
Home and Beauty	1950	St. Martin's	180
Knights of Madness	1950	Victoria Palace	1361
Latin Quarter 1950 (2)	1950	Casino	456
Lili Marlene	1950	Stratford East	
Music at Midnight	1950	His Majesty's	
Rhyme & Reason	1950	Torch	
Ring Round the Moon	1950	Globe	682
Sauce Piquante	1950	Cambridge	
Take It From Us	1950	Adelphi	570
Touch & Go	1950	Prince of Wales	352
After the Show (2)	1951	St. Martin's	
And So to Bed	1951	New	323
Fancy Free	1951	Prince of Wales	370
Fol-de-Rols	1951	St. Martin's	98
Folies Bergère Revue 1951	1951	Hippodrome	579
Gay's the Word	1951	Saville	504
Kiss Me Kate	1951	Coliseum	501
Late Night Extra	1951	Watergate	
Latin Quarter of 1951 (3)	1951	Casino	468
Lyric Revue	1951	Lyric Hammersmith/Globe	454
My Lucky Day	1951	Gateway	
Penny Plain	1951	St. Martin's	443
Rainbow Square	1951	Stoll	146
See You Later	1951	Watergate	
South Pacific	1951	Drury Lane	792
Zip Goes a Million	1951	Palace	544
Bells of St Martin's	1952	St. Martin's	107
Bet Your Life	1952	Hippodrome	362
Call Me Madam	1952	Coliseum	486
Globe Revue	1952	Globe	
Latin Quarter 4 Excitement	1952	Casino	419
London Laughs	1952	Adelphi	1113
Love From Judy	1952	Saville	594
Paris to Piccadilly	1952	Prince of Wales	850
Porgy & Bess	1952	Stoll	142
Rendezvous	1952	Comedy	28
Ring Out the Bells	1952	Victoria Palace	987
See You Again	1952	Watergate	
Wonderful Time	1952	Palladium	344
Airs on a Shoestring	1953	Royal Court	772
At the Lyric	1953	Lyric Hammersmith	
Boy Friend	1953	Players'/Wyndham's	2084
Braziliana	1953	Stoll	32
Buccaneer	1953	Watergate	short run
Cloakroom Ticket No 3	1953	New Lindsey	
Fun & the Fair	1953	Palladium	9 weeks
Girl of the Year	1953	Gateway	
Glorious Days	1953	Palace	255
Guys & Dolls	1953	Coliseum	555
Happy as a King	1953	Prince's	26
High Spirits	1953	Hippodrome	
King & I	1953	Drury Lane	946
Lucky Boy	1953	Winter Garden	3
Over the Moon	1953	Piccadilly/Casino	156
Paint Your Wagon	1953	Her Majesty's	477
Pardon My French	1953	Prince of Wales	758
Three Cheers	1953	Casino	14 weeks
Wish You Were Here	1953	Casino	282
1954 Palladium Show	1954	Palladium	549
After the Ball	1954	Globe	188
Can Can	1954	Coliseum	394
Cockles & Champagne	1954	Saville/Piccadilly	118
Duenna	1954	Westminster	134
Evening with Beatrice Lillie	1954	Globe	195
Going to Town	1954	St. Martins	68
Happy Holiday	1954	Palace	31
Intimacy at 8.30	1954	Criterion	551
Jokers Wild	1954	Victoria Palace	911
Joyce Grenfell Requests the Pleasure of Your Company	1954	Fortune	1 year
Light Fantastic	1954	Lyric Hammersmith	2 weeks
Noddy in Toyland	1954	Stoll/Prince's	Christmas
Off the Record	1954	Victoria Palace	702
Pal Joey	1954	Prince's	245
Pay the Piper	1954	Saville	20
Salad Days	1954	Vaudeville	2329
Talk of the Town	1954	Adelphi	656
Wedding in Paris	1954	Hippodrome	411
You'll Be Lucky	1954	Adelphi	436
Burning Boat	1955	Royal Court	12
Cranks	1955	St. Martin's/Duchess/Lyric H	217
Girl Called Jo, A	1955	Piccadilly	141
Jazz Train	1955	Piccadilly	
Kismet	1955	Stoll	648
Listen to the Wind	1955	Arts	48
May Fever	1955	New Lindsey	Christmas
Meet Me on the Corner	1955	Hippodrome	25 weeks
Noddy in Toyland	1955	Prince's	Christmas
Painting the Town	1955	Palladium	373
Pajama Game	1955	Coliseum	578
Paris By Night	1955	Prince of Wales	890
Plume de Ma Tante, La	1955	Garrick	700
Punch Revue	1955	Duke of York's	
Romance in Candlelight	1955	Piccadilly	53
Such Is Life	1955	Adelphi	548
Twenty Minutes South	1955	St. Martin's	101
Water Gypsies	1955	Winter Garden	239
Wild Thyme	1955	Duke of York's	52
Wonderful Town	1955	Prince's	205
Cloudcuckooland	1956	Arts	season
Comedy of Errors	1956	Arts	season
Fanny	1956	Drury Lane	333
For Amusement Only	1956	Apollo	698
Fresh Airs	1956	Comedy	163
Grab Me a Gondola	1956	Lyric	673
Harmony Close	1956	Lyric Hammersmith	62
Jubilee Girl	1956	Victoria Palace	53
Plain and Fancy	1956	Drury Lane	217
Rocking the Town	1956	Palladium	397
She Smiled at Me	1956	St. Martin's	4
Summer Song	1956	Prince's	90
Sweet William	1956	Irving	season
These Foolish Kings	1956	Victoria Palace	882
Threepenny Opera	1956	Royal Court	140
Trevallion	1956	Palace	4
United Notions	1956	Adelphi	
Vanishing Island	1956	Westminster	
Wild Grows the Heather	1956	Hippodrome	28
Wonderful Lamp	1956	Palladium	159
Antarctica	1957	Players'	season
At the Drop of a Hat	1957	New Lindsey/Fortune	759
Bells Are Ringing	1957	Coliseum	292
Crystal Heart	1957	Saville	6
Damn Yankees	1957	Coliseum	861
Dublin Pike Follies	1957	Lyric Hammersmith	
Free As Air	1957	Savoy	417
Harvest Time	1957	New Lindsey	season
Joyce Grenfell	1957	Lyric Hammersmith	
Meet Me by Moonlight	1957	Aldwych	148
Oh, My Papa!	1957	Garrick	45
Pleasures of Paris	1957	Prince of Wales	850
School	1957	Prince's	22
Share My Lettuce	1957	Lyric H'th/Comedy/Garrick	301
We're Having a Ball	1957	Palladium	305
Zuleika	1957	Saville	124
Cinderella	1958	Coliseum	season
Expresso Bongo	1958	Saville	316
Gentleman's Pastime	1958	Players'	18
Hostage	1958	Stratford East	
Irma la Douce	1958	Lyric	1512
For Adults Only	1958	Strand	292
Keep Your Hair On	1958	Apollo	20
Lady at the Wheel	1958	Lyric Hamm'th/Westminster	65
Large As Life	1958	Palladium	382
Living for Pleasure	1958	Garrick	370
Mister Venus	1958	Prince of Wales	16
My Fair Lady	1958	Drury Lane	2281
Pink Champagne	1958	Scala	
Pot Luck	1958	Victoria Palace	7 weeks
Simply Heavenly	1958	Young Vic	16
Valmouth	1958	Lyric Hammersmith	84
Wally Pone	1958	Unity	season
West Side Story	1958	Her Majesty's	1040
Where's Charley?	1958	Palace	404
Aladdin	1959	Coliseum	143
Blue Magic - revue	1959	Prince of Wales	436
Candide	1959	Saville	60
Chrysanthemum	1959	Palace	148
Clown Jewels	1959	Victoria Palace	803
Crooked Mile	1959	Cambridge	164
Demon Barber	1959	Lyric Hammersmith	39
Fings Aint What They Used To Be	1959	Stratford East/Garrick	897
Hooray for Daisy	1959	Lyric Hammersmith	51
Kookaburra	1959	Prince's	42
Lock Up Your Daughters	1959	Mermaid	330
Love Doctor	1959	Piccadilly	16

Title	Year	Theatre	Run
Make Me an Offer	1959	New	267
Marigold	1959	Savoy/Saville	77
One to Another	1959	Lyric Hammersmith	
Pieces of Eight	1959	Apollo	429
Quiz Kid	1959	Lyric Hammersmith	31
Swinging Down the Lane	1959	Palladium	343
When in Rome	1959	Adelphi	298
World of Paul Slickey	1959	Palace	47
World of Suzie Wong	1959	Prince of Wales	821
And Another Thing	1960	Fortune	
Art of Living	1960	Criterion	12 months
Billy Barnes Revue	1960	Lyric Hammersmith	
Call It Love	1960	Wyndham's	short run
Dancing Heiress	1960	Lyric Hammersmith	2 weeks
Don't Shoot, We're English	1960	Cambridge	short run
Flower Drum Song	1960	Palace	+300
Follow That Girl	1960	Vaudeville	211
Golden Touch	1960	Piccadilly	12
Innocent as Hell	1960	Lyric Hammersmith	13
Johnny the Priest	1960	Prince's	14
Joie de Vivre	1960	Queen's	4
Lily White Boys	1960	Royal Court	45
Look Who's Here	1960	Fortune	
Mine Fair Sadie	1960	Wyndham's	
Most Happy Fella	1960	Coliseum	464
Mr. Burke, MP	1960	Mermaid	114
Music Box Show	1960	Palladium	
New Cranks	1960	Lyric Hammersmith	
Oliver!	1960	New	2618
Once Upon a Mattress	1960	Adelphi	38
Stars In Your Eyes	1960	Palladium	season
Tom Sawyer	1960	Stratford East	18
Young in Heart	1960	Victoria Palace	
Belle or Ballad of Dr. Crippen	1961	Strand	44
Beyond the Fringe	1961	Fortune/May Fair	2200
Bye Bye Birdie	1961	Her Majesty's	8 months
Do Re Mi	1961	Prince of Wales	
Fantasticks	1961	Apollo	44
Four to the Bar	1961	Arts	
Glory Be!	1961	Stratford East	
Goldfaden Dream, A	1961	Prince's	season
King Kong	1961	Prince's	6 months
Let Yourself Go	1961	Palladium	
Little Old King Cole	1961	Palladium	205
Lord Chamberlain Regrets	1961	Saville	
Music Man	1961	Adelphi	395
On the Brighter Side	1961	Phoenix	
One Over the Eight	1961	Duke of York's	
Sound of Music	1961	Palace	2385
Stop the World, I Want to Get Off	1961	Queen's	478
Three Caskets	1961	Players'	season
Vie Parisienne, La	1961	Sadler's Wells	
We're Just Not Practical	1961	Stratford East	21
Wildest Dreams	1961	Vaudeville	76
Anna Russell	1962	St. Martin's	
Black & White Minstrel Show	1962	Shepherds Bush/Vic.Palace	4344
Black Nativity	1962	Criterion	60
Blitz!	1962	Adelphi	568
Cindy-Ella, or I Gotta a Shoe	1962	Garrick/New Arts	
Clap Hands	1962	Lyric H'smith/Prince Charles	
Do Somethin' Addy Man	1962	Stratford East	25
Fiorello!	1962	Piccadilly	56
Gentlemen Prefer Blondes	1962	Prince's	223
Joyce Grenfell	1962	Haymarket	
Little Mary Sunshine	1962	Comedy	44
Not To Worry	1962	Garrick	
Palladium Variety	1962	Palladium	
Pied Piper	1962	Stratford East	42
Premise	1962	Comedy	172
Sail Away	1962	Savoy	252
Scapa	1962	Adelphi	44
Space Is So Startling	1962	Westminster	
Thurber Carnival	1962	Savoy	
Twists	1962	Arts	
Vanity Fair	1962	Queen's	70
What a Crazy World	1962	Stratford East	48
All Square	1963	Vaudeville	
At the Drop of Another Hat	1963	Haymarket/Globe	12 months
Boys from Syracuse	1963	Drury Lane	3 months
Cambridge Circus	1963	New Arts	
Carnival	1963	Lyric	28
Enrico	1963	Piccadilly	2 months
Funny Thing Happened on the Way to the Forum, A	1963	Strand	762
Half a Sixpence	1963	Cambridge	679
House of Cards	1963	Players'/Phoenix	27
How to Succeed in Business Without Really Trying	1963	Shaftesbury	520
In the Lap of the Gods	1963	New Lindsey	
Looking For Action	1963	Prince Charles	
Man in the Moon	1963	Palladium	
No Strings	1963	Her Majesty's	short run
Oh, What a Lovely War!	1963	Stratford East/Wyndham's	501
On the Town	1963	Prince of Wales	63
On Your Toes	1963	Prince of Wales	53
Pickwick	1963	Saville	694
Pocahontas	1963	Lyric Hammersmith	12
Round Leicester Square	1963	Piccadilly	
See You Inside	1963	Duchess	
So Much to Remember	1963	Vaudeville	short run
Six of One	1963	Adelphi	
Swing Along	1963	Palladium	
Three Musketeers	1963	Lyric Hammersmith	
Virtue in Danger	1963	Mermaid/Strand	121
What Goes Up	1963	Stratford East	42
Aladdin & His Wonderful Lamp	1964	Palladium	
All in Love	1964	May Fair	22
Camelot	1964	Drury Lane	518
Chaganog	1964	Vaudeville/St. Martin's	
Comedy in Music	1964	Shaftesbury	
Divorce Me Darling!	1964	Players'/Globe	178
Give a Dog a Bone	1964	Westminster	
High Spirits	1964	Savoy	93
Instant Marriage	1964	Piccadilly	366
Late Joys	1964	Prince Charles	
Little Me	1964	Cambridge	334
Maggie May	1964	Adelphi	501
Nights at the Comedy	1964	Comedy	
Our Man Crichton	1964	Shaftesbury	208
Robert & Elizabeth	1964	Lyric	957
Rose and the Ring	1964	Stratford East	Christmas
She Loves Me	1964	Lyric	189
Wait a Minim	1964	Fortune	656
Wayward Way	1964	Lyric Ham'smith/Vaudeville	36
4000 Brass Halfpennies	1965	Mermaid	
Anyone for England?	1965	Lyric Hammersmith	
Babes in the Wood	1965	Palladium	
Charlie Girl	1965	Adelphi	2,202
Happy End	1965	Royal Court	short run
Hello Dolly	1965	Drury Lane	794
How Now Brown Cow?	1965	Lyric Hammersmith	
Joyce Grenfell	1965	Queen's	
Klondyke	1965	Old Vic	
Nymphs and Satires	1965	Apollo	short run
Passion Flower Hotel	1965	Prince of Wales	148
Something Nasty in the Woodshed	1965	Stratford East	20
Twang!	1965	Shaftesbury	43
Cinderella	1966	Palladium	
Come Spy With Me	1966	Whitehall	468
Decline & Fall	1966	Criterion	
Four Degrees Over	1966	Mermaid/Fortune	2 months
Funny Girl	1966	Prince of Wales	109
Joey, Joey	1966	Saville	22
Jorrocks	1966	New	181
London Laughs	1966	Palladium	
Man of Magic	1966	Piccadilly	135
Matchgirls	1966	Globe	119
On the Level	1966	Saville	118
Strike a Light	1966	Piccadilly	30
Three Musketeers	1966	New Arts	
110 in the Shade	1967	Palace	101
Annie	1967	Westminster	398
Black New World	1967	Strand	4 weeks
Boy Friend - rev.	1967	Comedy	365
Fiddler on the Roof	1967	Her Majesty's	2030
Four Musketeers	1967	Drury Lane	462
Marie Lloyd Story	1967	Stratford East	
Mrs. Wilson's Diary	1967	Stratford East/Criterion	
Oliver!	1967	Piccadilly	331
Present from the Corporation, A	1967	Fortune	3
Queenie	1967	Comedy	20
Sweet Charity	1967	Prince of Wales	484
Who's Pinkus? Where's Chelm?	1967	Cochrane	10
Cabaret	1968	Palace	316
Canterbury Tales	1968	Phoenix	2080
Cindy	1968	Lyric	short run
Forty Years On	1968	Apollo	
Golden Boy	1968	Palladium	118
Gulliver's Travels	1968	Mermaid	
Hair	1968	Shaftesbury	1999
I Do! I Do!	1968	Lyric	166
Jacques Brel Is Alive & Well & Living in Paris	1968	Duchess	41
Man of La Mancha	1968	Piccadilly	253
Man With a Load of Mischief	1968	Comedy	short run
Mr. & Mrs.	1968	Palace	44
Viva Viva	1968	Arts	17
Young Visiters	1968	Piccadilly	63
You're a Good Man Charlie Brown	1968	Fortune	116

134

Title	Year	Theatre	Perf.
Ann Veronica	1969	Cambridge	44
Anne of Green Gables	1969	New	300
As Dorothy Parker Once Said	1969	Fortune	
Belle Starr	1969	Palace	short run
Dames at Sea	1969	Duchess	short run
High Diplomacy	1969	Westminster	172
Mame	1969	Drury Lane	443
Martin Luther King	1969	Greenwich	
Phil the Fluter	1969	Palace	125
Promises, Promises	1969	Prince of Wales	560
Stiffkey Scandals of 1932	1969	Queen's	12
Two Cities	1969	Palace	44
Your Own Thing	1969	Comedy	42
1776	1970	New	168
At the Palace	1970	Palace	
Catch My Soul	1970	Roundhouse	+400
Erb	1970	Strand	38
Great Waltz	1970	Drury Lane	+600
Isabel's a Jezebel	1970	Duchess	short run
Lie Down, I Think I Love You	1970	Strand	13
Mandrake	1970	Criterion	12
Oh! Calcutta!	1970	Roundhouse/Royalty/Duchess	+2300
Sing a Rude Song	1970	Greenwich/Garrick	71
Winnie the Pooh	1970	Phoenix	season
Ambassador	1971	Her Majesty's	
Anything to Declare?	1971	Westminster	
Corunna	1971	Royal Court	12
Godspell	1971	Roundhouse/Wyndham's/Phoenix	1128
His Monkey Wife	1971	Hampstead	28
Joe Lives	1971	Greenwich	
Last Sweet Days of Isaac	1971	Old Vic	
Maybe That's Your Problem	1971	Roundhouse	18
Romance	1971	Duke of York's	6
Showboat	1971	Adelphi	909
Tale of Istanbul	1971	Aldwych	
Tyger	1971	New	
What a Way to Run a Revolution	1971	Young Vic	season
Applause	1972	Her Majesty's	382
Company	1972	Her Majesty's	344
Costa Packet	1972	Stratford East	65
Cowardy Custard	1972	Mermaid	
Gone With the Wind	1972	Drury Lane	398
Good Old, Bad Old Days	1972	Prince of Wales	309
Hullaballoo	1972	Criterion	
I and Albert	1972	Piccadilly	120
Jacob's Journey	1972	Albery	
Jesus Christ Superstar	1972	Palace	3358
Jumpers	1972	National	
Liberty Ranch	1972	Greenwich	26
Little Giant	1972	Greenwich	
Londoners	1972	Stratford East	63
Mother Earth	1972	Roundhouse	
Once Upon a Time	1972	Duke of York's	26
Popkiss	1972	Globe	65
Pull Both Ends	1972	Piccadilly	36
Rock Carmen	1972	Roundhouse	
Samarkand	1972	Richmond	season
Smilin' Through	1972	Prince of Wales	28
Stand and Deliver	1972	Roundhouse	14
Tom Brown's Schooldays	1972	Cambridge	76
Trelawny	1972	Sadlers Wells/Prince of Wales	177
Card	1973	Queen's	130
Carry On London	1973	Victoria Palace	630
Decameron '73	1973	Roundhouse	69
Grease	1973	New London	236
Gypsy	1973	Piccadilly	300
G.B.	1973	Westminster	
Is Your Doctor Really Necessary?	1973	Stratford	68
Joseph & the Amazing Technicolor Dreamcoat	1973	Roundhouse/Albery	243
Kingdom Coming	1973	Roundhouse	14
Larry the Lamb in Toytown	1973	Shaw	season
Lonesome Stone	1973	Rainbow	
Man From the East	1973	Roundhouse	short run
Me Nobody Knows, The	1973	Shaw	45
No, No, Nanette	1973	Drury Lane	277
Pippin	1973	Her Majesty's	2 months
Rocky Horror Show	1973	Royal Court/Comedy	2960
Treasure Island	1973	Mermaid	season
Two Gentlemen of Verona	1973	Phoenix	237
Water Babies	1973	Royalty	62
Zorba	1973	Greenwich	short run
3p Off Opera	1974	Half Moon	season
Billy	1974	Drury Lane	904
Bordello	1974	Queen's	2 months
Chox — revue	1974	Comedy	
Cole	1974	Mermaid	
Deja Revue	1974	New London	
Dick Deterred	1974	Bush/ICA	season
Dracula	1974	Stratford East	77
Evening with Hinge & Bracket	1974	Royal Court/May Fair	
Gentlemen Prefer Anything	1974	Stratford East	34
Good Companions	1974	Her Majesty's	252
Hans Andersen	1974	Palladium	+300
Jack the Ripper	1974	Ambassadors/Cambridge	228
John, Paul, George, Ringo & Bert	1974	Lyric	
Land of the Dinosaurs	1974	Stratford East	season
Sammy Cahn's Songbook	1974	New London	
At the Sign of the Angel	1975	Players'	short run
Black Mikado	1975	Cambridge	472
Cranford	1975	Stratford East	26
Dad's Army	1975	Shaftesbury	
Farjeon Reviewed	1975	Mermaid	
Follow the Star	1975	Westminster	
Gulliver's Travels	1975	Mermaid	season
Happy as a Sandbag	1975	Ambassadors	
Ipi Tombi	1975	Her Majesty's	
Jeeves	1975	Her Majesty's	38
Kwa Zulu	1975	New London/Piccadilly	
Lady or the Tiger	1975	Orange Tree/Fortune	52
Little Night Music, A	1975	Adelphi	406
Look Out, It's Sir	1975	Stratford East	season
Nickleby & Me	1975	Stratford East	44
Oh! Coward	1975	Criterion	
Pilgrim	1975	Roundhouse	short run
Tarantara-Tarantara	1975	Westminster/Phoenix	
Teeth 'n' Smiles	1975	Royal Court	
Thomas and the King	1975	Her Majesty's	short run
Venus & Superkid	1975	Roundhouse	season
Yobbo Nowt	1975	Shaw	
Betjemania	1976	Shaw	
Bitch	1976	Little	season
Chorus Line	1976	Drury Lane	903
Elidor	1976	Cochrane	season
Irene	1976	Adelphi	
Leave Him To Heaven	1976	New London	
Liza of Lambeth	1976	Shaftesbury	110
Magic of Young Houdini	1976	Phoenix	40
Mardi Gras	1976	Prince of Wales	212
Point	1976	Mermaid	season
Ride! Ride!	1976	Westminster	
Rip-Off	1976	Windmill	1940
Showman	1976	Stratford East	47
Side by Side by Sondheim	1976	Mermaid/Wyndham's	781
T. Zee	1976	Royal Court	38
Very Good Eddie	1976	Piccadilly	411
What's a Nice Country Like U.S. Doing in a State Like This?	1976	May Fair	
Boom! Boom!	1977	Victoria Palace	
Bubbling Brown Sugar	1977	Royalty	
Curse of the Werewolf	1977	Stratford East	24
Dean	1977	Casino	35
Drake's Dream	1977	Shaftesbury/Westminster	82
Edith Piaf, Je Vous Aime	1977	King's Head	
Elvis	1977	Astoria	
Fire Angel	1977	Her Majesty's	42
Gingerbread Man	1977	Old Vic	season
I Love My Wife	1977	Prince of Wales	401
Jericho	1977	Young Vic	season
Lionel	1977	New London	
Maggie	1977	Shaftesbury	42
Magic Man, The	1977	May Fair	24
Oh Mr Porter	1977	Mermaid	
Oliver!	1977	New	1152
Privates on Parade	1977	Aldwych	208
Sleak	1977	Roundhouse	27
Volpone	1977	National	
Annie	1978	Victoria Palace	1485
Bar-Mitzvah Boy	1978	Her Majesty's	77
Beyond the Rainbow	1978	Adelphi	6 months
Every Good Boy Deserves Favour	1978	Mermaid	
Evita	1978	Prince Edward	3176
Great American Backstage Musical	1978	Regent	
Kingdom Come	1978	King's Head	41
Kings and Clowns	1978	Phoenix	34
Lark Rise	1978	National	
Travelling Music Show	1978	Her Majesty's	short run
Troubadour	1978	Cambridge	76
Wren	1978	May Fair	34
Adventures of a Bear Called Paddington	1979	Royalty	
Ain't Misbehavin'	1979	Her Majesty's	
Aladdin	1979	Lyric Hammersmith	
Beatlemania	1979	Astoria	
Chicago	1979	Cambridge	+600
Colette	1979	Comedy	47
Day in Hollywood, A, Night in the Ukraine, A	1979	May Fair	168
Faust	1979	Young Vic	26

Title	Year	Venue	Run
Fearless Frank	1979	King's Head	52
Flowers for Algernon	1979	Queen's	29
Grease	1979	Astoria	124
King & I	1979	Palladium	538
Never Mind the Bullocks	1979	May Fair	season
Oh Boy!	1979	Astoria	
Songbook	1979	Globe	208
Tin Pan Ali	1979	Shaftesbury/Cochrane	2 weeks
Tommy	1979	Queen's	118
Barnardo	1980	Royalty	43
Biograph Girl	1980	Phoenix	57
Colette	1980	Colette	47
Mummy's Tomb	1980	Stratford East	
Nicholas Nickleby aka Smike	1980	Aldwych	
Only in America	1980	Roundhouse	
On the Twentieth Century	1980	Her Majesty's	165
Streets of London	1980	Her Majesty's	122
Swan with Topping	1980	Ambassadors	short run
Sweeney Todd	1980	Drury Lane	157
They're Playing Our Song	1980	Shaftesbury	
Tomfoolery	1980	Criterion	
Umbrellas of Cherbourg	1980	Phoenix	12
Barnum	1981	Palladium	655
Billy Bishop Goes to War	1981	Comedy	6 weeks
Captain Beaky	1981	Apollo	season
Cats	1981	New London	+9000
Chorus Girls	1981	Stratford East	4 weeks
Eastward Ho!	1981	Mermaid	45
Gavin & the Monster	1981	Westminster	78
Hiawatha	1981	National	
I'm Getting My Act Together & Taking It On the Road	1981	Apollo	8 weeks
Meg & Mog Show	1981	Arts	season
Mitford Girls	1981	Globe	12 weeks
Mrs. Tucker's Pageant	1981	Stratford East	49
One Mo' Time	1981	Cambridge/Phoenix	12 months
One Night Stand	1981	Apollo	47
Restoration	1981	Royal Court	62
Swan Down Gloves	1981	Aldwych	22
Suburban Strains	1981	Roundhouse	31
Tap Dance on a Telephone Line	1981	Tricycle	6 weeks
Wild, Wild Women	1981	Orange Tree	7 weeks
Wonderland	1981	King's Head	35
Worzel Gummidge	1981	Cambridge	8 weeks
Andy Capp	1982	Aldwych	99
Boogie, Woogie, Bubble 'n' Squeak	1982	May Fair	3 weeks
Destry Rides Again	1982	Donmar Warehouse	40
Hollywood Dreams (Binns)	1982	Gate	3 weeks
Jingle Jangle	1982	Shaw	1 week
Marry Me a Little	1982	King's Head	22
Mata Hari	1982	Lyric	4 weeks
Me, Myself & I	1982	Orange Tree	2 seasons
Masquerade	1982	Young Vic	31
Mysteries	1982	National	
Nightingale	1982	Lyric Hammersmith	4 weeks
Poppy	1982	Barbican	97
Song & Dance	1982	Palace	781
Star is Torn	1982	Stratford East	4 weeks
Underneath the Arches	1982	Prince of Wales	63 weeks
Wild, Wild Women	1982	Astoria	7 weeks
Windy City	1982	Victoria Palace	250
Abbacadabra	1983	Lyric Hammersmith	84
Any Minute Now	1983	Stratford East	3 weeks
Bashville	1983	Regent's Park Open Air	season
Blondel	1983	Old Vic	292
Blood Brothers	1983	Lyric	224
Bugsy Malone	1983	Her Majesty's	300
Countess Maritza	1983	Sadler's Wells	
Daisy Pulls It Off	1983	Gielgud	3 years
Dancin'	1983	Drury Lane	88
Dear Anyone	1983	Cambridge	65
Greatest Show on Legs	1983	Gate	
Hi-De-Hi	1983	Victoria Palace	84
His Master's Voice	1983	Half Moon	5 weeks
Incidental Music	1983	Orange Tree	7 weeks
Iron Harvest	1983	Old Red Lion	1 week
James & the Giant Peach	1983	Sadler's Wells	1 week
Jean Seberg	1983	National	short run
John, Paul, George, Ringo & Bert	1983	Young Vic	2 months
Jukebox	1983	Astoria	5 months
Little Shop of Horrors	1983	Comedy	813
Marilyn!	1983	Adelphi	5 months
Merrily We Roll Along	1983	Bloomsbury	24
Mr. Cinders (rev)	1983	Fortune	+500
Noel & Gertie	1983	King's Head	4 weeks
Our Day Out	1983	Young Vic	4 weeks
Singin' in the Rain	1983	Palladium	894
Snoopy — The Musical	1983	Duchess	14 months
Swan Esther & the King	1983	Young Vic	26
Two Ronnies	1983	Palladium	
Yakety Yak	1983	Astoria	4 weeks
42nd Street	1984	Drury Lane	4.5 years
Blockheads	1984	Mermaid	short run
Hired Man	1984	Astoria	164
Humpty Dumpty	1984	Dominion	
Importance	1984	Ambassadors	29
Little Me	1984	Prince of Wales	334
Peg	1984	Phoenix	146
Pump Boys & Dinettes	1984	Piccadilly	50 weeks
Ratepayers Iolanthe	1984	Queen Elizabeth Hall	2 months
Return to the Forbidden Planet	1984	Tricycle	1516
Six for Gold	1984	King's Head	30
Starlight Express	1984	Apollo Victoria	7406
Starting Here, Starting Now	1984	Richmond	4 weeks
Secret Diary of Adrian Mole, Aged 13¾	1984	Wyndham's	61 weeks
West Side Story	1984	Her Majesty's	571
Wiz	1984	Lyric Hammersmith	7 weeks
Are You Lonesome Tonight?	1985	Phoenix	47 weeks
Cradle Will Rock	1985	Old Vic	3 weeks
Gigi	1985	Lyric	242
Judy	1985	Greenwich	6 weeks
Kern Goes to Hollywood	1985	Donmar Warehouse	2 months
Lennon	1985	Astoria	28 weeks
Les Miserables	1985	Barbican/Palace/Queen's	+7500
Me & My Girl	1985	Adelphi	3303
Metropolitan Mikado	1985	Queen Elizabeth Hall	2 weeks
Mr. Men Musical	1985	Vaudeville	
Mutiny	1985	Piccadilly	60 weeks
Peter Pan	1985	Aldwych	73
Seven Brides for Seven Brothers	1985	Old Vic	extended
Songs for Stray Cats	1985	Donmar Warehouse	3 weeks
Tess of the D'Urbevilles	1985	Latchmere	3 weeks
What a Way to Run a Revolution	1985	Young Vic	11
Who Plays Wins	1985	Vaudeville	5 weeks
Adventures of Mr. Toad	1986	Bloomsbury	Christmas
Chess	1986	Prince Edward	1209
Comic Relief	1986	Shaftesbury	
Elmer Gantry	1986	Gate	4 weeks
Gambler	1986	Hampstead/Comedy	10 weeks
Heyday	1986	King's Head	4 weeks
Jeanne	1986	Sadler's Wells	3 weeks
La Cage aux Folles	1986	Palladium	301
Line One	1986	Shaw	2 weeks
Marlowe	1986	King's Head	4 weeks
Nightshriek	1986	Shaw	3 weeks
Noel & Gertie	1986	Donmar Warehouse	3 weeks
Old Man of Lochnagar	1986	Sadler's Wells	1 week
Phantom of the Opera	1986	Her Majesty's	+5000
Rebel	1986	Albany	3 weeks
Time	1986	Dominion	1 year
Wonderful Town	1986	Queen's	31 weeks
Blues in the Night	1987	Donmar Wareh'se/Piccadilly	5 weeks
Evening with Alan Jay Lerner	1987	Drury Lane	
Fascinating Aida	1987	Donmar Warehouse	6 weeks
Follies	1987	Shaftesbury	522
Girlfriends	1987	Playhouse	5 weeks
High Society	1987	Victoria Palace	47 weeks
It's a Girl	1987	Bush	4 weeks
Lady Day	1987	Donmar Wareh'se/Piccadilly	5 weeks
Lyle the Crocodile	1987	Lyric Hammersmith	season
March of the Falsettos	1987	Albery	3 weeks
Mystery of Edwin Drood	1987	Savoy	68
Nunsense	1987	Fortune	9 months
Pacific Overtures	1987	Coliseum	10 months
Secret Garden	1987	King's Head	5 months
Stop! In the Name of Love	1987	Piccadilly	12 weeks
What About Luv?	1987	Lyric Hammersmith	3 weeks
Wizard of Oz	1987	Barbican	9 weeks
Blood Brothers	1988	Albery/Phoenix	+7300
Budgie	1988	Cambridge	89
Mack and Mabel	1988	Drury Lane	
Phantom Violin	1988	Almeida	4 months
Ragged Child	1988	Sadler's Wells	
Re:Joyce	1988	Fortune	6 months
Rink	1988	Cambridge	38
South Pacific	1988	Prince of Wales	1 year
Sugar Babies	1988	Savoy	4 months
Winnie	1988	Victoria Palace	3 months
Ziegfeld	1988	Palladium	5 months
Aspects of Love	1989	Prince of Wales	1325
Buddy	1989	Victoria Palace/Strand	+5000
Forbidden Broadway	1989	Fortune	3 months
Metropolis	1989	Piccadilly	6 months
Miss Saigon	1989	Drury Lane	3840
Sherlock Holmes	1989	Cambridge	3 months
Slice of Saturday Night, A	1989	King's Head/Arts/Strand	21 months
Be-Bop the Ruler	1990	Finborough	3 weeks
Bernadette	1990	Dominion	3 weeks

Show	Year	Venue	Run
Five Guys Named Moe	1990	Stratford East/Lyric	4 weeks
Frogs	1990	Brentford	2 weeks
Glory	1990	Lyric Hammersmith	3 weeks
Heaven's Up	1990	Playhouse	5 weeks
Into the Woods	1990	Phoenix	186
Just So	1990	Tricycle	2 months
King	1990	Piccadilly	4 weeks
Someone Like You	1990	Strand	4 weeks
Sophie! The Last of the Red Hot Mommas	1990	New End	3 months
Sunday in the Park with George	1990	Lyttelton	4 months
70 Girls, 70	1991	Vaudeville	13 weeks
Blue Angel	1991	Stratford East/Globe	5 weeks
Carmen Jones	1991	Old Vic	season
Children of Eden	1991	Prince Edward	3 months
Days of Hope	1991	Hampstead	6 weeks
Good Golly Miss Molly	1991	Arts	16 weeks
Hunting of the Snark	1991	Prince Edward	7 weeks
Joseph & the Amazing Technicolor Dreamcoat	1991	Palladium	923
Jumping Red Lights	1991	Lilian Baylis	4
Leave It To Me	1991	Arts/Cambridge	
Little Match Girl	1991	Orange Tree	8 weeks
Matador	1991	Queen's	13 weeks
Nutmeg & Ginger	1991	Orange Tree	8 weeks
Out of this World	1991	Guildhall	10
Assassins	1992	Donmar Warehouse	9 weeks
Between the Lines	1992	Etcetera	20
Cotton Club	1992	Aldwych	6 months
Do I Hear a Waltz?	1992	Guildhall	12
From a Jack to a King	1992	Ambassadors	14 weeks
Grand Hotel	1992	Dominion	135
In the Midnight Hour	1992	Young Vic	3 weeks
Josephine	1992	Battersea	8 weeks
Judgement in Stone	1992	Lyric Hammersmith	3 weeks
Kiss of the Spiderwoman	1992	Shaftesbury	390
Moby Dick	1992	Moby Dick	15 weeks
Once Upon a Song	1992	King's Head	3 weeks
Oscar	1992	Tricycle	2 weeks
Some Like It Hot	1992	Prince Edward	12 weeks
Spread a Little Happiness	1992	Whitehall	3 weeks
Valentine's Day	1992	Globe	3 weeks
Which Witch	1992	Piccadilly	8 weeks
Babes	1993	Shaw	5
City of Angels	1993	Prince of Wales	30 weeks
Crazy for You	1993	Prince Edward	3 years
Eurovision	1993	Vaudeville	2 weeks
Forever Plaid	1993	Apollo	
Hot Stuff	1993	Cambridge	25 weeks
Leonardo	1993	Strand	5 weeks
Love in the Country	1993	Almeida	
Robin, Prince of Sherwood	1993	Piccadilly	
Sunset Boulevard	1993	Adelphi	1529
Cheryomushki	1994	Lyric Hammersmith	
Copacabana	1994	Prince of Wales	18 months
Great Balls of Fire	1994	Lyric Hammersmith	
Hot Shoe Shuffle	1994	Queen's	
Oliver!	1994	Palladium	600
Once On This Island	1994	Royalty	145
Out of the Blue	1994	Shaftesbury	
Patsy Cline	1994	Whitehall	
Peter Pan	1994	Cambridge	
She Loves Me	1994	Savoy	
Stairway to Heaven	1994	King's Head	
Sweet Lorraine	1994	Piccadilly	
Wednesday Matinee	1994	Shaw	
Whistle Down the Wind	1994	Riverside	
By Jeeves	1995	Duke of York's	3 months
Fame	1995	Cambridge/Aldwych	long run
Jolson	1995	Victoria Palace	5 months
Little Night Music, A	1995	Olivier	1 year
Mack & Mabel	1995	Piccadilly	270
Calamity Jane	1996	Sadler's Wells	
Dames at Sea	1996	Ambassadors	
Elvis, the Musical	1996	Prince of Wales	
Ferry Cross the Mersey	1996	Lyric	1 month
Fields of Ambrosia	1996	Aldwych	23
Kiss the Sky	1996	Shepherds Bush Empire	
Martin Guerre	1996	Prince of Wales	6 months
Nine	1996	Donmar Warehouse	3 months
Passion	1996	Queen's	232
Scrooge	1996	Dominion	3 months
Smokey Joe's Café	1996	Prince of Wales	2 months
Voyeurz	1996	Whitehall	3 months
Who's Tommy	1996	Shaftesbury	1 year
Always	1997	Victoria Palace	6 weeks
Beauty & the Best	1997	Dominion	
Carnaby Street	1997	Arts	
Centralia	1997	Brixton	3 weeks
Chicago	1997	Adelphi	long run
Dorian	1997	Arts	
Fix (Dempsey/Rowe)	1997	Donmar Warehouse	4 weeks
Heathcliff	1997	Apollo Hammersmith	3 months
Maddie	1997	Lyric	5 weeks
Saturday Night	1997	Bridewell	38
Slow Drag	1997	Whitehall	
Street Cries	1997	Camden	5 weeks
Summer Holiday	1997	Apollo	3 months
Boogie Nights	1998	Savoy	5 months
Dr. Dolittle	1998	London Apollo	1 year
Kat & the Kings	1998	Tricycle/Vaudeville	6 months
No Way to Treat a Lady	1998	Arts	3 weeks
Personals	1998	New	4 weeks
Rent	1998	Shaftesbury	6 months
Saturday Night Fever	1998	Palladium/Apollo Victoria	long run
Saucy Jack & the Space Vixens	1998	Queen's	2 months
Whistle Down the Wind	1998	Aldwych	+1000
Boyband	1999	Gielgud	3 months
Casper the Musical	1999	Shaftesbury	3 months
Escape from Pterodactyl Island	1999	Pleasance	4 weeks
Honk!	1999	Olivier	9 months
Lion King	1999	Lyceum	+2000
Mamma Mia	1999	Prince Edward	+2000
Oh, What a Night	1999	London Apollo	10 weeks
Saint, She Ain't, A	1999	Apollo	5 months
Spend, Spend, Spend	1999	Piccadilly	11 months
Tess of the D'Urbervilles	1999	Savoy	2 months
West Side Story	1999	Prince of Wales	12 months
Beautiful Game	2000	Cambridge	12months
Cava, La	2000	Victoria Palace/Piccadilly	6 months
Fosse	2000	Prince of Wales	12 months
Hard Times	2000	Haymarket	3 months
Hedwig & the Angry Inch	2000	Playhouse	
King & I	2000	Palladium	20 months
Lautrec	2000	Shaftesbury	short run
Merrily we Roll Along	2000	Donmar Warehouse	3 months
Napoleon	2000	Shaftesbury	4 months
Notre Dame de Paris	2000	Dominion	5 months
Witches of Eastwick	2000	Drury Lane	7 months
All You Need Is Love	2001	Queen's	
Closer to Heaven	2001	Arts	6 months
Kiss Me Kate	2001	Victoria Palace	extended
Peggy Sue Got Married	2001	Shaftesbury	2 months
Secret Garden	2001	Aldwych	4 months
Song of Singapore	2001	May Fair	10 weeks
Bombay Dreams	2002	Apollo Victoria	extended
Chitty Chitty Bang Bang	2002	Palladium	extended
Daisy Pulls It Off	2002	Lyric	
Follies at Royal Festival Hall	2002	Festival Hall	
Handful of Keys	2002	May Fair	1 week
Little Women	2002	Bloomsbury	1 week
My One and Only	2002	Piccadilly	
Our House	2002	Cambridge	extended
Riverdance	2002	Apollo, Hammersmith	
Shockheaded Peter	2002	Albery	2 months
Space Family Robinson	2002	Pleasance	
Stomp	2002	Sadler's Wells/Vaudeville	extended
Sweeney Todd	2002	Sadler's Wells/Whitehall	long run
We Will Rock You	2002	Dominion	long run
Cliff	2003	Prince of Wales	
Cyberjam	2003	Queen's	3 months
Money to Burn	2003	Venue	2
Pacific Overtures	2003	Donmar Warehouse	
Ragtime	2003	Piccadilly	
Tell Me on a Sunday	2003	Gielgud	
Thoroughly Modern Millie	2003	Shaftesbury	
Tonight's the Night	2003	Victoria Palace	extended
Zip	2003	Duchess	
Bat Boy	2004	Shaftesbury	
Brighton Rock	2004	Almeida	
Festen	2004	Lyric	
Grand Hotel	2004	Donmar Warehouse	
Jailhouse Rock	2004	Piccadilly	
Little Women	2004	Duchess	
Mary Poppins	2004	Prince Edward	
Murderous Instincts	2004	Savoy	1 week
Producers	2004	Drury Lane	
Oscar	2004	Shaw	1
Rat Pack, Live from Las Vegas	2004	Strand	
Simply Heavenly	2004	Whitehall	
Woman in White	2004	Palace	
Acorn Antiques	2005	Haymarket	
Billy Elliot	2005	Victoria Palace	
Far Pavilions	2005	Shaftesbury	
On the Town	2005	Coliseum	

APPENDIX 3

LONDON SHOWS & MUSICALS WITH RUNS OVER 400

This list does not claim to be comprehensive or infallible, indeed publicity agents often use different criteria when estimating the length of run. It is also impossible to compare like with like because theatre sizes vary enormously in size, ranging from small private clubs of around 40 seats to cavernous auditoriums in excess of 2,000 such as the Palladium and Drury Lane. It is also debatable as to what exactly constitutes a London West End theatre. Should it be simply the well-known venues or should it include those such as the fringe Moss Empires, some of which seated more than 3,000? A compromise was both inevitable and necessary, and we leave it to our readers to interpret the facts as best they can.

For those really keen to work out the actual figures, purposeful reference may be made to Appendix 4 which lists all the major theatres together with their approximate seating capacity.

Whatever the shortcomings of such a list we still hope it proves useful.

Cats	1981	9000	Chorus Line, A	1976	903
Les Miserables	1985	+7500	Fings Aint What They Used To Be	1959	897
Starlight Express	1984	7406	Singin' in the Rain	1983	894
Blood Brothers	1988	+7300	Paris By Night	1955	890
Buddy	1989	+5000	Bless the Bride	1947	886
Phantom of the Opera, The	1986	+5000	These Foolish Kings	1956	882
Black & White Minstrel Show, The	1962	+4000	Folies Bergère Revue	1949	881
Miss Saigon	1989	3840	King's Rhapsody	1949	881
Jesus Christ Superstar	1972	3358	Sweeter and Lower	1944	870
Me & My Girl	1985	3303	Damn Yankees	1957	861
Evita	1978	3176	Rose Marie	1925	851
Rocky Horror Show, The	1973	2960	Paris to Piccadilly	1952	850
Oliver!	1960	2618	Pleasures of Paris, The	1957	850
Sound of Music, The	1961	2385	World of Suzie Wong, The	1959	821
Salad Days	1954	2329	Little Shop of Horrors, The	1983	813
Oh Calcutta	1970	+2300	Better 'Ole, The	1917	811
My Fair Lady	1958	2281	Arcadians, The	1909	809
Chu Chin Chow	1916	2238	Clown Jewels	1959	803
Charlie Girl	1965	2202	Boy, The	1917	801
Beyond the Fringe	1961	2200	Hello Dolly	1965	794
Boy Friend, The	1953	2084	South Pacific	1951	792
Canterbury Tales	1968	2080	Sweetest and Lowest	1946	791
Fiddler on the Roof	1967	2030	Side by Side by Sondheim	1976	781
Lion King, The	1999	+2000	Song & Dance	1982	781
Mamma Mia	1999	+2000	Merry Widow, The	1907	778
Chicago	1997	+1600	Piccadilly Hayride	1946	778
Hair	1968	1999	Airs on a Shoestring	1953	772
Rip-Off	1976	1940	San Toy	1899	768
Me and My Girl	1937	1646	Funny Thing Happened on the Way		
Together Again	1947	1566	to the Forum, A	1963	762
Oklahoma!	1947	1543	Geisha, The	1896	760
Sunset Boulevard	1993	1529	At the Drop of a Hat	1956	759
Return to the Forbidden Planet	1984	1516	Pardon My French	1953	758
Irma la Douce	1958	1512	Lilac Domino	1918	747
Annie	1978	1485	Country Girl, A	1902	729
Beggar's Opera, The	1920	1463	Joy-Bells	1919	723
Knights of Madness	1950	1361	Cloches de Corneville, Les	1878	705
Maid of the Mountains, The	1917	1352	Off the Record	1954	702
Aspects of Love	1989	1325	Plume de Ma Tante, La	1955	700
Annie Get Your Gun	1947	1304	For Amusement Only	1956	698
Chess	1986	1209	Get a Load of This	1941	698
Dancing Years, The	1939	1156	Belle of New York, The	1898	697
Oliver!	1977	1152	Bitter Sweet	1929	697
Godspell	1972	1128	Pickwick	1963	694
London Laughs	1952	1113	Night & the Music, The	1945	686
Chinese Honeymoon, A	1901	1075	Brigadoon	1949	685
West Side Story	1958	1040	Ring Round the Moon	1950	682
Perchance to Dream	1945	1022	Half a Sixpence	1963	679
Whistle Down the Wind	1998	+1000	Toreador, The	1901	675
Ring Out the Bells	1952	987	Grab Me a Gondola	1956	673
Robert & Elizabeth	1964	957	Mikado, The	1885	672
King & I, The	1953	946	No, No, Nanette	1925	665
Happy & Glorious	1944	938	Under the Counter	1945	665
Dorothy	1886	931	Blue for a Boy	1950	664
Joseph & the Amazing Technicolor			Strike a New Note	1943	661
Dreamcoat	1991	923	Talk of the Town	1954	656
Jokers Wild	1954	911	Wait a Minim	1964	656
Showboat	1971	909	Barnum	1981	655
Billy	1974	904	White Horse Inn	1931	651

Starlight Roof	1947	649	Stop the World, I Want to Get Off	1961	478
Kismet	1955	648	Paint Your Wagon	1953	477
Zig-Zag	1917	648	Leap Year	1924	471
Our Miss Gibbs	1909	636	Round in 50	1922	471
Carry On London	1973	630	It's Foolish But It's Fun	1943	469
Whirl of the World, The	1924	627	Come Spy With Me	1966	468
Lilac Time	1922	626	Full Swing	1942	468
Yes, Uncle!	1917	626	Latin Quarter (3)	1951	468
Box 'O Tricks	1918	625	Madame Pompadour	1923	467
Catch of the Season, The	1904	621	Tails Up	1918	467
Black Velvet	1939	620	Olivette	1880	466
Buzz Buzz	1918	612	Here, There & Everywhere	1947	466
Waltzes from Vienna	1931	607	Most Happy Fella	1960	464
Chicago	1979	+600	Apple Sauce	1941	462
Great Waltz, The	1970	+600	Four Musketeers	1967	462
Oliver!	1994	600	Miss Hook of Holland	1907	462
Love From Judy	1952	594	Little Dog Laughed	1939	461
Brighter London	1923	593	Tonight's the Night	1915	460
Runaway Girl, A	1898	593	Latin Quarter (2)	1950	456
Folies Bergère	1951	579	Florodora	1899	455
Fine Feathers	1945	578	Latin Quarter (1)	1949	455
Pajama Game, The	1955	578	Lyric Revue, The	1951	454
Patience	1881	578	Hullo, Ragtime	1912	451
Poupée, La	1897	576	Gate Revue, The	1939	449
Going Up	1918	574	Mercenary Mary	1925	446
Follow the Girls	1945	572	Mame	1969	443
Follies at the Apollo	1908	571	Penny Plain	1951	443
HMS Pinafore	1878	571	Whirligig	1919	441
West Side Story	1984	571	Pantomime Rehearsal	1891	438
Balalaika	1936	570	Strike It Again	1944	438
High Time	1946	570	Blue Magic	1959	436
Take It From Us	1950	570	You'll Be Lucky	1954	436
Blitz!	1962	568	Black Vanities	1941	435
Carousel	1950	566	As You Were	1918	434
Punch Bowl	1924	565	Sauce Tartare	1949	433
Bing Boys on Broadway, The	1918	562	Desert Song, The	1927	432
Promises, Promises	1969	560	Girl from Kay's, The	1902	432
Orchid, The	1903	559	Kissing Time	1919	430
Guys & Dolls	1953	555	Bubbly	1917	429
Gondoliers, The	1889	554	Casanova	1932	429
Intimacy at 8.30	1954	551	Messenger Boy, The	1900	429
1954 Palladium Show	1954	549	Pieces of Eight	1959	429
Such Is Life	1955	548	A to Z	1921	428
Shop Girl, The	1894	546	Dollar Princess, The	1909	428
Zip Goes a Million	1951	544	Tulip Time	1935	425
King & I, The	1979	538	Bing Boys Are Here, The	1916	424
Quaker Girl, The	1910	536	Cigale, La	1890	423
Gangway	1941	535	Marriage Market, The	1913	423
Mr. Cinders	1929	528	Yeomen of the Guard, The	1888	423
Song of Norway	1946	526	Girl Friend, The	1927	421
Follies at the Apollo	1910	521	Little Christopher Columbus	1893	421
How to succeed in business without			Peep Show, The	1921	421
really trying	1963	520	Latin Quarter 4 (Excitement)	1952	419
Camelot	1964	518	Stop Flirting	1923	418
Under Your Hat	1938	512	Free As Air	1957	417
Clowns in Clover	1927	508	Belle of Mayfair, The	1906	416
Lady of the Rose	1922	507	Little Revue, The	1939	415
Katja the Dancer	1925	505	Bran Pie	1919	414
Gay's the Word	1951	504	Gaiety Girl, The	1893	413
Theodore & Co	1916	503	Gay Rosalinda	1945	413
Up and Doing	1940	503	Wedding in Paris	1954	411
Madame Favart	1879	502	Joy-land	1915	409
Kiss Me Kate	1951	501	Razzle-Dazzle	1916	408
Maggie May	1964	501	Twenty to One	1942	408
Oh, What a Lovely War!	1963	501	Little Night Music, A	1975	406
Chocolate Soldier, The	1910	500	Cavalcade	1931	405
Carissima	1948	488	Nine Sharp	1938	405
Cheep	1917	488	Where's Charley	1958	404
Call Me Madam	1952	486	I Love My Wife	1977	401
Hullo, Tango	1913	485	Lady Behave	1941	401
Sweet Charity	1967	484	Little Michus	1905	401
French Maid, The	1897	480	Spring Chicken, The	1905	401
Vagabond King, The	1927	480	Catch My Soul	1970	+400

For the best use of this table see also Appendix 1 (**Alphabetical and Composers etc.**);
Appendix 2 (**Chronological and Venues**); and Appendix 4 (**Theatre Statistics**).

APPENDIX 4

SOME LONDON THEATRES & CONCERT HALLS

It is hoped this list may prove a useful source of reference but it does not pretend to be comprehensive. The difficulty of finding accurate information means that some of the statistics may also be out of date. Some theatres changed their name several times, especially during the 19th Century, and many were cosmetically reconstructed as well as being rebuilt. The problem of what constitutes a theatre, as opposed to a music hall, cinema or night club, inevitably meant subjective judgements had to be used, while geographical location was also a major difficulty which had to be addressed. In the end, where to draw the line proved an impossible conundrum to solve! Missing statistics include where contemporary theatres failed to answer phone calls or correspondence, where a theatre apparently vanished without trace, or where inconclusive evidence occurred.

THEATRE	APPROXIMATE CAPACITY
Adelphi 1930, Strand (1st 1806 Sans Pareil; 2nd 1858 Theatre Royal New Adelphi; 3rd 1901 Century; prefix "Royal" dropped in 1940)	1480
Albany 1980, Deptford (1st 1968)	350
Albery, 1973, St. Martin's Lane (formerly New 1903 q.v., renamed Albery in 1973)	872
Aldwych 1905, Aldwych	1176
Alexandra 1740, Highbury Park (closed 1871)	1900
Alexandra 1873, Camden Town (burnt down 1881 — rebuilt as Royal Park theatre)	
Alexandra 1897, Stoke Newington (closed 1935, reopened as a cinema and boxing venue, closed 1950 and then demolished)	3000
Alexandra Palace 1873, Wood Green (burnt down within two weeks then rebuilt) a) Great Hall b) West Hall	7008 & 2500
Alhambra 1854, Leicester Square (originally the 3500 seat Royal Panopticon of Science and Art, then a music hall, rebuilt as a theatre in 1883 and also known as the Alhambra Palace — reopened 1912 — demolished then rebuilt as Odeon cinema, 1937)	1650
Almeida 1990, Islington (refurbished 2000)	321
Ambassadors 1913, West Street (originally designed as a pair with St Martin's, renamed New Ambassadors in 1998)	450
Apollo 1901, Shaftesbury Avenue	775
Apollo Victoria 1979, Victoria (formerly a cinema opened in 1930)	1524
Apollo, Hammersmith 1995 (formerly the Hammersmith Gaumont Palace cinema 1932)	2400
Arcola 2000, Hackney (2 studio theatres)	
Arts 1927, Great Newport Street	240
Astley's (see Olympic)	
Astoria 1977, Charing Cross Road (built as a cinema in 1927)	1121
Astoria, Brixton (see Brixton Academy)	
Astoria, Finsbury Park (see Rainbow)	
Avenue (see Playhouse)	
Balham Empire 1890, High Road (converted swimming pool, then a cinema)	766
Balham Hippodrome 1899, High Road, Balham (later Duchess Palace)	2000
Barbican 1982, Silk Street (includes the smaller Pit q.v.)	1166
Barnes 1925 (located in Barnes, it closed the following year)	
Barons Court 1990, Comeragh Road, Hammersmith	60
Battersea Arts Centre (BAC) 1980, Lavender Hill (contains 3 theatres & 2 halls)	total 1360
Battersea Palace 1886, York Road (closed 1924)	600
Beck 1977, Hayes	600
Bedford 1824, Camden High Street (closed 1950 and demolished 1969)	1110
Bijou 1 1862, Haymarket (burnt down 1876)	
Bijou 2 1863 Bayswater (opened as Victoria Hall, later renamed Century & Twentieth Century lasting until 1930s)	
Blackfriars 1576 (demolished 1655)	
Blackheath Concert Halls 1895 (and recital hall)	700 & 220
Bloomsbury 1968 (run by University College London, opened as the Collegiate)	550
Boar's Head, Whitechapel (16th Century inn & theatre)	
Bob Hope 1982, Eltham (formerly Eltham Little)	182
Boltons 1947, South Kensington (reverted to cinema)	240
Borough 1896, Stratford (became a cinema in 1933, now closed)	3000
Bow Palace, Bow Road 1855 (rebuilt 1892, in use as a cinema by 1923)	2000
Bower 1837, Lambeth (closed 1877)	
Bridewell 1994, Fleet St. (converted Victorian swimming pool)	160
Britannia 1841, Hoxton (later a cinema which was bombed in the Blitz)	4000
Brixton Academy 1985 , Stockwell Road (originally the Astoria Theatre which was opened in 1929 — reopened with a large ground floor which caters for 4500 unseated, but with seats in balcony however)	
Brixton Theatre & Opera House 1896, Coldharbour Lane (renamed Melville shortly before being bombed in 1940)	1504
Broadgate Arena, Exchange Square (ice rink)	3000
Broadway 2000, Lewisham (formerly the Lewisham 1932, first known as the Town Hall extension, — plus studio theatre)	850 & 100
Bull 1978, Barnet (plus studio theatre)	177 & 100
Bullion Room 2001 (next to the Hackney Empire)	250
Bush 1972, Shepherds Bush	105
Cadogan Hall 2004, Sloane Terrace (converted church)	900
Camberwell Empire 1894, Denmark Hill (closed 1924, demolished 1937)	2000
Camberwell Palace 1899, Denmark Hill (closed 1956)	2000
Cambridge 1930, Seven Dials	1283
Camden 1 1901, Camden High St. (cinema in 1924)	2500
Camden 2 1994, Hampstead Road	60
Canterbury Music Hall 1852, Lambeth (rebuilt 1876, blitzed 1942 & demolished 1950s)	1500
Carlton 1927, Haymarket (converted to a cinema in 1930)	1150
Casino (see London Casino)	
Chanticleer 1937, South Kensington (closed 1940)	
Chapterhouse, Merton (semi open air with moveable seating)	
Charing Cross 1872 (demolished 1895 to make way for Charing Cross Hospital)	
Chelsea Palace 1903, King's Road (closed 1957)	2500
Chepstow — see Gate 3	
Chicken Shed 1994, Southgate (plus studio theatre)	286 & 85
Children's 1927, Holborn (closed 1931)	
Chiswick Empire 1912 (demolished 1959)	1948
Churchill 1977, Bromley	785
City of London 1835, Bishopsgate (destroyed by fire 1871)	
Clock Tower 1995, Croydon	
Cochrane 1963, Southampton Row	300
Cockpit 1 1609 (also called Phoenix), Drury Lane (closed 1665)	

△ *The Playhouse near Charing Cross was used extensively by the BBC before reverting to a traditional theatre in 1987.*

▷ *A smart piece of detective work established this picture of Daly's Theatre in Leicester Square as being taken in 1937, the year it was closed to make way for a new cinema.*

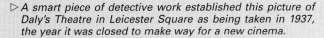

◁ *Above left: King's Theatre, Hammersmith had 3,000 seats and was one of many places of entertainment in the area. It was demolished in 1963.*

△ *There have been four major London opera houses. D'Oyly Carte opened the Palace as the Royal English Opera House for Sullivan's grand works; Covent Garden is subtitled The Royal Opera House; the Lyceum was once known as the English Opera House; and (above) the Stoll opened in 1911 as the London Opera House before being renamed four years later. It was demolished in 1957 to make way for the new Royalty Theatre.*

◁ *The second Globe Theatre shared a back wall with the Opera Comique and together they were known as the Rickety Twins. It was demolished in 1902 to make way for the Aldwych redevelopment scheme. This picture was taken in 1901 and shows husband-and-wife team Fred Terry and Julia Neilson starring in* **Sweet Nell of Old Drury**, *a play about Nell Gwynn.*

Cockpit 2 1970, Gateforth Street	200
Coliseum 1904, St. Martin's Lane (formerly London Coliseum, changed name 1931)	2358
Collins's 1862, Islington Green (closed 1958)	1400
Colour House 1995, Merton Abbey Mills	70
Comedy 1881, Panton Street	796
Conway Hall 1929, Holborn (plus smaller hall)	500 & 100
Coronet 1898, Notting Hill (closed 1923 and became a cinema)	
Cottesloe (see National)	
Court 1870, Chelsea (also called New Chelsea, demolished 1887) see also Royal Court	
Covent Garden, Royal Opera House 1858, Bow Street (1st 1732; 2nd 1809)	2156
Criterion 1874, Piccadilly Circus	591
Croydon Empire c.1900 (demolished)	
Croydon Hippodrome 1867 (also called Theatre Royal — demolished)	
Crystal Palace 1874, Sydenham (closed)	1700
Curtain 1577, Shoreditch (16th & 17th Century theatre)	
Dalston 1898, Hackney (became a cinema — closed)	1000
Daly's 1893, Leicester Square (demolished 1937, replaced by Warner cinema, 1938)	1225
Dominion 1929, Tottenham Court Road (converted into a cinema in 1932, later converted back to joint use)	2171
Donmar Warehouse 1960, Covent Garden (converted brewery & banana warehouse in regular use since 1981)	252
Dorset Garden 1671 (see Duke's 2)	
Drill Hall 1981, Chenies Street (built 1882 as a drill hall for the Bloomsbury Rifles)	200
Drury Lane, Theatre Royal 1812 (1st 1663; 2nd 1674; 3rd1794)	2205
Duchess 1929, Aldwych	470
Duke of York's 1892, St. Martin's Lane (opened as Trafalgar Square, Trafalgar 1894, renamed Duke of York's in 1895)	650
Duke's 1 1661, Lincoln's Inn Fields	
Duke's 2 1671, Dorset Garden	
Duke's 3 (see Holborn Theatre Royal)	
Ealing Hippodrome 1899	
Earl's Court Arena 1937, Earl's Court (very large exhibition centre)	
East London 1834, Whitechapel Rd (briefly renamed Effingham during 1850s, closed 1897)	2150
Edward Alderton 1976, Bexleyheath	85
Elephant & Castle 1872, New Kent Road (cinema by 1928)	2000
Eltham Little 1946 (now the Bob Hope q.v.)	198
Embassy 1928, Hampstead (became the Central School of Speech & Drama in 1957)	678
Emery 1994, Poplar	100
Empire 1884, Leicester Square (replaced by Empire cinema 1928, site of later Empire cinema, 1928 & ballroom, 1963)	3000
Empress, Brixton 1898, Brighton Terrace	1250
Etcetera 1986, Camden High Street	50
Everyman 1920, Hampstead (became a cinema in 1947 — closed)	
Fairfield Halls 1962, Croydon (includes Ashcroft Theatre)	1700
Finborough 1991, Earls Court	50
Finsbury Park Empire 1910 (closed 1960, demolished 1965)	2000
Folly (see Toole's)	
Fortune 1 1623-1661, Cripplegate (1st 1600-1621)	
Fortune 2 1924, Russell Street	440
Gaiety 1 1864, Strand (opened as Strand Musick Hall, rebuilt 1868 as the Gaiety, demolished 1903 for road redevelopment)	
Gaiety 2 1903, Aldwych (closed 1939, demolished 1957)	1264
Gallery of Illustration 1856, Regent Street (closed 1875)	
Garrick 1 1854 1881, Whitechapel (1st 1831 burned down 1846)	460
Garrick 2 1889, Charing Cross Road	678
Gate 1 1925, Floral Street, Covent Garden (converted warehouse — moved two years later to Gate 2)	96
Gate 2 1927, Villiers Street (blitzed 1941)	
Gate 3 1944 Kensington, also called Gateway/Chepstow	
Gate 4 1979, Notting Hill Gate	
Gateway (see Gate 3)	
Gatti's Over the Arches 1865, Westminster Bridge Road (also known as Gatti's Palace of Varieties, closed 1924)	1183
Gatti's Under the Arches 1866, Hungerford Bridge (later Hungerford Music Hall, then Charing Cross Music Hall — became a cinema in 1910)	
Geoffrey Whitworth 1952, Crayford	151
Gielgud 1995, Shaftesbury Avenue (formerly Hicks/Globe q.v., renamed Gielgud in 1995)	900
Globe 1 1599, Southwark (destroyed by fire 1613, rebuilt but closed by Puritans in 1642)	
Globe 2 1867, Newcastle Street (closed and demolished 1902 — shared a wall with the Opera Comique its "Rickety Twin")	1800
Globe 3 1906 (opened as Hicks, Globe 1909 — became the Gielgud in 1995)	907
Globe 4 1997, Bankside	1600
Golders Green Hippodrome 1913 (ground floor now used by BBC Concert Orchestra with seats in balcony)	700
Grace 1992, Battersea (see Latchmere)	80
Grafton 1930, Tottenham Court Road (became a BBC wartime studio - now closed)	
Grand, Clapham 1900, St John's Hill (now a club with 3 dance halls)	3000
Grand, Croydon 1896 (demolished)	
Grand, Fulham 1897 (Fulham 1906, then Shilling — demolished)	2200
Grand, Islington 1870 (Philharmonic Music Hall/Islington Empire — 3 separate buildings destroyed by fire, rebuilt as cinema1932, demolished 1962)	3000
Granville 1898, Fulham Broadway (closed 1956, demolished1971)	1500
Great Queen Street (see Kingsway)	
Grecian 1825, Shoreditch (closed 1882)	1750
Greenford Hall, Greenford	580
Greenwich 1969, Crooms Hill (1st 1871 as Crowder's Music Hall, Parthenon, Barnard's, Greenwich Hippodrome)	426
Greenwood 1975, Guy's Hospital, Weston St.	450
Hackney Empire 1901, Hackney	1500
Half Moon 1972, Whitehorse Road	80
Hammersmith Palace 1880s, King Street (rebuilt 1898 & 1910)	2825
Hampstead 1962, Swiss Cottage	174
Hampton Hill Playhouse 1998 (plus studio theatre)	200
Harrow Arts Centre 1988 (plus Travellers Studio)	612 & 130
Haymarket, Theatre Royal 1821 (1720 Little Theatre in the Hay Market)	905
Hen & Chickens, Highbury (reopened 1998)	50
Her Majesty's (His Majesty's) 1897, Haymarket (1st 1705 14 Queen's then 1714 1837 Kings; 2nd 1791; 3rd 1869)	1216
Hicks 1906 (see Globe 3)	
Hippodrome (see London Hippodrome)	
Holborn Empire 1857, High Holborn (1857 Weston's Music Hall, 1887 Royal Holborn, rebuilt as Holborn Empire 1905, blitzed 1841 demolished 1960)	2000
Holborn Theatre Royal 1866, High Holborn (renamed Mirror, then Duke's before being burnt down & demolished 1880s)	
Holland Park c.1960	826
Holloway Empire 1899, Holloway Rd (cinema in 1924, demolished 1953)	1200
Hope 1613, Southwark (demolished 1687)	

Hoxton Hall 1864, Hoxton	
ICA (Institute of Contemporary Arts) 1948, The Mall	
Ilford Hippodrome 1908, Ilford (blitzed 1941)	3000
Imperial 1876, Westminster (opened as Royal Aquarium — demolished 1907 now site of Westminster Central Hall)	
Intimate 1935, Palmers Green	458
Irving 1951, Leicester Square (closed 1964)	
Islington Empire (see Grand, Islington)	
Jermyn St. 1994, Westminster	70
Judi Dench 1971, Crouch Hill (studio theatre)	
Kenneth More 1974, Ilford	365
Kennington 1898, Kennington Park Rd. (sold for flats 1950)	1350
Kenwood House Open Air, Hampstead Lane (open air summer concerts in neo-classical mansion)	
Kilburn Empire 1906, Kilburn High Rd.	2000
Kilburn Palace 1866, Belsize Rd.	500
King's (see Her Majesty's)	
King's, Hammersmith 1902, Hammersmith Road (later a BBC theatre, demolished1963)	1700
King's Cross 1830, Liverpool St. (demolished 1880)	360
King's Cross Coach Station 2001 (converted coach station)	
King's Head 1970s, Islington	
King's Road 1910, Chelsea	438
Kingsway 1907, Great Queen Street (opened as the Novelty theatre in 1882, then Folies Dramatiques/Jodrell/New Queen's/Great Queen Street, rebuilt as Kingsway 1907, damaged in the Blitz, demolished 1956)	564
Landor 1995, Clapham	
Latchmere 1982, Battersea Park Road	
Leicester Square 1930 (2000 on opening but quickly converted into a cinema with 1763 seats)	2000
Lewisham (see Broadway)	
Lewisham Hippodrome 1911, Catford (demolished1961)	2500
Lilian Baylis (see Sadler's Wells)	200
Lincoln's Inn Fields 1 1656 (closed 1705)	
Lincoln's Inn Fields 2 1714 (closed 1744, demolished 1848)	
Little 1910, John Street (damaged by bombs 1917 — reopened 1920, blitzed 1941 — demolished1949)	377
Little 1938, North Street, Bromley	112
London Apollo (see Apollo Hammersmith)	
London Arena 1989 (Docklands redevelopment project)	500-12500
London Casino (see Prince Edward)	1800
London Hippodrome 1900, Leicester Square (1958 renamed Talk of the Town — closed 1982 & became a night club)	1340
London Palladium 1910, Argyll Street (1st Hengler's Grand Circque 1871)	2286
London Pavilion 1891, Piccadilly Circus (1st 1861; 2nd 1885; 3rd converted to a 1180 seater cinema in 1934, 1980s night club complex)	1080
Lyceum 1904, Wellington Street (1st 1771 destroyed by fire 1831; 2nd 1834 closed 1903) (named Theatre Royal, English Opera House, Royal Lyceum on different occasions — closed 1939, became a dance hall in 1945 then theatre again in 1996)	2200
Lyric 1888, Shaftesbury Avenue	932
Lyric, Hammersmith 1895 (1889 Lyric Hall; rebuilt 1890 as Lyric Opera House, demolished 1972 — rebuilt 1979)	550
Lyttelton (see National)	
MacOwan 1963, Logan Place (LAMDA theatre)	110
Man in the Moon c. 1980, Chelsea (closed 2004)	
Marlborough 1903, Islington (became a cinema in 1919, closed 1957, demolished 1962)	
Mary Wallace 1961, Twickenham	96
Marylebone Music Hall 1857 (closed 1894)	
May Fair 1963, Berkeley Square (originally the hotel ballroom)	310
Melville (see Brixton)	
Mercury 1933, Ladbroke Road	130
Mermaid 1959, Blackfriars	498
Metropolitan 1897, Edgware Road (1st 1862 as Turnham's Grand Concert Hall seating 4000, demolished1963)	1800
Middlesex (see Winter Garden)	
Mile End Empire 1885, Stepney (1st Lusby's Music Hall destroyed by fire in 1884, opened as the Paragon, renamed in 1912)	2000
Millfield 1988, Edmonton	300
Mirror (see Holborn Theatre Royal)	
National, South Bank (Lyttelton 1976/Olivier 1976/Cottesloe 1977)	900/1100/350
National Film 1952, South Bank	
Network 1992 (formerly New Arch — under Waterloo Station)	70
New 1, 1810, Tottenham Street (see Scala)	
New 2, 1903, St. Martin's Lane (renamed the Albery 1972 q.v.)	938
New Ambassadors (see Ambassadors)	
New Cross Empire 1899, New Cross Road (also known as Deptford Empire, demolished late 1950s)	3000
New End 1974, Hampstead (former 19th century mortuary, refurbished 1986)	84
New Lindsey 1949, Kensington (demolished)	164
New London 1973, Drury Lane (on site of Winter Garden q.v.)	1102
New Oxford (see Oxford)	
New Prince's 1911 (see Shaftesbury 2)	
Newington Butts 1572 (now Elephant & Castle site)	
Novelty (see Kingsway)	
Old Barn 1960, Sidcup (part of Rose Bruford College)	96
Old Vic 1818, Waterloo Road (Royal Coburg 1818, Royal Victoria 1833, New Victoria Palace, Royal Victoria Hall, Coffee Tavern)	1067
Olivier (see National)	
Olympia, Kensington 1886 (very large exhibition centre)	
Olympic 1890, Strand (1st Olympic Pavilion 1806, subsequent names included Astley's, Middlesex Amphitheatre, New Pavilion; 2nd rebuilt after fire 1849, demolished 1889; 3rd 1890, closed 1899 & demolished 1905)	
Open Air 1932, Regent's Park (rebuilt 1976 & 2000, originally 3000 in deckchairs)	1182
Opera Comique 1870, Aldwych (closed 1899, demolished 1902 — shared a wall with the Globe 2, its "Rickety Twin")	
Opera House (see Covent Garden, Lyceum, Palace & Stoll)	
Orange Tree 1971, Richmond	170
Oxford 1861, Tottenham Court Road (opened as Oxford Music Hall, renamed New Oxford 1921, closed 1926, demolished 1928)	
Palace 1891, Cambridge Circus (formerly the Royal English Opera House 1891, Palace Theatre of Varieties 1892, Palace 1911)	1400
Palladium & Pavilion (see London Palladium and London Pavilion)	
Paragon (see Mile End Empire)	
Paris, Lower Regent Street (opened as a cinema but quickly taken over by the BBC as a recording studio, demolished c.2000)	500
Parkhurst 1890, Holloway Rd. (closed 1909)	600
Paul Robeson 1989, Hounslow	280
Pavilion 1828, Whitechapel (rebuilt 1856 & 1874 — known as the Drury Lane of the East, damaged in the Blitz, demolished 1961)	
Peacock 1960, Portugal Street	1010
Peckham Hippodrome 1898, Peckham High St. (cinema 1912)	2600
Penge Empire 1915 (later the Essoldo cinema, demolished 1960)	

People's Palace 1886, Mile End Rd, Stepney	1600
Philharmonic (see Grand, Islington)	
Phoenix 1930, Charing Cross Road	1000
Piccadilly 1928, Piccadilly Circus	1200
Pit 1982 (a smaller theatre within the larger Barbican q.v.)	200
Place 1969, Duke's Road, WC1	
Players 1867, Villiers Street (1st 1867 The Arches, renamed 1946 rebuilt in 1990, closed 2002)	258
Playhouse 1907, Charing Cross (1st 1882 Royal Avenue, rebuilt in 1907 — became a BBC studio in 1951 — reverted to a public theatre in 1987)	800
Playhouse 1999, Hampton Hill (plus studio theatre)	198 & 50
Playhouse 1949, Erith	200
Pleasance 1996, Caledonian Road	288
Polish 1982, Kings St, Hammersmith	
Polka 1979, Wimbledon	
Poplar Hippodrome 1905 (converted to cinema 1925, bombed, demolished in 1950)	2500
Portfolio Playhouse 1937, Baker Street (blitzed in the Second World War)	
Prince Charles 1962, Leicester Sq. (converted to cinema 1969)	420
Prince Edward 1930, Old Compton Street (renamed London Casino 1936, cinema 1954-1978, reopened as theatre under original name)	1618
Prince of Wales's 1937, Coventry Street (1st 1884 Prince's, changed to Prince of Wales in 1886)	1100
Prince's 1, 1840 (see St. James's)	
Prince's 2, 1884 (see Prince of Wales)	1062
Prince's 3, 1911 (opened as New Prince's, also see Shaftesbury)	1726
Princess's 1880, Oxford Street (1st 1836 demolished 1880; 2nd 1880 rebuilt as Royal Princess's, closed 1902, demolished 1931)	
Purcell Room 1951, Belvedere Road	370
Putney Hippodrome c.1905, Felsham Rd. (closed 1920s)	1900
Q 1924, north side of Kew Bridge (formerly Prince's Hall, closed 1956)	497
Queen Elizabeth Hall 1951, South Bank	917
Queen's 1 18th Century, Long Acre (opened as St. Martin's Hall, converted into a theatre 1867, closed 1878)	
Queen's 2 1907, Shaftesbury Avenue (blitzed in Second World War, rebuilt 1959)	990
Queen's Royal Opera House 1897, Crouch End (blitzed in Second World War)	
Queen's, Hornchurch 1975 (formerly converted 1913 cinema, opened 1953, demolished 1975)	
Queen's, Poplar 1856 (demolished 1964)	
Queen's Hall, 1895 Langham Place, plus Queen's Small Hall (blitzed 1941)	3000 & 500
Questors 1964, Ealing (plus studio)	350 & 100
Rainbow 1970s (formerly the Astoria, Finsbury Park — closed 1990s and converted into a church)	1500
Red Bull 1605, Clerkenwell (demolished in the 1660s)	
Regent 1 c.1850, Westminster	1500
Regent 2 1922, Kings Cross (opened as Euston Palace of Varieties, 1900 — became a cinema in 1930, demolished 1971)	1300
Regent 3 1974, Regent Street (originally Marlborough Hall 1838 — rebuilt 1911, Polytechnic Great Hall, Polytechnic Theatre, Cameo Poly Cinema)	518
Regent's Park (see Open Air)	
Richmond 1899, Richmond on Thames	840
Riverside Studios 1974, Hammersmith (formerly film and BBC TV studios — now two separate studio theatres)	400 & 156
Rose & Crown, Hampton Wick	
Rose 1587, Bankside (demolished 1605)	
Rose 1994, Sidcup (part of Rose Bruford College)	331
Rotherhithe Hippodrome 1899, Lower Road, Rotherhithe	2000
Round House 1969, Chalk Farm (converted 1847 railway engine shed, closed)	500
Royal Albert Hall 1871, Kensington	5250
Royal Artillery 1863, Woolwich (converted from barracks chapel, reopened after fire in 1905, blitzed in Second World War, closed 1954)	
Royal Connaught 1873, Holborn (also known as Royal Amphitheatre closed 1886 — blitzed and demolished 1941)	
Royal Court 1888, Sloane Square (1st 1870 New Chelsea/ Belgravia/Court on nearby site — split into two theatres in 1969 — Upstairs/Downstairs)	70/395
Royal Festival Hall 1951, South Bank — also includes Queen Elizabeth Hall & Purcell Room	2930
Royal Opera House (see Covent Garden)	
Royal Strand 1831 (see Strand)	
Royalty 1 1787, Well Street (East London Theatre 1813; 2nd Royal Brunswick 1828 collapsed within 3 days of opening)	
Royalty 2 1840, Dean Street (Royal Soho 1840, New Opera House 1850, New Royalty 1861, Royalty 1883, closed 1938, blitzed, demolished 1955)	450
Royalty 3 1960, Kingsway (built on site of London Opera House/ Stoll)	1000
Rudolf Steiner 1926, Park Road, Regents Park	
Sadler's Wells 1931, Rosebery Avenue (1st 1683 Sadler's Musick House; 2nd 1765 rebuilt several times, includes Lilian Baylis Theatre 1980)	1500/200
Salisbury Court 1620s, Fleet Street (burnt down 1666)	
Saville 1931, Shaftesbury Avenue (rebuilt as 2 cinemas 1970)	1200
Savoy 1881, Strand (rebuilt 1929)	1158
Scala 1905, Charlotte Street (1st 1772 King's Concert Room/New/Tottenham Street Theatre/Regency/West London/Fitzroy/Prince of Wales closed 1884, demolished 1903 — then rebuilt as Scala, closed 1968, demolished 1972)	1139
Shaftesbury 1 1888, Shaftesbury Avenue (blitzed 1941)	1240
Shaftesbury 2 1911, Shaftesbury Avenue (New Prince's/ Prince's, renamed Shaftesbury 1963)	1404
Shakespeare 1896, Lavender Hill (cinema 1920s, demolished 1957)	1205
Shaw 1971, Euston Road (closed mid 1990s, reopened 2004)	450
Shepherds Bush Empire 1903, Hammersmith (became the BBC TV Theatre from 1953 1995 before returning to its original public theatre role)	1638
Shoreditch Empire 1894 (opened as South London Music Hall 1856, demolished 1935)	1000
Shoreditch Olympia 1837, Shoreditch High St. (rebuilt twice after fire in 1866 — cinema in 1920s, demolished 1940)	2500
Soho 2000, Dean Street (plus studio theatre)	144 & 85
South London Palace 1860, Lambeth (rebuilt after 1869 fire, blitzed 1940, demolished 1955)	4000
South London 1967, Norwood (two theatres, Bell & Prompt Corner)	100 & 65
Space 1996, Isle of Dogs (converted church)	100
Spitalfields Market (closed mid 1990s)	
St George's Hall 1867, Langham Place (opened as St. George's Theatre/Opera House Matinee 1897, Maskelyne's 1922 — acquired by BBC in 1933 & housed BBC theatre organ, blitzed September 1940)	1500
St. James' Hall, Piccadilly (demolished 1893 and replaced by the Piccadilly Hotel)	
St. James's 1835, King Street, Piccadilly (briefly renamed Prince's 1840-2, sold 1957 and demolished)	950
St. John's, Smith Square 1728, Westminster (deconsecrated church now used for BBC concerts and recitals)	780
St. Martin's 1916, Shaftesbury Avenue (the second of a pair, the other being the Ambassadors in 1913)	550
Standard 1830s, Shoreditch (rebuilt 1866 after fire, became Olympia Music Hall, cinema 1926, bombed & demolished 1940)	2090
Stoll 1911, Kingsway (opened as London Opera House, cinema 1917, theatre again 1941, demolished 1957, now site of Royalty 3 q.v.)	2090
Strand 1, 1832 (renamed Punch's Playhouse 1850, rebuilt 1882 as Royal Strand,demolished 1905, now site of Aldwych underground station)	
Strand 2, 1905, Aldwych (opened as Waldorf, then Whitney 1911 & renamed Strand in 1913)	1067
Stratford East (see Theatre Royal, Stratford East)	500
Streatham Hill 1929 (now an ice rink)	2900
Surrey, Blackfriars Road 1809 (originally called Royal Circus, rebuilt after fire in 1865, demolished 1934)	
Swan 1595, Bankside (closed 1630s)	
Talk of the Town (see London Hippodrome)	
Tavistock House, Tavistock Square (mid 19th Century private theatre at the home of Charles Dickens)	
Terry's 1887, Strand (closed 1910 and became a cinema demolished 1923)	888

Theatre 1576, Shoreditch (removed 1598 to form the Globe)
Theatre 62, West Wickham (see Wickham)
Theatre Royal (see Covent Garden, Drury Lane & Haymarket)
Theatre Royal 1884, Stratford East (rebuilt 1902) 500
Tivoli 1890, Strand (cinema erected on site in 1923, demolished 1957) 1000
Toole's 1869, Strand (opened as Royal Charing Cross, reopened as the Folly 1876, Toole's 1892, demolished 1896) . . . 600
Torch 1938, Knightsbridge (closed 1954)
Tower 1952, Islington 156
Trafalgar Square (see Duke of York's)
Tricycle 1980, Kilburn Road (rebuilt after fire in 1987) 225
Trocadero 1820, Great Windmill St. (became a restaurant)
UCL, University College London (see Bloomsbury)
Unity 1937, St Pancras (burnt down 1975)
Upstairs at the Gatehouse 1997, Highgate Village (opened 1895 as Highgate Hall)
Vanbrugh 1954, Gower Street (RADA theatre) 200
Variety 1870, Hoxton (cinema after 1910) 800
Vaudeville 1926, Strand (1st 1870; 2nd 1891) 690
Vauxhall (17th & 18th Century pleasure gardens with an open air theatre — closed 1859)
Venue, Leicester Square 2002 350
Victoria Palace 1911, Victoria Street (1st Moy's Music Hall 1840, Royal Standard Music Hall 1863) 1517
Waldorf (see Strand)
Wapping 2000 (converted power station)
Warehouse 1977, Croydon 100
Watergate 1949, Strand (closed 1956)
Watermans Arts Centre, Brentford 1991 239
Wembley Arena 1934 11000
Wembley Conference Centre 1976 (Grand Hall) 2700
West London, Edgware Road 1832 (Royal Pavilion/Portman/Royal West London/Marylebone/Royal Alfred, then cinema, blitzed 1941, burnt down 1962)
Westminster 1931, Palace Street 646
Westminster Central Hall 1912 (main hall & several auditoriums including Lecture Room/Library each seating 500 — site of former Imperial theatre) . . . 2350
White Bear 1988, Kennington Park Road 45
Whitefriars 1605, Fleet Street (closed 1629)
Whitehall 1930, Whitehall (became the Trafalgar Studios in 2004 with 380 and 100 seat spaces) 628
Whitney (see Strand 2)
Wickham (Theatre 62)1973, West Wickham 80
Wigmore Hall 1901, Wigmore Street 540
Willesden Hippodrome 1907, (opened as Willesden Empire, blitzed 1940)
Wilton's Music Hall 1858, Whitechapel
Wimbledon 1910, Broadway (plus studio theatre) . . . . 2000 & 80
Winchester Music Hall 1856, Southwark (opened as Surrey Music Hall 1848, demolished 1878)
Windmill 1931, Great Windmill Street (converted from cinema Palais de Luxe 1910, cinema 1964, now a night club) . . . 322
Winter Garden 1919, Drury Lane (1st 1851 Middlesex Music Hall; 2nd New Middlesex Theatre of Varieties, rebuilt 1919, demolished 1965,
    now site of New London q.v.) 1640
Wood Green Empire 1912 2000
Woolwich Empire 1900 ((rebuilt from Theatre Royal c.1880, also known as Barnard's, closed 1958, demolished 1960) . . . 1800
Woolwich Hippodrome 1900 (converted to cinema by 1925) 1700
Wyndham's 1899, Charing Cross Road 750
Young Vic 1970, Lambeth 450

◁ This splendid picture of the Old Vic (built in 1818) was taken in 1922 and shows a marked resemblance to a railway warehouse. It was also known as the Royal Victoria Hall as painted on the side of the building. Although primarily associated with Shakespeare and grand opera, and despite being south of the Thames, it has always been regarded as a West End theatre. It is difficult to know exactly what the piles of rubble are but tramlines can be clearly seen on the cobbled street. In 1970 the Young Vic theatre company was built on a former bomb site nearby and opened by Sybil Thorndike. John Pearce was the original Victorian proprietor of the in-house temperance restaurant, later nicknamed "Pearce and Plenty" because of large portions and good value for money. It closed in the late-Twenties when London Council demanded greater financial accountability.

▷ The Alexandra at Stoke Newington was typical of many places of mass entertainment in the London suburbs. Designed by Frank Matcham and built in 1897 when theatre going was at its height, there was never a thought that its 2,000 seats might become a liability. However, firstly wind-up gramophone records in the early-20th Century followed by radio in the 1920s, meant that the audience could now hear their favourite stars in their own home. The advent of television sounded the death knell for many similar venues and although it staggered along as a post-war boxing venue and cinema this picture shows a forlorn building up for sale, soon to be demolished and replaced by flats.

APPENDIX 5

FIRST PRODUCTIONS OF FAMOUS LONDON PANTOMIMES

Aladdin (The Wonderful Lamp)	Covent Garden	1788
Babes in the Wood	Haymarket	1793
Beauty and the Best	Adelphi	1821
Blue Beard	Covent Garden	1791
Cinderella	Drury Lane	1804
Dick Whittington	Covent Garden	1814
Fair One with the Golden Locks (Goldilocks)	Haymarket	1843
Forty Thieves (Ali Baba)	Drury Lane	1806
Goody Two Shoes	Sadler's Wells	1803
Gulliver's Travels	Covent Garden	1817
Hop o' My Thumb	Covent Garden	1831
House That Jack Built	Olympic	1817
Humpty Dumpty	Sadler's Wells	1832
Jack and Jill	Lyceum	1812
Jack and the Beanstalk	Drury Lane	1819
Jack the Giant Killer	Sadler's Wells	1803
Little Bo-Peep	Adelphi	1831
Little Jack Horner	Drury Lane	1816
Little Red Riding Hood	Sadler's Wells	1803
Mother Goose	Covent Garden	1806
Old Mother Hubbard	Covent Garden	1833
Peter Pan	Duke of York's	1904
Puss in Boots	Covent Garden	1832
Robinson Crusoe	Drury Lane	1781
Sinbad the Sailor	Royalty	1805
Sleeping Beauty	Surrey	1812
Valentine and Orson	Sadler's Wells	1795
White Cat	Lyceum	1811
Yellow Dwarf	Astley's Royal Amphitheatre	1807

SOME FAMOUS PANTOMIME DAMES

Nat Jackley   Norman Evans   Jon Pertwee   Reg Dixon

Billy Dainty   Cyril Fletcher   Danny La Rue   Arthur Askey

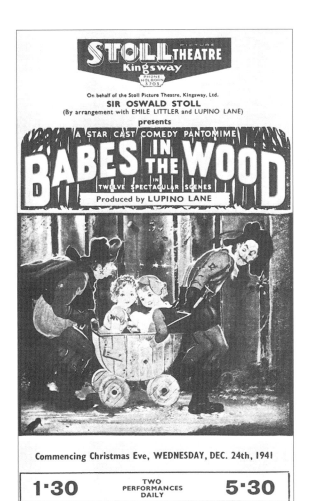

△ An illustration from the first ever production of "Puss in Boots" at Covent Garden in 1832.

◁ A wartime offering of "Babes in the Wood". Hitler destroyed several London theatres but was unable to stop the British public from enjoying their pantomimes. The Stoll was opened in 1911 as the London Opera House but was demolished in 1957. Part of the site is now occupied by the Royalty theatre.

◁ No prizes for guessing that in 1959 "Humpty Dumpty" was played by Harry Secombe.

▽ Part of the magic of pantomime is slapstick comedy. Here, Bill Tasker pours cold water inside the trousers of Shadows' Hank Marvin (left) and John Rostill during "Cinderella" at the Palladium in 1966.

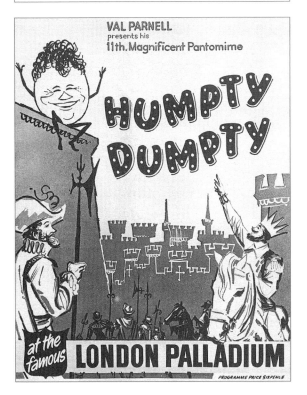

APPENDIX 6

SOME FAMOUS COMPOSERS, LIBRETTISTS, IMPRESARIOS, MUSICAL DIRECTORS AND ENTERTAINERS INVOLVED WITH LONDON MUSICALS

Abbott, Russ 1947-
Ackland, Joss 1928-
Adams, Cliff 1923-2001
Addinsell, Richard 1904-1977
Addison, John 1920-1998
Adler, Richard 1921-
Adrian, Max 1903-1973
Ager, Milton 1893-1979
Ahlers, Anny 1906-1933
Ainsworth, Alyn 1924-1990
Albery, Bronson 1881-1971
Albery, Donald 1914-1988
Albery, James 1838-1889
Allen, Chesney 1894-1982
Allgood, Sara 1879-1950
Alpar, Gitta 1900-1991
Alwyn, Kenneth 1928-
Ambrose, Bert 1897-1971
Anderson, Daphne 1922-
Andrews, Julie 1935-
Angers, Avril 1922-
Ansell, John 1874-1948
Archer, Harry 1888-1960
Arkell, Reginald 1882-1959
Arlen, Harold 1915-1986
Armitage, Richard 1928-
Arnaud, Yvonne 1892-1958
Arne, Thomas 1710-1778
Arnold, Doris 1904-1969
Arnold, Tom 1893-1969
Asche, Oscar 1871-1936
Ashcroft, Peggy 1907-1991
Ashley, Henry 1831-1890
Ashley, Robert ?-c1945
Askey, Arthur 1900-1982
Astaire, Adele 1898-1981
Astaire, Fred 1899-1987
Atkin, Pete 1945-
Augarde, Adrienne 1882-1913
Augarde, Amy 1868-1959
Austin, Frederic 1872-1952
Ayckbourn, Alan 1939-
Ayer, Nat 1887-1952
Bacharach, Burt 1928-
Bacon, Max 1906-1969
Baddeley, Hermione 1906-1986
Baker, George 1885-1976
Baker, Hylda 1905-1986
Balfe, Michael 1808-1870
Ball, Michael 1962-
Banks, Leslie 1890-1952
Barbour, Joyce 1901-1977
Barker, Ronnie 1929-
Barnard, Ivor 1887-1953
Barnes, Binnie 1903-1998
Barnes, Sally 1922-1985
Barrie, JM (James Matthew) 1860-1937
Barrington, Rutland 1853-1922

Barry, John 1933-
Bart, Lionel 1930-1999
Baskcomb, AW 1880-1939
Bass, Alfie 1921-1987
Bates, Thorpe 1883-1958
Bath, Hubert 1883-1945
Batt, Mike 1950-
Baxter, Stanley 1926-
Baynes, Sidney 1879-1938
Beaumont, Hugh 'Binkie' 1908-1973
Beaumont, Roma 1913-2001
Beckwith, Reginald 1908-1965
Belmore, Bertha 1882-1953
Benatzky, Ralph 1884-1957
Benedictus, David 1938-
Benjamin, Louis 1922-1994
Bennett, Alan 1934-
Bennett, Billy 1887-1942
Benson, George 1943-
Bentine, Michael 1922-1996
Bentley, Dick 1907-1995
Berkeley, Ballard 1904-1988
Berlin, Irving 1888-1989
Bernstein, Leonard 1918-1990
Berry, WH 1872-1951
Best, Edna 1900-1974
Bidgood, Harry 1898-1957
Bigg, Julian 1961-
Birtwistle, Harrison 1934-
Black, Cilla 1943-
Black, Don 1936-
Black, George 1890-1945
Black, Stanley 1913-2002
Blackman, Honor 1927-
Blair, Lionel 1931-
Blakeley, James 1873-1915
Blaney, Norah 1896-1983
Blessed, Brian 1936-
Blezard, William 1921-2003
Blore, Eric 1887-1959
Bock, Jerry 1928-
Bolton, Guy 1884-1979
Bond, Jessie 1853-1942
Booth, Connie 1944-
Booth, Webster 1902-1984
Borge, Victor 1909-2000
Borodin, Alexander 1833-1887
Boublil, Alain 1941-
Boughton, Rutland 1878-1960
Boulter, John 1931-
Bovill, CH 1891-1930?
Boyd-Jones, Ernest 1869-1904
Boyle, Billy 1945-
Bradfield, Louis 1866-1913
Bragg, Melvyn 1939-
Braham, Philip 1882-1934
Brahms, Caryl 1901-1882
Brandon, Johnny 1926-

Brandram, Rosina 1846-1907
Brandreth, Gyles 1948-
Breeze, Alan 1909-1980
Brel, Jacques 1929-1978
Brent, Romney 1902-1976
Bresslaw, Bernard 1934-1993
Bretherton, Freddy 1908-1954
Brett, Jeremy 1933-1995
Bricusse, Leslie 1931-
Bridgewater, Leslie 1893-1975
Bright, Gerald alias Geraldo, q.v.
Brightman, Sarah 1960-
Brisson, Carl 1895-1958
Britton, Tony 1924-
Brodszky, Nicholas 1905-1958
Bron, Eleanor 1938-
Bronhill, June 1927-
Brooke-Taylor, Tim 1940
Broones, Martin 1892-1971
Brown, Georgia 1933-1992
Brown, Joe 1941-
Browne, Irene 1896-1965
Bruce, Carol 1919-
Bryan, Dora 1924-
Brynner, Yul 1915-1985
Buchanan, Jack 1891-1957
Burke, Marie 1894-1988
Burke, Patricia 1917-2003
Burke, Tom 1890-1969
Burnaby, Davy 1881-1949
Burton, Richard 1925-1984
Butterworth, Clara 1890-1999
Butterworth, Peter 1919-1979
Bygraves, Max 1922-
Byng, Douglas 1893-1987
Byng, George 1862-1932
Cadell, Jean 1884-1967
Cadell, Simon 1950-1996
Caesar, Irving 1895-1996
Cahn, Sammy 1913-1993
Cairncross, James 1915-
Caldicot, Richard 1908-1995
Calloway, Cab 1907-1994
Calthrop, Donald 1888-1940
Calthrop, Gladys 1894-1980
Cameron, Violet 1863-1919
Campbell, Judy 1916-2004
Cannon, Esma 1892-1972
Cardew, Phil 1903-1960
Carlisle, Elsie 1897-1977
Carmichael, Hoagy 1899-1981
Carmichael, Ian 1920-
Carne, Judy 1939-
Carr, Frank Osmond 1858-1916
Carr, Jane 1909-1957
Carr, Michael 1904-1968
Carrott, Jasper 1945-
Carson, Jean 1925-
Carte, Richard D'Oyly 1844-1901
Carter, Desmond 1895-1939
Caryll, Ivan 1860-1921
Cass, Ronald 1923-
Castle, Roy 1932-1994
Catley, Gwen 1906-1996
Cavanagh, Peter 1914-1981
Cellier, Alfred 1844-1891
Cellier, Frank 1884-1948
Chapman, Edward 1901-1977
Chapman, Graham 1941-1989
Chappelle, Frederick 1895-?
Charig, Phil 1902-1960
Charisse, Cyd 1922-
Charlot, André 1882-1956
Charnin, Martin 1934-
Chatto, Tom 1920-1982
Chester, Betty 1895-1943
Chevalier, Maurice 1888-1972
Childs, Gilbert 1866-1931
Chisholm, George 1915-1998
Churchill, Diana 1913-1994
Clark, Petula 1932-
Clay, Frederic 1838-1889
Cleese, John 1939-

Lionel Bart

Arthur Schwartz

Howard Dietz

Clements, John 1910-1989
Cliff, Laddie 1891-1937
Clifton, Bernard 1902-1970
Clinton-Baddeley, VC (Victor Clifford) 1900-70
Clutsam, GH (George) 1866-1951
Clyde, June 1909-1987
Coates, Eric 1886-1957
Cochran C.B. (Charles Blake)1872-1951
Cochrane, Peggy 1902-1988
Coffin, Hayden 1862-1935
Coghill, Nevill 1899-1980
Cole, George 1925-
Coleman, Cy 1929-2004
Coles, Jack ?-1991
Collingwood, Lawrence 1887-1982
Collins, Anthony 1893-1963
Collins, Jose 1887-1958
Collins, Lottie 1866-1910
Collinson, Francis M 1898-1985
Comber, Bobbie 1890-1942
Comden, Betty 1919-
Compton, Fay 1894-1978
Connelly, Reg 1895-1963
Connolly, Billy 1942-
Connor, Kenneth 1916-1993
Conrad, Con 1891-1938
Conti, Italia 1874-1946
Conti, Tom 1941-
Cook, Peter 1937-1995
Cooper, Gladys 1889-1971
Cooper, Terence 1933-1997
Cooper, Tommy 1921-1984
Coote, Robert 1909-1982
Corbett, Ronnie 1930-
Coslow, Sam 1902-1982
Cotton, Billy 1899-1969
Coupland, Diana 1929-
Courtneidge, Cicely 1893-1980
Courtneidge, Robert 1859-1939
Covington, Julie 1947-
Coward, Noel 1899-1973
Coyle, John E 1894-1964
Coyne, Joseph 1867-1941
Cranko, John 1927-1973
Craven, Gemma 1950-
Crawford, Michael 1942-
Cribbins, Bernard 1928-
Crisham, Walter 1906-1985
Croft, David 1922-
Crook, John 1852-1922
Croom-Johnston, Austen 1909-1964
Crowther, Leslie 1933-1996
Cryer, Barry 1935-
Currie, Finlay 1878-1968
Curry, Tim 1946-
Cutler, Kate 1870-1955
Cuvillier, Charles 1877-1955
D'Abo, Mike 1944-
D'Amato, Chappie 1897-1976
Dahl, Roald 1916-1990
Dainty, Billy 1927-1986

Dale, Jim 1935-
Dall, Evelyn 1918-
Dane, Clemence 1888-1965
Daniels, Bebe 1901-1971
Dankworth, John 1927-
Darbyshire, Michael ?-1979
Dare, Phyllis 1890-1975
Dare, Zena 1885-1975
Darewski, Herman 1883-1947
Darewski, Max 1894-1929
David, Hal 1921-
Davidson, Jim 1954-
Davies, Betty Ann 1910-1955
Davies, Irving 1926-2002
Davies, Tudor 1892-1958
Davies, Windsor 1930-
Davis, Carl 1936-
Davis, Harry 1901-1996
Day, Edith 1896-1971
Day, Frances 1908-1984
Dean, Basil 1888-1978
De Courville, Albert 1888-1960
De Sylva, Buddy 1895-1950
De Valois, Ninette 1898-2001
Decker, Diana 1926-
Delfont, Bernard 1909-1994
Delgado, Roger 1918-1973
Delysia, Alice 1889-1979
Dench, Judi 1934-
Desmond, Florence 1905-1993
Desmonde, Jerry 1908-1967
Dibdin, Charles 1745-1814
Dickson, Barbara 1947-
Dickson, Dorothy 1893-1995
Dietz, Howard 1896-1983
Dixon, Adele 1908-1992
Dixon, Conway 1874-1943
Dixon, Reg 1914-1983
Docker, Robert 1918-1992
Dodds, Jamieson 1885-1942
Dods, Marcus 1918-1984
Dolin, Anton 1904-1983
Dolman, Richard 1895-?
Drake, Charlie 1925-
Drayton, Alfred 1881-1949
Dring, Madeleine 1923-1977
Driver, Betty 1920-
Duffield, Kenneth 1885-1958
Duke, Vernon 1903-1969
Duna, Steffy 1910-1992
Dunhill, Thomas 1877-1946
Dunn, Clive 1920-
Duprez, Fred 1884-1938
Dvorak, Anton 1841-1904
Dyall, Valentine 1908-1985
Dyrenforth, James 1895-1973
Eaton, Shirley 1937-
Eaton, Wallas 1917-1995
Ebb, Fred 1932-2004
Eddington, Paul 1927-1995
Edgar, Marriott 1880-1951

Ediss, Connie 1871-1934
Edwardes, George 1852-1915
Edwards, Jimmy 1920-1988
Elizalde, Fred 1908-1979
Elliot, TS (Thomas Stearns) 1888-1965
Elliott, Madge 1898-1955
Ellis, Mary 1897-2003
Ellis, Vivian 1903-1996
Elsie, Lily 1886-1962
Elton, Ben 1959-
Emmanuel, Ivor 1927-
Emney, Fred 1900-1980
Essex, David 1947-
Etting, Ruth 1897-1978
Evans, Jessie 1918-1993
Evans, Norman 1901-1962
Eysler, Edmund 1874-1949
Eyton, Frank 1894-1962
Fairbrother, Sydney 1872-1941
Fall, Leo 1873-1925
Fancourt, Darrell 1888-1953
Faris, Alexander 1921-
Farjeon, Herbert 1887-1945
Farjeon, Violetta 1881-1965
Farnie, HB (Harold Bulwer) 1820-1889
Farrar, Gwen 1899-1944
Felix, Hugo 1866-1934
Felton, Felix 1911-1972
Ferguson, Lester 1917-1995
Fenoulhet, Paul 1906-1979
Fiander, Lewis 1938-
Field, Sid 1904-1950
Fielding, Harold 1916–2003
Fielding, Fenella 1934-
Fields, Dorothy 1904-1974
Fields, Gracie 1898-1979
Fields, Herbert 1897-1958
Fields, Joseph 1885-1966
Fields, Lew 1867-1941
Fields, Tommy 1908-1988
Filippi, Rosina 1867-1930
Finck, Herman 1872-1939
Finlay, Frank 1926-
Flanagan, Bud 1896-1968
Flanders, Michael 1922-1975
Fletcher, Cyril 1913-2005
Fletcher, Percy 1879-1932
Flotsam, see BC Hilliam
Formby, George 1904-1961
Formby, George Sr. 1877-1921
Forsyth, Bruce 1928-
Fortune, John 1939-
Fosse, Bob 1927-1987
Fox, Roy 1901-1982
Francis, Dai 1930-2003
Francis, Dick 1889-1949
Frankau, Ronald 1894-1951
Frankel, Benjamin 1906-1973
Fraser, Bill 1908-1987
Fraser-Simson, Harold 1878-1944
Frece, Lauri de 1881-1921

149

Freed, Arthur 1894-1973
French, Harold 1897-1997
French, Hugh 1910-1976
French, Percy 1854-1920
Friedlander, William B 1885-1968
Friml, Rudolf 1879-1972
Frohmann, Charles 1861-1915
Fry, Christopher 1907-
Fry, Stephen 1957-
Furber, Douglas 1885-1961
Gail, Zoe 1920-
Galton, Ray 1930-
Galvani, Dino 1890-1960
Garden, Grahame 1943-
Gardiner, Reginald 1903-1980
Garrick, David 1717-1779
Garrick, John 1902-1966
Gawthorne, Peter 1884-1962
Gay, John 1685-1732
Gay, Maisie 1883-1945
Gay, Noel 1898-1954
Gayson, Eunice 1931-
Geraldo, 1904-1974
Gerard, Teddie 1892-1942
German, Edward 1862-1935
Gerrard, Gene 1892-1971
Gershwin, George 1898-1937
Gershwin, Ira 1896-1983
Gesner, Clark 1938-2002
Gibbons, Carroll 1903-1954
Gideon, Melville 1884-1933
Gielgud, John 1904-2000
Gilbert, William Schwenk 1836-1911
Gilbert, Jean 1879-1942
Gilbert, Olive c1900-1981
Gilliam, Terry 1940-
Gilliland, Helen 1897-1942
Gilmore, Peter 1931-
Gingold, Hermione 1897-1987
Glanville, Brian 1931-
Godfrey, Arthur 1868-1939
Goehr, Walter 1903-1960
Goffin, Cora 1902-2004
Gold, Jimmy 1886-1967
Gonella, Nat 1908-1998
Goodall, Howard 1958-
Gordon, Hal 1894-1946
Gordon, Marjorie 1893-1983
Gordon, Noele 1923-1985
Gould, Elliott 1938-
Gowers, Patrick 1936-
Grable, Betty 1916-1973
Grade, Lew 1906-1998

Graham, Harry 1874-1936
Grainer, Ron 1922-1981
Grattan, Harry 1867-1951
Graves, George 1876-1949
Graves, Peter 1911-1994
Gray, Dolores 1924-2002
Gray, Dulcie 1919-
Gray, 'Monsewer' Eddie 1898-1969
Gray, Sally 1918-
Green, Adolph 1915-2002
Green, Benny 1927-1998
Green, Danny 1903-1973
Green, Johnny (John) 1908-1989
Green, Phil 1911-1982
Greenbank, Harry 1865-1899
Greenbank, Percy 1878-1968
Greenbaum, Hyam 1901-1942
Greene, Evie 1878-1917
Greenwood, Charlotte 1892-1977
Gregg, Hubert 1914-2004
Grenfell, Joyce 1910-1979
Grey, Clifford 1887-1941
Grieg, Edvard 1843-1907
Griffiths, Derek 1946-
Grimaldi, Joseph 1792-1809
Grimaldi, Marion 1926-
Grossmith, George 1847-1912
Grossmith, George Jr. 1874-1935
Grossmith, Lawrence 1877-1944
Grun, Bernard 1901-1972
Guest, Val 1911-
Guetary, Georges 1915-1997
Gwenn, Edmund 1875-1959
Gwynne, Nell 1642-1687
Gwyther, Geoffrey 1890-1944
Hackforth, Norman 1908-1996
Hackney, Pearl 1916-
Haddon, Peter 1898-1962
Hague, Albert 1920-2001
Hahn, Reynaldo 1875-1947
Haigh, Kenneth 1931-
Hale, Binnie 1899-1984
Hale, Robert 1874-1940
Hale, Sonnie 1902-1959
Hall, Adelaide 1901-1993
Hall, Henry 1898-1989
Hamilton, Ord 1899-1955
Hammerstein, Oscar II 1895-1960
Hampshire, Susan 1937-
Hancock, Sheila 1933-
Handl, Irene 1901-1987
Hanley, Jimmy 1918-1970
Hanson, John 1921-1998

Harbach, Otto 1873-1963
Hardwicke, Cedric 1893-1964
Hardy, Robert 1925-
Hare, Doris 1905-2000
Hare, Robertson 1891-1979
Harper, Gerald 1929-
Harnick, Sheldon 1924-
Harris, Augustus 1852-1896
Harris, Jack 1901-1976
Harris, Jet 1939-
Harris, Richard 1930-2002
Harrison, George 1943-2001
Harrison, Rex 1908-1990
Hart, Charles 1962-
Hart, Lorenz 1895-1943
Harvey, Laurence 1927-1973
Harvey, Maurice 1877-1944
Hassall, Christopher 1912-1963
Hatch, Tony 1940-
Hawk, Jeremy 1918-2002
Hawkins, John 1949-
Hawthorne, Nigel 1929-2001
Hawtrey, Charles 1858-1923
Hawtrey, Charles 1914-1988
Hayes, Melvyn 1935-
Hayes, Patricia 1909-1998
Hayter, James 1907-1983
Hazell, Hy 1919-1970
Heal, Joan 1922-1998
Hearne, Richard 1909-1979
Heath, Ted 1900-1969
Hedley, HB 1890-1931
Helier, Ivy St. 1890-1971
Hemmings, David 1941-2003
Henderson, Dickie 1922-1985
Henderson, Ray 1896-1970
Heneker, David 1906-2001
Henson, Leslie 1891-1957
Heppner, Sam 1913-1983
Herbert, AP (Alan Patrick) 1890-1971
Herbert, Victor 1859-1924
Herman, Jerry 1933-
Heslop, Charles 1883-1966
Hess, Nigel 1955-
Hicks, Seymour 1871-1954
Hill, Richard 1942-
Hill, Ronnie 1911-1991
Hill, Rose 1914-2003
Hilliam, BC (Bentley Collingwood)1890-1968
Hird, Thora 1911-2003
Hirsch, Hugo 1884-1961
Hirsch, Louis 1887-1924
Hobbs, Jack 1893-1968
Hobson, Valerie 1917-1998
Hockridge, Edmund 1922-
Hodge, Patricia 1946-
Hoey, Iris 1885-1979
Hoffman, Al 1902-1960
Holland, Jeffrey 1946-
Hollingshead, John 1827-1904
Holloway, Laurie 1938-
Holloway, Stanley 1890-1982
Holmes, Leslie 1901-1960
Holmes A'Court, Janet 1943-
Holmes A'Court, Robert 1937-1990
Hood, Basil 1864-1917
Hopkins, Antony 1921-
Horan, Edward 1898-?
Horwitt, Arnold 1918-1977
Houston, Billie 1906-1961
Houston, Renee 1902-1980
Howard, Norah 1901-1968
Howard, Sydney 1885-1946
Howerd, Frankie 1917-1992
Howes, Bobby 1895-1972
Howes, Sally Ann 1930-
Hudd, Roy 1936-
Hulbert, Claude 1900-1964
Hulbert, Jack 1892-1978
Hulme-Beaman, SG (Sydney George)
    1887-1932
Humphries, Barry 1934-
Huntley, GP 1868-1927
Huntley, GP Jr. 1904-1971
Huntley-Wright, Betty 1911-
Hutch, see Leslie Hutchinson
Hutchinson, Leslie (Hutch) 1900-1969
Hyden, Walford 1892-1959
Hylton, Jack 1892-1965
Idle, Eric 1943-
Ifield, Frank 1937-

Frank Loesser

150

Irons, Jeremy 1948-
Irving, Ethel 1869-1963
Jackley, Nat 1909-1988
Jackson, Jack 1907-1978
Jacobi, Victor 1883-1921
Jacobs, Howard 1900-1977
James, Jimmy 1892-1965
James, Sidney 1913-1976
Janis, Elsie 1889-1956
Jay, Isabel 1886-1927
Jeans, Ronald 1887-1973
Jeans, Ursula 1906-1973
Jetsam, see Malcolm McEachern
Jewell, Jimmy 1909-1995
Johnson, Bill 1918-1957
Johnson, Laurie 1927-
Johnstone, Clarence 1885-1953
Jones, Guy 1874-1959
Jones, Leslie Julian 1910-
Jones, Sidney 1861-1946
Jones, Terry 1942-
Jones, Trefor 1902-1965
Jonson, Ben 1573- 1637
Josephs, Wilfred 1927-1997
Joyce, Archibald 1873-1963
June (June Tripp), 1901-1945
Junkin, John 1930-
Kahn, Gus 1886-1941
Kalman, Emmerich 1882-1953
Kalmar, Bert 1884-1947
Kander, John 1927-
Karlin, Miriam 1925-
Katscher, Robert 1894-1942
Kaufman, George 1889-1961
Kaye, Stubby 1918-1997
Kearns, Allen 1894-1956
Keel, Howard (Harold) 1917-2004
Kellam, Ian 1934-
Kendall, Henry 1897-1962
Kennedy, Cheryl 1947-
Kennedy, Jimmy 1902-1984
Kenwright, Bill 1945-
Kerker, Gustave 1857-1923
Kern, Jerome 1885-1945
Kernan, David 1938-
Kerr, Bill 1922-
Kester, Max lyricist ?-1991
Ketelbey, Albert 1875-1959
Keys, Nelson 1886-1939
King, Denis 1939-
Kingsley, Ben 1943-
Kinnear, Roy 1934-1988
Kirkwood, Pat 1921-
Knight, Esmond 1906-1987
Knox, Teddy 1894-1974
Korris, Harry 1891-1971
Kretzmer, Herbert 1925-
Kunneke, Edward 1885-1953
Kunz, Charlie 1896-1958
Kyte, Sydney 1896-1981
La Rue, Danny 1927-
Laine, Cleo 1927-
Lanchester, Elsa 1902-1986
Landis, Jessie Royce 1904-1972
Lane, Lauri 1921-1986
Lane, Lupino 1892-1959
Lang, Harold 1923-1970
Langford, Bonnie 1964-
Lansbury, Angela 1925-
Lapotaire, Jane 1944-
Laurie, John 1897-1980
Lavender, Ian 1946-
Lawrence, Gertrude 1898-1952
Lawson, Wilfrid 1900-1966
Laye, Dilys 1934-
Laye, Evelyn 1900-1996
Layton, Turner 1894-1978
Le Mesurier, John 1912-1983
Lee, Benny 1916-1995
Lee, Bert 1881-1946
Lee, Vanessa 1920-
Lefeuvre, Guy 1883-1950
Legrand, Michel 1932-
Lehar, Franz 1870-1948
Lehmann, Liza 1862-1918
Lehrer, Tom 1928-
Leigh, Mitch 1928-
Leigh, Rowland 1903-1963
Leigh, Walter 1905-1942
Lennon, John 1940-1980
Lennox, Vera 1904-1984

Leno, Dan 1860-1904
Leonard, Queenie 1905-2002
Lerner, Alan Jay 1918-1986
Leslie-Smith, Kenneth 1897-1993
Leslie, Fred 1880-1945
Leslie, Lew 1886-1963
Lester, Mark 1876-?
Levin, Bernard 1928-2004
Levy, Louis 1893-1957
Lillie, Beatrice 1894-1989
Lincke, Paul 1866-1946
Lindo, Olga 1899-1968
Lindsay, Robert 1949-
Lipman, Maureen 1946-
Lipton, Celia 1923-
Lipton, Sydney 1906-1995
Lister, Laurier 1907-
Littler, Emile 1903-1985
Littler, Prince 1901-1973
Littlewood, Joan 1914-2002
Livesey, Jack 1901-1961
Lloyd, Hugh 1923-
Lloyd, Jeremy 1932-
Lloyd, Marie 1870-1922
Lloyd Webber, Andrew 1948-
Lloyd Webber, William 1914-1982
Lockwood, Margaret 1916-1990
Loesser, Frank 1910-1969
Loewe, Frederick 1904-1988
Logan, Ella 1913-1969
Logan, Jimmy 1928-2001
Lom, Herbert 1917-
Lonsdale, Frederick 1881-1954
Loraine, Violet 1886-1956
Losch, Tilly 1904-1975
Loss, Joe 1909-1990
Lotis, Dennis 1925-
Lovat, Nancie 1900-1946
Lowe, Arthur 1915-1982
Lubbock, Mark 1898-1986
Lupino, Barry 1882-1962
Lupino, Stanley 1894-1942
Lupino, Wallace 1898-1961
Lynn, Ralph 1882-1962
Lynne, Carol 1918-
Lyon, Ben 1901-1979
Lytton, Henry 1867-1936
MacColl, Ewan 1915-1989
MacCunn, Hamish 1868-1916
MacDermot, Galt 1928-
MacDermot, Robert 1910-
MacFarland, Dorothea 1920-1988
Macfarlane, Elsa 1899-1975
Mackey, Percival 1894-1950
Mackinder, Lionel 1868-1915
Mackintosh, Cameron 1946-
Madoc, Ruth 1943-
Malleson, Miles 1888-1969
Malo, Gina 1909-1963
Mandel, Frank 1884-1958
Manning, Ambrose 1861-1940
Mantovani, Annunzio 1905-1980
Margetson, Arthur 1887-1951
Markova, Alicia 1910-
Marks, Alfred 1921-1996
Marsden, Betty 1919-1998
Marsden, Gerry 1942-
Martin, Mary 1913-1990
Martin, Millicent 1934-
Marvin, Hank 1941-
Maschwitz, Eric 1901-1969
Massey, Daniel 1933-1988
Matthews, Jessie 1907-1981
May, Edna 1878-1948
May, Hans 1880-1959
Mayerl, Billy 1902-1959
McCartney, Paul 1942-
McEachern, Malcolm 1885-1945
McEwan, Geraldine 1932-
McHugh, Jimmy 1894-1969
McKenna, Virginia 1931-
McQueen-Pope, WJ 1888-1960
Melachrino, George 1909-1965
Melford, Austin 1884-1971
Melford, Jack 1899-1972
Melville, Alan 1910-1983
Mendelssohn, Felix 1911-1952
Menken, Alan 1949-
Mercer, Johnny 1909-1976
Merman, Ethel 1909-1984
Merrill, Bob 1921-1998

Jerome Kern

Merson, Billy 1881-1947
Messager, Andre 1853-1929
Mesurier, John Le 1912-1983
Metaxa, George 1899-1950
Meyer, George 1884-1959
Meyer, Joseph 1894-1987
Michell, Keith 1928-
Middleton, Guy 1908-1973
Miles, Bernard 1907-1991
Millar, Gertie 1879-1952
Miller, Gary 1924-1968
Miller, Jonathan 1934-
Miller, Max 1895-1963
Miller, Ruby 1889-1976
Milligan, Spike 1918-2002
Millocker, Karl 1842-1899
Mills, Florence 1895-1927
Mills, John 1908-
Milton, Billy 1905-1989
Milton, Harry 1900-1965
Mitchell, George 1917-2002
Mitchell, Warren 1926-
Mollison, Clifford 1897-1986
Monckton, Lionel 1861-1924
Monkhouse, Bob 1928-2003
Monkman, Phyllis 1892-1976
Moody, Ron 1924-
Moore, Dudley 1935-2002
More, Julian 1928-
More, Kenneth 1914-1982
Morgan, Diana 1910-1986
Morley, Robert 1908-1992
Morley, Sheridan 1941-
Morrison, Jack 1887-1948
Morton, Hugh 1865-1916
Mount, Peggy 1915-2001
Moya, Stella 1916-2003
Mozart, Amadeus 1756-1791
Murdoch, Richard 1907-1990
Myers, Richard 1901-?
Nainby, Robert 1869-1948
Nash, Heddle 1896-1961
Naughton, Charlie 1886-1976
Neagle, Anna 1904-1986
Nervo, Jimmy 1989-1975
Nesbitt, Harry 1905-1968
Nesbitt, Max 1903-1966
Nesbitt, Robert 1906-1995
Newell, Raymond 1894-1972
Newley, Anthony 1931-1999
Newman, Greatrex 1892-1984
Newton, Robert 1905-1956
Nicholls, Horatio 1888-1964
Nichols, Beverley 1898-1983

Nichols, Joy 1927-1992
Nimmo, Derek 1930-1999
Noble, Dennis 1899-1966
Noble, Ray 1903-1978
Norman, Monty 1928-
Norton, Frederic 1875-1946
Novello, Ivor 1893-1951
Noyes, Alfred 1880-1958
Nugent, Moya 1901-1954
O'Brien, Richard 1942-
O'Connor, Des 1932-
O'Neal, Zelma 1903-1989
O'Toole, Peter 1932-
Oddie, Bill 1941-
Offenbach, Jacques 1819-1880
Oldham, Derek 1892-1968
Oliver, Stephen 1950-1992
Oliver, Vic 1898-1964
Olivier, Laurence 1907-1989
Orchard, Julian 1930-1979
Ornadel, Cyril 1924-
O'Shea, Tessie 1913-1995
Owen, Bill 1914-1999
Oxenford, Daphne 1920-
Paddick, Hugh 1915-2000
Page, Rita 1905-1954
Paige, Elaine 1951-
Palin, Michael 1943-
Paramor, Norrie 1914-1979
Park, Phil 1907-1978
Parker, Jim 1934-
Parker, Ross 1914-1974
Parnell, Jack 1923-
Parnell, Val 1894-1972
Parr Davies, Harry 1914-1955
Parsons, Donovan 1888-1980
Parsons, Nicholas 1923-
Pasco, Richard 1926-
Passmore, Walter 1867-1946
Paul, Betty 1921-
Payn, Graham 1918-
Payne, Edmund 1865-1914
Payne, Jack 1899-1969
Peach, L. du Garde 1890-1976
Pearce, Vera 1896-1966
Pelissier, HG (Harry Gabriel) 1874-1913
Pepper, Harry S. 1891-1970
Percival, Horace 1886-1961
Percival, Lance 1933-
Percy, Esme 1887-1957
Perry, Jimmy 1923-
Pertwee, Bill 1926-
Pertwee, Jon 1919-1996
Phillips, Montague 1885-1969
Phillips, Van 1905-1992
Phillips, Woolf 1919-2003
Phipps, Nicholas 1913-1980
Pils, Jacques 1906-1970
Pitt, Archie 1895-1940
Pitt, Percy 1869-1932
Planquette, Robert 1848-1903
Playfair, Arthur 1869-1918
Pleydell, Ronnie 1913-1994
Plowright, Joan 1929-
Pola, Eddie 1907-1995
Pollard, Su 1949-
Porter, Cole 1891-1964
Posford, George 1906-1976
Pounds, Courtice 1862-1927
Pounds, Louie 1872-1970
Praed, Michael 1960-
Preager, Lou 1906-1978
Previn, Andre 1929-
Printemps, Yvonne 1895-1977
Prowse, Juliet 1936-1996
Purcell, Harold 1907-1977
Purdell, Reginald 1896-1953
Quatro, Suzie 1950-
Quayle, Anna 1936-
Quilley, Denis 1927-
Quilter, Roger 1877-1953
Rabinowitz, Harry 1916-
Randolph, Elsie 1904-1981
Ray, Robin 1934-1998
Raye, Carol 1923-
Read, Al 1909-1987
Read, Mike 1952-
Reader, Ralph 1904-1982
Reece, Brian 1913-1962
Reed, Oliver 1938-1999
Reed, Thomas German 1817-1888

Reeve, Ada 1874-1966
Regan, Joan 1929-
Reid, Beryl 1920-1996
Reid, Billy 1902-1974
Retford, Ella 1885-1962
Revel, Harry 1905-1958
Reynolds, Alfred 1884-1969
Reynolds, Dorothy 1913-1978
Rhys-Jones, Griff 1953-
Rice, Tim 1944-
Richard, Cliff 1940-
Richardson, Ian 1934-
Richardson, Ralph 1902-1983
Ridley, Arnold 1896-1984
Rigby, Arthur 1900-1971
Riscoe, Arthur 1896-1954
Risque, WH ?-1916
Ritchard, Cyril 1897-1977
Roberts, Rachel 1927-1980
Robeson, Paul 1898-1976
Robey, George 1869-1954
Robin, Leo 1900-1985
Robins, Phyllis 1910-1982
Robinson, Cardew 1923-1992
Robinson, Eric 1909-1974
Rodgers, Anton 1933-
Rodgers, Richard 1902-1979
Roebuck, Janine 1954-
Rogers, Anne 1933-
Rogers, Clodagh 1947-
Rogers, Eric 1921-1978
Rogers, Ginger 1911-1995
Romberg, Sigmund 1887-1951
Rome, Harold 1908-1996
Ros, Edmundo 1910-
Rose, Clarkson 1890-1968
Rosenthal, Harry 1900-1953
Rosenthal, Jack 1931-2004
Ross, Adrian 1859-1933
Ross, Annie 1930-
Ross, Jerry 1926-1955
Rossington, Norman 1928-1999
Rostill, John 1942-1973
Routledge, Patricia 1929-
Roy, Derek 1922-1981
Roy, Harry 1900-1971
Royston, Roy 1898-1976
Rubach, Edward 1912-1971
Rubens, Paul 1875-1917
Ruby, Harry 1895-1974
Rushton, Willie 1937-1996
Russell, Kennedy ?-1954
Russell, Willy 1941-
Rutherford, Margaret 1892-1972

Santley, Joseph 1889-1971
Sarony, Leslie 1897-1985
Sayle, Alexei 1952-
Scala, Primo alias Harry Bidgood, q.v.
Scales, Prunella 1932-
Schmidt, Harvey 1929-
Schonberg, Claude-Michel 1944-
Schubert, Franz 1797-1828
Schwab, Laurence 1893-1951
Schwartz, Arthur 1900-1984
Scofield, Paul 1922-
Scott, Terry 1927-1994
Scott-Wood, George 1903-1978
Seal, Elizabeth 1933-
Secombe, Harry 1921-2001
Segal, George 1934-
Sellers, Peter 1925-1980
Selten, Morton 1860-1939
Sewell, Danny 1930-2001
Shacklock, Constance 1913-1999
Shakespeare, William 1564-1616
Shane, Paul 1940-
Shaw, George Bernard 1856-1950
Shephard, Firth 1891-1949
Sheridan, Richard Brinsley 1751-1816
Sherman, Richard 1928-
Sherman, Robert 1925-
Sherrin, Ned 1931-
Sherwin, Manning 1902-1974
Shield, William 1748-1829
Shiner, Ronald 1903-1966
Shulman, Milton 1913-2004
Sievier, Bruce 1894-1953
Simmons, Jean 1929-
Simon, Neil 1927-
Sims, Joan 1930-2001
Sinclair, Peter 1901-1995
Sirmay, Albert 1918-1967
Skellern, Peter 1947-
Slade, Julian 1930-
Slaughter, Walter 1860-1908
Sleep, Wayne 1948-
Smith, Maggie 1934-
Smith, 'Whispering' Jack 1898-1950
Smithson, Florence 1884-1936
Snow, Valaida 1900-1956
Somers, Debroy 1890-1952
Sondheim, Stephen 1930-
Sonin, Ray 1907-1991
Sowande, Fela 1905-1987
Spear, Bernard 1919-2003
Speight, Johnny 1920-1998
Spinetti, Victor 1933-
Squire, JH 1880-1956

Alan J. Lerner (left) and Frederick Loewe

Squires, Dorothy 1915-1998
Squires, Rosemary 1928-
St Helier, Ivy 1890-1971
St John, Florence 1854-1912
Stamp-Taylor, Enid 1904-1946
Stanley, Phyllis 1914-
Stardust, Alvin 1942-
Starkie, Martin 1925-
Starr, Ringo 1940-
Steafel, Sheila 1935-
Steele, Tommy 1936-
Stennett, Stan 1925-
Stephenson, Pamela 1949-
Sterndale Bennett, Joan 1914-1996
Stevens, James 1923-
Stevens, Ronnie 1925-
Stevens, Shakin' 1948-
Stewart, Ian 1908-1989
Stewart, Michael composer 1929-
Stilgoe, Richard 1943-
Stoll, Oswald 1866-1942
Stolz, Robert 1880-1975
Stone, Lew 1898-1969
Stoppard, Tom 1937-
Stothart, Herbert 1885-1949
Strachey, Jack 1894-1972
Stratton, Eugene 1861-1918
Straus, Oscar 1870-1954
Strauss, Johann I 1804-1849
Strauss, Johann II 1825-1899
Streisand, Barbara 1942-
Stritch, Elaine 1925-
Strouse, Charles 1928-
Stuart, Leslie 1864-1928
Stubbs, Una 1937-
Studholme, Marie 1875-1930
Styne, Jule (Julius Stein) 1905-1994
Sullivan, Arthur 1842-1900
Summerfield, Eleanor 1921-2001
Sutherland, Gavin 1972-
Swain, Hal 1894-1966
Swann, Donald 1923-1994
Swanstrom, Arthur 1888-1940
Swinburne, Nora 1902-2000
Talbot, Howard 1865-1928
Tanner, James 1850-1915
Tarbuck, Jimmy 1940-
Tate, Harry 1872-1940
Tate, James 1875-1922
Tauber, Richard 1892-1948
Tempest, Marie 1864-1942
Temple, Nat 1913-
Tennent, HM 1879-1941
Ternent, Billy 1899-1977
Terriss, Ellaline 1871-1971
Terry-Thomas 1911-1990
Teyte, Maggie 1888-1976
Thatcher, Heather 1896-1987
Thesiger, Ernest 1879-1961
Thomas, Terry, see Terry-Thomas
Thompson, Emma 1959-
Thompson, Fred 1884-1949
Thorburn, Billy 1900-1971
Thorndike, Sybil 1882-1967
Thornton, Frank 1921-
Tierney, Harry 1890-1965
Tilley, Vesta 1864-1952
Timothy, Christopher 1940-
Titheradge, Dion 1889-1934
Took, Barry 1928-2002
Topol 1935-
Tours, Frank 1877-1963
Townshend, Pete 1945-
Toye, Wendy 1917-
Travers, Ben 1886-1980
Tree, Lady 1863-1937
Trent, Bruce 1912-1995
Tresmand, Ivy 1898-1980
Trevor, Austin 1897-1978
Trinder, Tommy 1909-1989
Trix, Helen 1886-1951
Trix, Josephine 1898-1952
Tucker, Sophie 1884-1966
Tunbridge, Joseph 1886-1961
Turner, John Hastings 1892-1956
Ustinov, Peter 1921-2004
Valentine, Dickie 1929-1971
Vaughan, Frankie 1928-1999
Vaughan, Norman 1927-2002
Verno, Jerry 1895-1975

Victoria, Vesta 1874-1951
Vincent, Robby 1895-1966
Von Tilzer, Albert 1878-1956
Vosburgh, Dick 1929-
Voss, Stephanie 1936-
Waddington, Patrick 1903-1987
Walbrook, Anton 1896-1967
Walker, Syd 1886-1945
Wall, Max 1908-1990
Wallace, Edgar 1875-1932
Wallace, Ian 1919-
Wallace, Nellie 1870-1948
Waller, Fats 1904-1943
Waller, Jack 1885-1957
Wallis, Bertram 1874-1952
Wallis, Shani 1933-
Walls, Tom 1883-1949
Walters, Julie 1950-
Walters, Thorley 1913-1991
Ward, Dorothy 1911-1988
Ward, Polly 1909-1987
Warner, John 1924-2001
Warren, C Denier 1889-1971
Warriss, Ben 1909-1993
Waterhouse, Keith 1929-
Waterman, Dennis 1948-
Watson, Betty Jane 1921-
Watson, Wylie 1889-1966
Wattis, Richard 1912-1975
Watts, Queenie 1926-1980
Wayne, Jeff 1944-
Wayne, Jerry 1921-
Wayne, Naunton 1900-1970
Webb, Clifton 1889-1966
Webb, Lizbeth 1926-
Webb, Marti 1944-
Weill, Kurt 1900-1950
Welch, Bruce 1941-
Welch, Elisabeth 1908-2003
Welchman, Harry 1886-1966
Welland, Colin 1934-
Wells, John 1936-1998
Wenham, Jane 1927-
Western, George 1895-1969
Western, Kenneth 1899-1963
Weston, RP (Robert Patrick) 1878-1936
Whelan, Albert 1875-1961

White, Sheila 1950-
Whitfield, David 1926-1980
Whitfield, June 1925-
Whiting, Jack 1901-61
Whitsun-Jones, Paul 1923-1974
Whitty, May 1865-1948
Whyton, Wally 1929-1997
Wilbur, Jay 1898-1969
Wildeblood, Peter 1923-1999
Wilding, Michael 1912-1979
Williams, Charles 1893-1978
Williams, Frank 1931-
Williams, Kenneth 1926-1988
Willson, Meredith 1902-1984
Wilson, Julie 1924-
Wilson, Sandy 1924-
Wilton, Robb 1881-1957
Wimperis, Arthur 1874-1953
Windeatt, George 1901-1959
Windsor, Barbara 1937-
Winn, Anona 1904-1994
Winnick, Maurice 1902-1962
Winstone, Eric 1915-1974
Winters, Bernie 1932-1991
Winters, Mike 1930-
Wisdom, Norman 1915-
Wodehouse, PG (Pelham Grenville) 1881-1975
Wood, Arthur 1875-1953
Wood, Haydn 1882-1959
Wood, Victoria 1953-
Woodforde-Finden, Amy 1860-1919
Woods, Aubrey 1928-
Woodward, Edward 1930-
Woolfenden, Guy 1937-
Wordsworth, Barry 1948-
Wright, Geoffrey 1912-
Wright, Hugh E 1879-1940
Wright, Huntley 1869-1943
Wright, Lawrence alias Horatio Nicholls, q.v.
Wylam, Wilfred aka Wilfred Josephs q.v.
Wylie, Julian 1878-1934
Wylie, Lauri 1880-1951
Yana 1932-1989
Yorke, Peter 1902-1966
Youmans, Vincent 1898-1946
Ziegler, Anne 1910-2003
Zwar, Charles 1911-1989

George (left) and Ira Gershwin

153

INDEX

△ ▷ *Like so many theatres built around the turn of the 20th Century, both the Coronet (opened 1898) in Notting Hill High Street (above) and the Camden (opened 1900) had relatively short lives hosting plays and musicals. With the advent of gramophone records, radio and films the demand for live performances rapidly diminished and by the 1920s both had become cinemas. There was a positive rash of new 'picture palaces' during the 1930s but the postwar television boom saw many of these off as well.*

◁ *The Prince of Wales in Coventry Street was opened in 1937 and is the second theatre on the site, the first having been erected in 1884 as the Prince's.* **The Witches of Eastwick** *was premiered at Drury Lane in 2000 before moving to the Prince of Wales the following year.*

△ ▽ *Following a spell as a dance hall the decorous Lyceum reopened as a theatre in 1996 and three years later hit the jackpot with* **The Lion King**.

BIBLIOGRAPHY

ABC of Show Business — Wolf Mankowitz (Oldbourne c.1958)
Book of Musicals (from Showboat to Evita) — Arthur Jackson (Mitchell Beazley 1979)
British Light Music — Philip Scowcroft (Thames, 1997)
British Musical Theatre Vol. 1 1865-1914 — Kurt Ganzl (Oxford 1986)
British Musical Theatre Vol. 2 1915-1984 — Kurt Ganzl (Oxford 1986)
British Theatre — Raymond Mander & Joe Mitchenson (Hulton 1957)
Cochran (Biography of C.B. Cochran) — James Harding (Methuen 1988)
Cock-a-Doodle-Do (Memoirs of Charles B. Cochran) — (Dent 1941)
Curtain Call for the Guv'nor (Biography of George Edwardes) — Ursula Bloom (Hutchinson 1954)
Dictionary of Theatre — David Pickering (Sphere 1988)
Encyclopedia of British Film — ed. Brian McFarlane (Methuen 2003)
Footlights Flickered (Theatre in the Twenties) — W.J. Macqueen-Pope (Herbert Jenkins 1959)
Footlights! — Robert Hewison (Methuen 1983)
Four Years at the Old Vic — Harcourt Williams (Putnam 1935)
Frank Matcham, Theatre Architect — ed. Brian Walker (Blackstaff 1980)
Gaiety & George Grossmith — Stanley Naylor (Stanley Paul 1913)
Gaiety Years — Alan Hyman (Cassell 1975)
Gaiety, Theatre of Entertainment — W.J. Macqueen-Pope (Allen 1949)
Gay Twenties — J.C. Trewin, Raymond Mander & Joe Mitchenson (MacDonald 1958)
Gertie Millar & the Edwardesian Legacy — Ken Reeves (private publication 2004)
Ghosts & Greasepaint — W.J. Macqueen-Pope (Robert Hale 1951)
Give Me Yesterday — W.J. Macqueen-Pope (Hutchinson 1957)
Goodbye Piccadilly — W.J. Macqueen-Pope (David & Charles 1972)
Haymarket, Theatre of Perfection — W.J. Macqueen-Pope (Allen 1948)
Indiscreet Guide to Theatreland — W.J. Macqueen-Pope (Muse Arts c.1950)
Ivor (Biography of Ivor Novello) — W.J. Macqueen-Pope (Allen 1951)
Ivor Novello, Man of the Theatre — Peter Noble (Falcon 1951)
London Musical Shows on Record 1889-1989 — Robert Seeley & Rex Bunnett (Gramophone 1989)
London's Theatres — Mike Kilburn, photographs Alberto Azoz (New Holland 2002)
London Theatres & Music Halls 1850-1950 — Diana Howard (Library Association 1970)
Lost Theatres of London — Raymond Mander & Joe Mitchenson (New English Library 1976)
Melodies Linger On, The — W.J. Macqueen-Pope (Allen 1950)
Musical Comedy — Raymond Mander & Joe Mitchenson (Peter Davies 1969)
Musical Theatre — Alan Jay Lerner (Collins 1986)
Nights of Gladness — W.J. Macqueen-Pope (Hutchinson 1956)
Noel (Biography of Noel Coward) — Charles Castle (Abacus 1974)
Noel Coward (Autobiography compilation) — (Methuen 1991)
Our Theatres in the Eighties — Sheridan Morley (Hodder & Stoughton 1990)
Oxford Companion to Popular Music — ed. Peter Gammond (Oxford 1991)
Penguin Encyclopaedia of Popular Music — ed. Donald Clarke (Penguin 1998)
Pillars of Drury Lane — W.J. Macqueen-Pope (Hutchinson 1955)
Revue — Raymond Mander & Joe Mitchenson (Peter Davies 1971)
Ring Up the Curtain — Ernest Short & Arthur Compton-Rickett (Herbert Jenkins 1938)
Romance of the English Theatre — Donald Brook (Rockcliff 1947)
Sondheim & Co. — Craig Zadan (Pavilion 1987)
Spread a Little Happiness (First 100 Years of the British Musical) — Sheridan Morley (Thames 1987)
Theatre Royal, Drury Lane — W.J. Macqueen-Pope ((Allen 1945)
Theatre World — magazines from Thirties to Fifties
Theatre World 1945-46 — ed. Daniel Blum (Guide, New York 1946)
Theatres of London — Raymond Mander & Joe Mitchenson (New English Library 1975)
Through Stage Doors — Sydney Blow (Chambers 1958)
Top Hat & Tails (The Story of Jack Buchanan) — Michael Marshall (Elm Tree 1978)
Turbulent Thirties — J.C. Trewin, Raymond Mander & Joe Mitchenson (MacDonald 1960)
Who's Who in the Theatre — John Parker (Pitman) several editions